The Ongo Book 2.0: everyday nonviolence

CATHERINE CADDEN & JESSE WIENS CHU

The Ongo Book 2.0: Everyday Nonviolence
Copyright © 2022 by Catherine Cadden and Jesse Wiens Chu

All rights reserved. No part of this book may be reproduced or redistributed in any form or by any electronic or mechanical means, including information storage and retrieval systems, without permission in writing from the authors, except by a reviewer who may quote brief passages in a review.

Use of the quotations in this book is done under the Fair Use copyright principle. All quotations remain the literary works and intellectual properties of their respective originators. Neither the publisher nor the authors of this work assert any claim of copyright for individual quotations. If any rights have inadvertently been infringed upon, the publisher asks that the omission be excused and agrees to make the necessary corrections in subsequent printings.

ISBN 979-8-9861731-0-8

Editor: Dennis Crean
Design: Hadley Gustafson and Jesse Wiens Chu
Cover Illustration: Jennifer Hewitson
Interior Illustrations: Kate Raffin

Published by Baba Tree International
P.O. Box 966
Bellevue, WA 98009
United States of America
www.babatree.org

The Ongo Book 2.0: Everyday Nonviolence

"In a hurried and harried world, here are some basic and potentially powerful ideas about how to remain stable and unrocked. My guess is they will become more valuable as our various external crises deepen, and some of the distractions on which we currently lean begin to show their shallowness."

– **Bill McKibben**, author of *The End of Nature* and *Deep Economy*
and Co-founder of 350.org

"*The Ongo Book: Everyday Nonviolence* is a beautiful and practical book balanced with inspiration, simple yet complete teachings, and practices on every aspect of an integrated spirituality. I find the practices clearly explained, guiding the dedicated practitioner with precise maps to the inner landscape and the landscape of interpersonal relationships. For many years, in my own evolution and teaching, it has been very clear to me that, in order to actualize our spiritual evolution, we need the support of a community who share our vision and values. *The Ongo Book* provides a practical support for this vision."

– **Robert Gonzales**, Founder of the Center for Living Compassion and
former board president of the Center for Nonviolent Communication

"The socially-engaged Buddhist peace movement adopted the slogan, 'There is no Way to peace, peace is the Way'. This is a call to live and embody the aspirational goals of a spiritual life. This book is a companion along the path. The contemplative exercises celebrate a peaceful, respectful way to listen deeply; build bridges of understanding; and develop clear, compassionate communication skills to live harmoniously with others."

– **Subhana Barzaghi**, Zen Roshi, Insight Meditation teacher,
and psychotherapist

"Never before have I experienced such a tangible, simple, yet transformative practice. In using these practices my heart has opened in a way I never imagined possible! If the entire world population could embark on this 12-week journey then we would inhabit a much kinder, wiser, and nonviolent place."

– **Melissa Bernstein**, Co-founder of Melissa & Doug and Lifelines

Get even more support for your practice of everyday nonviolence.

The Ongo Companion Website is a free sanctuary online for all *Ongo Book* practitioners, offering a wealth of additional resources for learning and connection. On it, you can:

- Download audio recordings of guided Ongo meditations
- Watch video recordings of Ongo teachings
- Find resources for joining or starting your own Ongo group
- Connect with other Ongo practitioners and groups around the world
- Sign up for one-on-one practice support with Catherine and Jesse
- and that's just the beginning!

Simply go online to **ongo.global** to join. We look forward to seeing you there.

Contents

Foreword by Shantum Seth	ix
Foreword by Lucy Leu	xi
Welcome to Ongo – An Invitation	1
How to Use This Book – The Quick-Start Guide	5
Solo Practices: General Directions	7
Preparing for Buddy Practice: Guidance for Ongo Buddies	9
Creating a Circle of Support: How to Start an Ongo Group	11
Leading Group Practice: Instructions for the Group Guide	13

WEEK 1

Group Gathering: The Ongo Circle	18
Buddy Practice: Safety, Trust, and Respect	26
Solo Practices: A Place to Start • Mindfulness of Breath • Mindfulness of Body	29

WEEK 2

Group Gathering: The Empathy Circle	40
Buddy Practice: Empathy	46
Solo Practices: Mindfulness of Needs • Meeting Needs • Being Needs	49

WEEK 3

Group Gathering: Self-Empathy ... 60

Buddy Practice: Joining Alliances with Comparing Mind ... 66

Solo Practices: To-Be List • Self-Empathy Journal • Self-Empathy Meditation ... 71

WEEK 4

Group Gathering: Turning Toward Suffering and a Power Greater Than Ourselves ... 84

Buddy Practice: Facing Suffering, Finding Serenity ... 90

Solo Practices: Life's Inbox • Daily Miracles • Calling on Our Ancestors ... 93

WEEK 5

Group Gathering: Core Beliefs ... 102

Buddy Practice: Empathy ... 110

Solo Practices: Unpacking Core Beliefs • Habit and Choice • Requests ... 113

WEEK 6

Group Gathering: Finishing Business ... 126

Buddy Practice: Understanding, Acceptance, and Belonging ... 132

Solo Practices: Seeing the Gift • Taking Inventory • Forgiveness Meditation ... 135

WEEK 7

Group Gathering: Forgiveness ... 146

Buddy Practice: Gratitude ... 154

Solo Practices: Gratitude List • Sharing Gratitude • Celebration and Mourning ... 157

WEEK 8

Group Gathering: Celebration and Mourning ... 166

Buddy Practice: Compassionate Boundaries ... 172

Solo Practices: Mindfulness of Shenpa • Turning Toward Shenpa • Asking for Help ... 175

WEEK 9

Group Gathering: Shenpa	186
Buddy Practice: Empathy	192
Solo Practices: Mindful Walking • Practicing for All Beings • Empathic Reflection	195

WEEK 10

Group Gathering: Speaking Truth	206
Buddy Practice: Speaking from the Heart	212
Solo Practices: The Courage to Speak • Connecting Requests • Right Speech	215

WEEK 11

Group Gathering: Dialogues of the Heart	228
Buddy Practice: The Hook	234
Solo Practices: Harvesting • Post-Ongo Support • You Are Here	239

WEEK 12

Group Gathering: Ongo Harvest	250
Buddy Practice: Pure Meeting	254
Solo Practices: Five Days to Live • Four • Three • Two • One Day to Live	255

Afterword – Continuing Ongo with Integrity   263

APPENDIX A

Needs Wheel	271
Feelings	272
Body Sensations	273
Self-Empathy (aka "What We're Bringing into the Room")	274
Communication Flow Chart	275
Needs Cards	276

APPENDIX B: LEADING GROUP PRACTICE ONLINE

How to Use this Appendix	281
Creating a Circle of Support: How to Start an Ongo Group	282
Leading Group Practice: Instructions for the Group Guide	282
Week 1 Group	286
Week 2 Group	290
Week 3 Group	293
Week 4 Group	296
Week 5 Group	298
Week 6 Group	302
Week 7 Group	303
Week 8 Group	304
Week 9 Group	305
Week 10 Group	308
Week 11 Group	310
Week 12 Group	310
About the Quotes: In Dedication to Our Teachers	312
Gratitudes	322
Gratitudes Continued	326
About the Authors	332

Foreword

Shantum Seth

I first met Jesse and Catherine ten years ago on a pilgrimage. This pilgrimage that I have been curating for 35 years is along the footsteps of the two historical figures that I think of as my two greatest teachers, the Buddha and Gandhi.

The photograph on the cover of the first edition of *The Ongo Book*, the planting of a Bodhi tree sapling, was taken on that journey. It is significant that the image is that of a sapling and not of a seed. Because the seed that came to us from the Buddha is already a healthy sapling. It is not something new that we are starting. We have been handed a sapling from a centuries-old tree, and all we have to do is to cultivate the sapling. With this book, we are being given the tools to do our part.

My other great teacher, Thich Nhat Hanh, often spoke of seeing the clouds, the rain, the sunshine, the earth, all in a leaf. If we took out one of those elements, then the leaf would not exist. This realization of what he calls "our inter-being," underlines our sense of interconnectedness and our universal responsibility. What we say, what we do, what we think, have repercussions beyond our imagination. On this fragile little planet, we are all interrelated and coexistent. If we destroy ourselves, then we take all other species with us. What's timely about *The Ongo Book* is that our survival is uncertain. It offers practices on how to live harmoniously and in loving community.

What I particularly like about this book is the way it offers practical exercises on how to build community – like conducting circle sharing in such a way that each person feels included and can share freely.

Both the authors, Catherine and Jesse, are natural facilitators, and their book can guide many others. There is a great sense of ease and playfulness that comes naturally to them. Catherine can connect effortlessly with young people, who grow to trust and love her very quickly. It's a gift – not everyone has this skill. Jesse has a certain stability, a rock-like center, which allows Catherine's dance.

We recognize a common bond between the four of us – the two authors, my wife, Gitu, and me. We all share the same aspiration to make the world a better place, not just for ourselves but for others and for future generations. We have a common idealism, a similar sense of purpose.

Over the years we've known them, Jesse and Catherine have connected us to other friends in their circle who share the same sense of purpose. Both Jesse and Catherine have a way of building trust, and people naturally gravitate to them. This, the making of a "Beloved community," a Sangha, built on practices in nonviolence, is what this book is about – helping each other to live and breathe easy, and creating a more harmonious and loving world.

We've been at war and in conflict for a long time, even within ourselves, and that has been a great cause of suffering in the world, for individuals, within families, and for society at large. There is much despair, anger, hatred, and brutality.

It is tough to keep the light of nonviolence alive in the midst of such darkness, skepticism, and ridicule. I know it to my own cost. How many times have people dismissed me with a scoff: "You're an idealist, the world is going to destroy itself anyway, this is the Kali Yuga."

But I do believe that the potential of basic goodness exists in all human beings. I also see that there is a basic human need to belong and to connect and to feel that connection. We can see it in the youngest of children. Our effort is to keep that goodness alive in ourselves and to touch it in others. It's what we were born to do. This book helps us to do that.

– Shantum Seth

March 2022

Shantum Seth received the 'lamp transmission' from Zen Master Thich Nhat Hanh ordaining him as a *Dharmacharya* (Teacher of the Dharma) in 2001, and he has been teaching in India and across the world. He has also been leading "In the Footsteps of the Buddha'" pilgrimages and other multifaith and transformative journeys since 1988 and is considered the foremost guide to the sites associated with the Buddha. He is actively involved in social, environmental, and educational programs, including work on cultivating mindfulness in society, with educators, the Central Reserve Police Force, and the corporate sector among others, pioneered by the non-profit trust Ahimsa, of which he is one of the founders. Previously having lived in England, the USA, and France (in a monastery) for over 14 years, he now resides with his wife, Gitanjali, and daughters in Dehradun, in the foothills of the Indian Himalayas.

Foreword

Lucy Leu

I live in a world where there is so much to learn, to read, to gain, to see, to do, and to acquire – a world of fast foods, quick fixes, new skills, the latest discoveries and promising techniques. I am sometimes overwhelmed, seeking to consume all the wisdom and knowledge I see out there in the world.

Catherine and Jesse offer something different here. Extending a gentle hand, they lead me into a journey where each step is its own reward. I am invited to pause, I find my footing, I encounter the unknown inside. I relax into a spaciousness where fresh understanding lands and seeps through the layers of who I am. I change from inside out. And my world changes.

This journey is, as the authors say, "for those who want to *be* nonviolence in the real world." The felt sense of nonviolence in the body is a relaxed, open state of goodwill grounded in a knowing that, in its essence, this self is not separate from other selves. Connection (or interconnectedness) is central to Nonviolent Communication (NVC) and the Dharma lineages reflected in *The Ongo Book*. However, nonseparation is not something that my brain (however smart) or my will (however strong) can accomplish. While I might study Buddhist concepts, read about nonviolence, or even master the use of words and expressions posited by Nonviolent Communication, my life and my world will only transform when the teachings spring into life from within the heart. Although the journey extends across a lifetime, *The Ongo Book* provides a sturdy 12-week scaffolding that allows me – alone, or even more powerfully, with the shared intention and presence of fellow travelers – to experiment with, experience, and integrate new ways of being and seeing offered by wise teachings.

To me, *The Ongo Book* is not a book to read in the usual sense. It is a clear, bright guide that takes me on a journey to discover myself being held in new light. If I am willing to take time to return again and again and look, I will see unfamiliar angles, facets, and potentials in that face I take to be me. I might realize that I am not the person I see in the mirror – not the (good, kind, competent, intelligent, strong) "self" I think I am nor the (bad, stupid) one I'd like not to be. There is simply the fullness of being, profound connectedness within and with "others," and a felt sense of belonging to a continuously changing and vibrant flow – this dynamic mystery we call Life.

I am inspired by the authors' inclusion and honoring of their many teachers and the humble acknowledgment that "there is nothing new here in this book." Though our sources of wisdom may be age-old, each generation longs to be addressed in their own language and through the forms and culture that have evolved in their lifetime. When I take the Ongo journey to embody the teachings, I transform not only myself and my world, but water the soil from which next generations will emerge. We are in an age of precipitous change – how we each live our one precious life will shape the future of humanity. I am so grateful that *The Ongo Book* is here to support us as a friend.

– Lucy Leu,
March 2022

Lucy Leu is the former board president of the Center for Nonviolent Communication, the editor of the internationally bestselling *Nonviolent Communication: A Language of Life*, author of the *Nonviolent Communication Companion Workbook*, and co-creator of the *NVC Toolkit for Facilitators*. She co-founded the Freedom Project, bringing NVC and mindfulness trainings to prison inmates and those reintegrating into society. Lucy began practicing Vipassana Insight Meditation in 1986. Introduced to relational meditation through Insight Dialogue in 2008, she has been actively engaged in practice and service with the Insight Dialogue Community. She is privileged to live on the unceded ancestral lands of the Coast Salish peoples (aka Vancouver, British Columbia).

"For our brief time on this wonderful planet,
we must bow deeply to one another,
to Earth,
and to all other sentient beings,
and resist with the power of love
anything that creates or stands as a barrier
between ourselves and the whole kingdom of life."
— Alycee J. Lane

Welcome to Ongo
An Invitation

"We are all just walking each other home."
– Ram Dass

Peace. Compassion. Wisdom.

When you read these words, what comes to mind?

Do you think of your life, or someone else's? Do you think of where you live and work, or somewhere removed from your daily experience? Do you think of something that you live daily, or something that you wish for?

As meditation teachers, nonviolent direct-action educators, and Nonviolent Communication Certified Trainers, we have led trainings on six continents and worked with thousands of people. Wherever we go, people generally ask us the same question in various ways: "What I'm learning today is great, but how can I practice it in my everyday life?"

What if peace, compassion, and wisdom weren't just nice words that you visit from time to time, but your actual day-to-day experience? What if your home was your temple and your life was your spiritual teacher?

For us, these aren't abstract concerns. We ask questions like these ourselves every day, in our marriage, and in our relationships with relatives, neighbors, and coworkers. As teachers, we feel a responsibility to explore in our own lives what we are inviting our students to do; to be present with our breath and our feelings in the middle of heated discussions; to face our emotional wounds and our deeply held beliefs and take ownership for how they affect our relationships with others; to empathize with the needs of others and speak up for our own, even when we're afraid.

What has become clear to us is that, though most of us generally enjoy the "get away" feeling of a workshop or retreat, the big learning begins when we return home. Enlightenment is a great idea, but we all really want to know how to have a compassionate discussion about money with our spouses, or how to wisely address basic issues in our communities. In Kabul, Afghanistan, in 2007, amidst an ongoing U.S.-led military invasion and Taliban suicide bombings, the hottest topic in our nonviolence training for peace leaders was how to have an honest conversation with one's neighbors about garbage and sewage.

Ongo was created in 2010 as our answer to this call to bring spiritual practice home. The term *Ongo* pays homage to the Japanese Zen tradition of "ango" (安居). Ango comes from the ancient Buddhist tradition of *Vassa*, a three-month period of intensive spiritual contemplation and practice, held during the Indian monsoon season. During the months when it was difficult to travel due to washed-out roads, and small animals and plants were most vulnerable to being invisibly trampled, the Buddha and his disciples would settle in one place to deepen their training in wisdom and compassion.

We have updated this tradition to meet the needs of ordinary people today. We call it "Ongo" as shorthand for *ongoing* spiritual practice. Although we recommend taking retreats or pilgrimages away from home and believe this can have powerful effects on one's life, we wanted to provide the support of a retreat within people's daily lives. We wanted to create a spiritual community whose care and connection could be felt even when someone was at home or at work. We wanted the teachings and practices we offered to make sense in the context of those everyday relationships and pressures.

Each day of our lives holds opportunity for us to awaken our hearts and minds to peace. You hold in your hands an invitation to discover that possibility of practice within your own life.

This book offers the "how to get there from here" while staying home. Within its pages are twelve weeks of inspiration, step-by-step guidance, and ways to create support and companionship. There are no prerequisites other than the willingness to say yes to the journey.

These practices were derived primarily from Buddhism, particularly Soto Zen and Vipassana, and Nonviolent Communication. Some of them also come from other bodies of wisdom and lineages, like Nonviolence, the Twelve Steps, the work of Stephen and Ondrea Levine, and Indigenous Elders with whom we have worked directly. We believe all the teachings we share are indigenous to many nations across the earth. We respect the carriers of these traditions. We also honor that there is nothing new here in this book. Like a story passed through generations, each retelling reflects the generation of its time and an evolution needed for humanity. In sharing this work, we honor the teachers who were called by compassion to share this wisdom with others. We honor those who came before them, who may have gone to great lengths to keep this wisdom alive.

Ongo does not require you to subscribe to any particular religion or belief system. In fact, our hope is that it opens up new depth and possibilities for you within your own faith or spiritual practice, whether that's prayer, meditation, yoga, or simply being kind to others.

Imagine living your spiritual practice in everything that you do – in movement and in stillness, in words and in silence. Imagine there being no separation between a spiritual retreat and your life. This book invites you into that reality through a progression of short, simple, and doable practices for you to incorporate into your daily life over the course of three months.

This book continues the evolution of Ongo and how we are sharing those practices. It's our best attempt at making the support, companionship, and wisdom of Ongo accessible to anyone, anywhere in the world. In its pages, we hope you will find more than answers for your life questions – we hope you will find a spiritual path where your questions deepen and the answers emerge through your own insights and discoveries.

You hold in your hands an invitation.

An invitation to step onto your path of peace, compassion, and wisdom.

An invitation to discover what this journey means to you.

How to Use This Book
The Quick-Start Guide

- **Read "Welcome to Ongo"** (page 1).

- **If doing Ongo on your own,** read "The Solo Practices: General Directions" (page 7). Then, choose a date to begin your twelve weeks of Ongo practice and start with "Week 1 Solo Practices" (page 29).

- **If doing Ongo with one other person,** both of you read "The Solo Practices: General Directions" (page 7) and "Preparing for Buddy Practice" (page 9). Then, together, choose a date to begin your twelve weeks of Ongo practice and start with the "Week 1 Buddy Practice" (page 26) and "Week 1 Solo Practices" (page 29).

- **If doing Ongo with an existing group,** read "The Solo Practices: General Directions" (page 7) and "Preparing for Buddy Practice" (page 9). After the first group gathering, you will begin with the "Week 1 Buddy Practice" (page 26) and "Week 1 Solo Practices" (page 29).

- **If you would like to do Ongo with a group, and there is no existing group,** read "Creating a Circle of Support: How to Start an Ongo Group" (page 11).

- **If doing Ongo with a group that is meeting online instead of in-person,** use the guidance offered in "Leading Group Practice Online" (page 281), in addition to the instructions above.

Solo Practices: General Directions

"For me, the practices are simple and so doable that I have continued many of them after Ongo. I am finding that, though simple, their cumulative effect is powerful."
– Franca N., Nigeria

The Solo Practices are the heartbeat of Ongo. They provide a consistent rhythm to lean into, five days a week, a rhythm that strengthens our connection to wisdom and compassion on a daily basis. We have found these relatively short moments of engagement each day to be energizing and more sustainable than the habit of waiting for "free time" to practice.

Ongo Solo Practices are designed for individual practice. Even if you are not practicing as part of a group, you can have a complete Ongo experience simply by following the guidance laid out in the Solo Practice sections of this book. When practiced in the order they are presented, these practices will take you on a journey that deepens your understanding and skill over the course of the twelve weeks of Ongo.

Each week offers a flow of three Solo Practices alternating with two Rememberings. Rememberings, in this book, are inspiring quotations that deepen and turn us toward the essence of the practices. They help us to remember the be-ing inside of the do-ing. In this way, even on days when we are not actively doing some practice, we are still contemplating how to *be* these practices inside of everything else we do. This is also designed to support flexibility and depth in your practice – you will always have the option to wait a day to do a particular Solo Practice or take two days to really dive in to a single practice.

How to get the most out of the Solo Practices:

🔥 **Schedule daily Ongo time.** Many have found that scheduling a regular time for their Solo Practice takes the stress out of trying to "make time" each day. We recommend scheduling a minimum of 30 minutes, three days a week. Most Solo Practices take less than 30 minutes to do, but many are rich enough that you can take more time with them when you feel the spaciousness to do so. On the other days, take a couple minutes to read and reflect on the Remembering to keep your connection to Ongo alive. Some people enjoy taking extra time on Remembering days to meditate as well.

🔥 **Do the practices (don't just read them).** These practices offer transformative experiences that go beyond a moment of intellectual inspiration. Give yourself that opportunity.

🔥 **Do the practices within the timeframe they are offered.** Rarely does that "perfect" moment come when there is nothing else pulling on our attention. The best time to practice is now. Also, these practices build on one another, so when initially learning them, they are best practiced in sequence.

🔥 **Follow the guidance that's offered**, even if you think you already know how to do that practice. The artist Georgia O'Keefe would paint the same flower over a hundred times to fully discover all she could about that flower. Each time we return to a practice, we may discover even more than we originally found. We may start to change how we practice it, as the practice changes us.

🔥 **Go gently.** The Buddha once advised a lute player who was struggling with their meditation practice to approach practice as they would approach tuning the strings of their lute – not too tight and not too slack. Practicing nonviolence means we cultivate nonviolence with ourselves as well as others.

🔥 **Some Solo Practices offer more possibilities**, noted with the following icons:

 Tips give advice for the practice, if you're having trouble with it.

 Audio or video versions of some practices are available online on the Ongo website at <u>ongo.global</u>.

 "Instant" practices offer one- to two-minute variations that can be done even in the middle of a busy day.

 "Deepening" practices offer experienced practitioners suggestions for how to explore a particular practice even further.

Preparing for Buddy Practice:
Guidance for Ongo Buddies

"I can't imagine I would have gotten even a fraction of the benefit I did from Ongo without [the] Buddy Practice. That was where the biggest learning took place. My capacity to take risks grew. I started to trust myself a little and to really love my buddies because we had the space and structure to be vulnerable with each other."
– Andi W., U.S.A.

Ongo Buddies are your close companions on the Ongo journey. They are there for empathy and support, and to deepen your learning in ways that are distinct from what is found when practicing on one's own or in a group. Some past participants have described Ongo Buddy Practice as both the most challenging and the most rewarding aspect of their Ongo journey.

The weekly one-hour Ongo Buddy Practice offers a safe space and structure to set down old habits and identities. It's a chance to practice new modes of being in the presence of another, your Ongo Buddy. If you are part of an Ongo group, you will have three different Ongo Buddies over the course of Ongo (guidance for how to choose them is included with the first, fifth, and ninth Group Gatherings). If you are not part of an Ongo group, you can still do Ongo Buddy Practices by inviting a willing friend or loved one to do them with you.

We offer the following suggestions for Ongo Buddies:

Before you meet with your Buddy:

- **Read through the Buddy Practice for that week** to have a sense of what you will be doing together. This supports clarity, ease of understanding, mutuality, and connection.

- **Set a time that works for you and your Buddy to meet** once a week for one hour. The Buddy Practices can be practiced on the phone, by video conference, or in person.

Bring to your Buddy Practice:

- Your journal or some paper
- Pens, pencils, or other writing utensils that you enjoy
- Your copy of *The Ongo Book*

During the Buddy Practice:

- **Meet (or take the call) in a quiet place** with few external distractions. Turn off notifications on your phone and other devices. Consider that you're co-creating a sacred meeting space.

- **Be with each other as you would in a sacred place.** These practices often bring up deep vulnerability and intimacy. Be with each other, from beginning to end, in a way that promotes safety, trust, and respect for yourselves.

- **Follow the format of the practice, as it is written**, so that there can be the opportunity to learn what it has to offer you both. Even if some of these practices are familiar to one of you from other contexts, you may find that they take on new meaning when practiced in the way they are written here.

- **Consciously choose your weights.** Some practices may bring up deep emotions and memories. When choosing which life material you want to work with in the presence of your Buddy, choose material that will stretch your learning *and* that you feel safe working with.

- **If the practice brings up feelings or memories that do not feel safe to share in the moment,** simply acknowledge that to your partner. Breathe deeply and feel the contact between your body and the earth supporting you. Make a plan to address what has arisen with a trusted friend or therapist so you can bring this important aspect of self into your Ongo journey.

- **Resist the impulse to fall into old habits of connecting** through commiserating, fixing, solving, giving advice, or telling old stories. Although there is nothing wrong with these ways of connecting, this time is set aside to practice ways of being that may feel more vulnerable, less familiar, and ultimately, more rewarding.

- **If you want to connect with your Buddy in a way that differs from the written practice, be sure to check with them first.** This supports a sense of mutual choice and consideration.

- **Remember that there's no "wrong" way to do any of this.** We're all just learning.

- **Relax and enjoy** your time together.

Creating a Circle of Support: How to Start an Ongo Group

"Ongo has made my feet touch the ground a little more firmly; I can walk the path of peace and presence that I long for with a little more frequency. I loved the daily support of knowing that I was sharing a journey with a group of seekers on a similar path."
– Adina R., U.S.A.

By engaging the practices in this book, you have already joined a worldwide community of Ongo practitioners. Even if you do only the Solo Practices without ever starting an Ongo group, you will still have a fulfilling experience of Ongo.

When you want a more direct sense of community and support, it may be time to create a circle of support locally or online. Gathering with others can deepen your solo journey and provide a place to share your struggles, celebrate your growth, and learn from others' experiences. An Ongo group that meets weekly creates a safe incubator for exploring practices that can, at times, feel too vulnerable to practice in other areas of your life. Sitting, meeting, and being with others, even in silence, can comfort us when we're feeling alone. Sharing wisdom in a group deepens our sense of companionship on the spiritual path.

If you would like to start an Ongo group, here's everything you need to know:

Suggestions and requests for group participants:

- **People joining the group are motivated by their own desire** to grow wisdom and compassion in their life, not by the pressure of others.

- **People joining the group have a sense of what Ongo is**, either through looking through the book themselves or having it explained to them by someone who's familiar with it.

- **Participants each need to have their own copy of this book** for the Solo and Buddy Practices. Those who only have the first edition of *The Ongo Book* can still practice together with those who have this second edition. There will be a few times when, for Buddy and Group practices, first edition users will need to refer to another participant's copy of the second edition for the most current guidance.

- **Participants are asked to commit and show up to the majority of the twelve weekly gatherings**, especially the opening and closing gatherings, to support the sense of connection and shared purpose.

- **Participants are asked to treat whatever is shared at the Group Gatherings and in Buddy Practices as confidential**, to care for the safety and trust of all.

- **Participants are asked to commit to their own spiritual and mental well-being**, and are willing to seek outside help if anything arises that needs additional support beyond what the Ongo group can offer.

Action steps for the group organizer:

- **Familiarize yourself with the structure of Ongo** by reading through the "Welcome to Ongo" and the introductory pages on "Solo Practices," "Preparing for Buddy Practices," and "Leading Group Practice." If your group will meet online, you will also be referencing the "Leading Group Practice Online" chapter at the back of the book.

- **Invite as few as three or as many as nineteen people to join you** in starting an Ongo group. With less than four participants total, some of the learning in the group practices may not be as rich. With more than twenty, some of the personal connection may be lost.

- **Choose a day and time that works for everyone to meet** weekly for the twelve weeks of Ongo for the one-and-a-half-hour Group Gatherings. (Larger groups may need two hours.) Ongo will start on the date of the first Group Gathering.

- [282] **Choose a quiet, comfortable, and easily accessible place** for the Group Gatherings to take place. Optionally, the meeting place can rotate among the homes of whomever's leading. For groups meeting online, see the additional guidance in the "Leading Group Practice Online" chapter, under the heading "Creating a Circle of Support". You can find it by turning to the page number shown in the computer icon at the left.

- **As the person organizing the Ongo group, you will be the Guide for the first Group Gathering.** This responsibility will be shared by the other participants for the rest of Ongo.

Leading Group Practice: Instructions for the Group Guide

> *"Ongo provided me with a community that chose to support each other with empathy, respect, trust, deep connection, nurturance, and support – with wise guidance. This was really important to me at this time in my life."*
> – Kate F., Australia

Taking the Ongo journey as a group gives friends, family, and community members an opportunity to travel the spiritual path together. Ongo groups meet once a week for fun, learning, and connection, using the guidance found in the group chapters in this book. Generally, each week's Group Gathering opens with a meditation, followed by a short teaching and activity for practice, then closes with sharing and gratitude. Each group will have a Group Guide. The Group Guide's role is to provide a sense of order and clarity of direction for the group. Over the course of twelve weekly Group Gatherings, each participant will take a turn at being the Group Guide.

Because of this shared power structure, there is no need to be shy about being in the lead and offering guidance when it is your turn to play that role for the group. In fact, your presence and initiative as Group Guide can support the community's desire to learn and their sense of safety.

The following pages list the responsibilities of the Group Guide. These, along with the group chapter for the week that you are leading, lay out, step-by-step, everything you need to know to act as Group Guide. No prior experience or knowledge is necessary. A few days before the Group Gathering, take the time to prepare yourself by reading them over – and remember to have fun!

If your group is meeting online instead of in person, look for this computer icon throughout the book. It will appear to the left of any section where there is additional guidance for online groups. Turn to the page number shown in the icon to find the additional guidance for that section.

Two or three days before the Group Gathering:

- **Read the Group Gathering instructions for the week that you will be guiding** so that you can have a sense of what will be happening and anything that you might need.

- **Remind everyone of the day, time, and place of the gathering as well as any preparation** they are being asked to do. See the section called "Preparation – All Participants" at the beginning of the Group Gathering instructions for the week you are guiding for this information. Not every Group Gathering has preparation for the participants to do.

- **Do any preparation noted under "Preparation – Group Guide,"** also found at the beginning of the Group Gathering instructions for the week you are guiding.

How to read the Group Gathering guidance:

What the activity is → **Opening Meditation**

What to do (in bold) → **After a moment of silence, read the guidance below to the group.**

How to do it (non-bold) → Read in a way that supports the group to relax into the guidance:

What to say (indented) → Settle in to where you are sitting. Sit comfortably and at ease.

- Each activity begins with a header title with a brushstroke behind it.

- Below the header are instructions for you, the Group Guide, to follow, in **bold text**. When needed, additional explanation is offered as non-bolded text, and examples are *italicized*.

- Indented text with a brushstroke beside it is meant to be read out loud to the group just as it's written.

 Bring to the Group Gathering:

- A small bell, chime, or other gentle instrument that can be used to signal the beginning and end of certain practices (like meditation)

- A watch or other device to keep time

- Paper or index cards

- Pens, pencils, markers, or other writing utensils (if possible, in a variety of colors)

- Your copy of *The Ongo Book*

- Starting with Week 2's Group Gathering, the deck of Needs Cards (Week 1's Group Guide can ignore this). See "Needs Cards" on page 276 in the Appendix for instructions.

On the day of the Group Gathering:

- **Arrange seating in a circle.** This enables every participant to easily see and be seen by every other participant and honors the equality of each participant's place.

- **Minimize distracting sights, sounds, and smells** to support everyone's focus and ease. For example, put away any unrelated books or media in the space. Ask participants to avoid wearing perfumes or scented products. Remind everyone to turn off their cell phones.

- **Consider placing something small and simple in the center of the circle** that invites a sense of welcome, inspiration, and coming together, without obstructing anyone's view of the other participants – for example, a few fresh flowers or a candle.

During the Group Gathering:

- **If this is your first time through Ongo, we highly suggest that you "stick to the script" and support the group to do the same**, following the guidance laid out for the week's Group Gathering exactly as it's written. Even if some of the teachings and practices are familiar to you from other trainings you've had, you may find they take on new meaning when practiced in the way we offer them here. That said, there are limitations to any form, including the ones offered in this book, and if this is the group's third or fourth time going through Ongo, then you may want to experiment with the guidance offered in "Continuing Ongo with Integrity" (page 263).

- **Step in to offer gentle guidance** whenever you have a sense that what's happening is straying from the collective purpose. One way to check your sense is to ask the group, "I notice that I'm starting to feel a bit distracted from our collective purpose in this moment, and I'm wondering, are others feeling that also?" It is also possible that what's happening is contributing to learning, even if it's not apparent to you or others at first. In those moments, your question can help bring that out. After getting a sense from the group, follow up with a proposal. Here's one simple and effective way to do that: "Based on what I'm hearing, I'd like to propose _____. Would anyone be unwilling to do that?" It could be a proposal to shift or to continue with what's happening for a certain amount of time. Either way, making a proposal helps to create clarity for the group.

- **Use "power-with" leadership.** Remember the power of silent empathy and taking a collective breath together when things get tough in the group sharing. As the guide, use the process and wisdom of Ongo, rather than be compelled to fix or know the answers. With regard to being asked questions as the guide or as a host of the group, remember that the wisdom is collective. Look together in *The Ongo Book* to see whether it answers the question, or discuss the question as a group.

- **If traumatic memories or current traumas reveal themselves for one or more participants,** stop the practice or discussion that's taking place and slow things down. One way to do this is to invite everyone to take three deep breaths together, and feel where the body is supported by the earth. Then offer the Loving-kindness Meditation from the Week One Group Practice (page 20). Afterwards, check in with the person to see whether they want to make a plan now with the group to take care of what has arisen or one-on-one with someone from the group after the group gathering. It is important that they make a plan, which may include getting professional support outside of the Ongo group, and that someone from the group supports them to follow through with care.

- **Keep track of time**, without worrying about time. Generally, by following the guidance written in that week's Group Practices, all the activities can happen within a one-and-a-half-hour gathering. For larger groups, plan for two hours. Whenever there is an activity that could take longer than the available time, instructions are offered for how to judge when to shift the group to the next activity.

- **Remember to have fun!** You came to Ongo to enrich your life, not to add one more burden to it. If the responsibility of being Group Guide is starting to weigh heavy on your mind, take a moment to breathe and relax. Smile. It's all going to be okay.

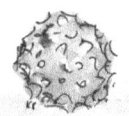

Week 1

WEEK 1 GROUP

The Ongo Circle

*"Entering an ango or practice period away from the busyness of life
is to stop and give honor to ancestors, family, and community.
It is a way to cultivate the light you inherited a thousand years ago
from the first awakened ones. It is a chance to offer
flowers and incense, to bow to the gift of life."*
– Zenju Earthlyn Manuel

Preparation – All participants:

- Bring to this first Group Gathering a written intention that expresses what calls you to Ongo at this moment in your life and what you are hoping to walk away with in your learning by the end of the Ongo journey.

- Bring your planner, calendar, or schedule book, if you use one.

Preparation – Group Guide (the organizer of this Ongo group):

- A day or two before the Group Gathering, remind everyone of the day, time, and place of the gathering and the invitation to bring an intention (see above).

- Read "Leading Group Practice" (page 13) and do the points listed under "Responsibilities of the Guide."

Opening Meditation

Invite everyone to take their seats in the circle.

Read the following, to the group:

> Welcome, everyone, to our Ongo Circle. We gather in a circle because on a circle, we each have a place and can all be equally seen and heard. Here, we all belong and we all matter.
>
> Let us begin by each saying our name into the circle. As each person speaks, welcome them with your presence by silently listening and allowing the length of a full breath before the next person says their name. I will start by sharing my name and taking a breath, and then we will continue around the circle to my left.

Say your name into the circle. Take a full breath. Silently invite the person to your left to continue the round by sharing their name.

Once everyone in the circle has shared their name, read:

> The purpose of the Ongo group is to offer learning, support, and companionship in our practice of wisdom and compassion. One of the ways that we support each other is through our consistent presence and commitment. We ask that we all show up to the majority of the Group Gatherings and Buddy Practices, and do the majority of the Solo Practices.
>
> Another way we support each other is by caring for the vulnerability that naturally comes with practicing something new and unfamiliar. We can create a safe and trusting space for sharing honestly about our learning process. To support that sense of safety and trust, we ask that whatever is shared in our Ongo Group Gatherings be treated as confidential and not spoken of outside these gatherings without permission from the person who shared. We ask that we support one another not to fall into habits of gossip, criticism, or unwanted advice. Instead, let us do our best simply to see each other's vulnerability and notice where it mirrors our own.
>
> A third way we can help each other is by stepping up and stepping back. What that means is that if you are hearing others' voices more often than your own, try stepping up and sharing more, and if you are hearing your own voice more often than others', step back and listen more. In this way, we support both an equality and diversity of voices in our group.
>
> Are you willing to agree to these three requests of commitment, confidentiality, and consideration for all voices?

Pause to check if all agree. If not all are in agreement, ask if there is a simple change to the agreement that would be acceptable for all. If there isn't, we suggest that, for ease and meaningful use of everyone's energy, the group continue only with those participants who are willing to agree to the requests described above. Our experience is that Ongo groups require some form of commitment, confidentiality, and consideration for participants to have a real sense of support from the group.

After all agree, read:

> Look around at your Ongo community. This will be our circle for the Ongo journey. On this journey, we support one another, and we each also take responsibility for our own seat. As we practice, deep material from our lives may come up to be practiced with. It is up to you to determine for yourself how much you are willing to work with in the

moment. Let yourself be stretched but not overwhelmed. If you do get overwhelmed, please let us know, so we can help hold that with you. One of the ways we can help is by offering loving-kindness.

Each week, our gatherings will begin with a meditation to help us arrive, settle, and remember our group purpose. Today, we will do a loving-kindness meditation together that we can return to whenever needed, including moments of individual or collective overwhelm. Loving-kindness is about connection, an offering of unconditional love for ourselves and others. In this, we are not trying to achieve a certain feeling or belief. We are gathering all our attention behind an intention: to connect to and offer the energy of love and kindness that already exists in life, and in our own heart.

Loving-kindness Meditation

Invite everyone to settle into a comfortable seated position.

Ring a bell to signal the beginning of the meditation.

After a moment of silence, read the guidance below to the group. Read in a way that supports the group to relax into the guidance, allowing space and breaths of silence between sentences.

> Close your eyes or simply let them soften, choosing a point where the gaze can rest. Let your energy settle into the body.
>
> Take a few deep breaths, then let the breath fall into its own comfortable rhythm.
>
> Wiggle your toes to gain a sense of where your feet are, and give your neck a stretch to awaken the spine, allowing more space.
>
> As we continue, anytime you feel disconnected or distracted, wiggle your toes to return to the sense of where you are sitting, right now, safe, and belonging in this circle.
>
> Let your belly soften with each breath.
>
> Now, turn your attention to the energy of loving-kindness that lives in you.
>
> Offering this energy of loving-kindness to yourself, say, in the quiet of your own heart, May I be safe. Be healthy. Be happy. Be at ease.
>
> Repeat these phrases to yourself in silence.

Allow a few minutes of silence, then read:

> If you get distracted, gently notice and return to the breath and the phrases, May I be safe. Be healthy. Be happy. Live with ease.
>
> Now, call to mind someone who has helped you. Maybe you have never even met them, but they have inspired you from afar. They could be an adult, a child, a pet.
>
> Offering this energy of loving-kindness, say to them in your heart, May you be safe. Be healthy. Be happy. Be at ease.

Allow a few more minutes of silence, then read:

> With the breath, notice the softening of your belly.
>
> Now, call to mind a dear friend. This can be the first friend that comes to mind.
>
> Turn the energy of loving-kindness towards them. Say in your heart to them, May you be safe. Be healthy. Be happy. Be at ease.

Allow a few more minutes of silence, then read:

> Now, a group of new friends. Turn your inner attention to this Ongo group.
>
> With the energy of loving-kindness, say to them, in the quiet of your heart, May you be safe. Be healthy. Be happy. Be at ease.
>
> May the support of this community, and the teachings and practices offered throughout Ongo, grow peace, wisdom, and compassion in our hearts, in our beings.

Allow a few more minutes of silence, then read:

> Now, let's turn our attention, our loving-kindness, to all beings everywhere.
>
> May all beings, known and unknown, be safe. Be healthy. Be happy. Be at ease.
>
> May all beings be free from suffering.
>
> I will now ring the bell three times: once to remember gratitude for ourselves, once to remember gratitude for each other, and once to remember gratitude for everything else that supports us to gather in this way together. After the third ring, we will close this meditation by putting our palms together in front of our hearts and offering a simple bow to express this gratitude. The bow is a gesture of humility and respect in many traditions.

Ring the bell three times, pausing the length of an inhalation in-between each strike of the bell.

Place your palms together in front of your heart and offer a bow to the circle.

Sharing and Listening

Read this guidance to the group:

> We each were invited to bring a written intention that expresses what calls you to Ongo at this moment in your life, and what you are hoping to walk away with in your learning by the end of the Ongo journey. Starting with whoever feels moved to share first, let's go around the circle now and hear from each other our Ongo intentions. When you share, say your name again and your intention. I ask that we support each other by listening with curiosity and full presence to whoever is sharing, rather than thinking about other things. I also ask that we do not crosstalk, ask questions, or comment on each other's sharing. To support everyone to have time to share, I suggest we keep our sharing to about three minutes each.
>
> Who feels moved to start?

Invite the person who starts to share their name and their Ongo intention.

Continue around the circle until everyone, including you, has shared.

Harvest

Ask the group, "What touched you while sharing and listening to one another?"
Invite anyone who feels moved, including you, to speak. It's okay if no one responds right away or if there is some silence between people sharing. In that silence, the energy may be gathering for someone to speak. Allow space for this by simply breathing and listening until you sense that there is nothing more that wants to be said.

Close by offering gratitude to everyone for their sharing and listening.

Setting up Ongo Buddy Practices

Read to the group:

> This week, we will meet with another Ongo member, either by phone or in person, for our first Ongo Buddy Practice. We will continue to meet once a week with that same person through Week 4 of Ongo. Each month, we will change Ongo Buddies so that we will have the opportunity to deepen our Ongo experience by working one-on-one with different community members

Today, we will select our first Ongo Buddies. Our only recommendation is that family members and life partners wait until the third month to be partnered together in order to care for the vulnerability at the beginning of the learning process and the deep bond of those relationships. Beyond that, the goal here is not to find "perfect pairings" but rather to let an intuitive process unfold. Let's each take a minute now in silence to breathe and imagine, from this circle, which three people you feel called to practice one-on-one with.

After a minute of silence, read:

Now, breathing into the vulnerability that can come with asking someone to be our friend, turn toward one of the three people. With this as our beginning, let's discuss who the pairings will be for this first month. We will have different Ongo Buddies in months two and three, and magic can happen when we don't over-think this process, so we'll just take five minutes for this discussion.

Keep track of time. Let the group know when there's just one minute left for the discussion.

After everyone has a Buddy, read:

After this meeting, please take a moment to connect with your Buddy to schedule your first meeting together. Be sure to read the pages on "Preparing for Buddy Practice" before your first Buddy meeting, if you haven't already. Finally, if in the coming weeks, you or your Buddy aren't showing up consistently for your Buddy Practice together, please reach out to the group and ask if someone else might be willing to be your backup for the month.

Setting up Ongo Solo Practices

Read to the group:

Each week, there are three Solo Practices that we will do on our own time and two Rememberings that expand on the teachings of those Solo Practices. Past Ongo participants found that having a consistent time for Solo Practice each day supported them to remember to practice and feel a greater sense of connection to Ongo throughout their week. We recommend setting aside 30 minutes, three days a week, for Solo Practices. We also recommend setting aside a few minutes for reflection on the days that there are Rememberings. Many find that early morning, before the start of the day, can be a clear and peaceful time for practice. Whenever you choose, aim to find times when you can be both rested and awake.

Invite everyone to take a few minutes to schedule their Solo Practice time for the week and create reminders in their calendar, phone, or on a piece of paper.

Remind everyone to read "Solo Practices: General Directions" (page 7), if they haven't already.

Closing

Ask for a volunteer to guide the group next week. That person will be the Group Guide for Week 2's Group Gathering.

Remind that volunteer to read the pages on "Leading Group Practice" (page 13) and Week 2's Group Gathering pages before the next meeting. Everything they need to know will be in those pages.

Invite everyone to take three full breaths in silence together.

Invite everyone to each share their name and one word that describes what they are taking with them from this first Ongo Group Gathering. Start with the person on your left and go around the circle clockwise until everyone, including you, has shared.

Safety, Trust, and Respect

*"The nonviolent approach does not immediately change the heart of the oppressor.
It first does something to the hearts and souls of those committed to it.
It gives them new self-respect;
it calls up resources of strength and courage they did not know they had."*
– Dr. Martin Luther King, Jr.

Opening Meditation

Take a few minutes to meet your new Buddy, perhaps sharing with them something that they may not know about you yet.

Decide who will read the guided meditation and who will time your silent sitting together.

Whoever is reading, read the following guidance, allowing a silent pause between paragraphs for both of you to follow the guidance being offered:

> Take a deep breath.
>
> Bring your attention to the body, feeling whatever sensations and feelings are present. If needed, take a moment to adjust your posture or seating for comfort and support.
>
> Take another deep breath. On the exhale, gently invite the body and mind to relax and settle.
>
> For the next few minutes, simply rest your attention on the breath, letting it be natural and fluid. If at any point you notice that your attention is lost in thoughts, gently bring it back to resting on the flow of the breath.

Sit together in meditation for 2 minutes.

Whoever is keeping time signals the other when 2 minutes have passed.

Close with a bow of appreciation to your Buddy for sitting with you.

Practicing Safety, Trust, and Respect

Taking turns, slowly read the following guidance out loud to each other:

> Often, when we gather for the first time with a new person or group, needs for safety, trust, and respect arise. Today, we will take the opportunity to turn toward each of

these and explore how they live in us, through a dyad meditation practice. There is no crosstalk or dialogue in this form. Instead, it is an invitation to simply be curious and present with yourself and your Buddy.

In a moment, we will take turns asking each other a few open-ended questions about safety, trust, and respect. When it is our turn to respond, we are invited to share freely whatever response comes. Allow it to be a full exploration, taking time to explore what the word we're being asked about means to us. How does it live in our bodies? What physical sensations and feelings do we associate with it? What is our relationship to it when we're alone, with others, and in a group? How is it when it's fulfilled and not fulfilled? And is there anything else that arises as a response to the question? If we notice that our attention is getting caught up in our own thoughts about what we're saying – for example, judgments about whether or not it's a "good" response, whether we're talking too much or too little, or even whether or not our response makes sense to our Buddy – simply notice, breathe, and return to presence with whatever wants to be spoken through us as a response to the question. We are allowing whatever arises from within to be given voice.

When it is our turn to listen, we are asked to listen in silence, with our full presence. If we notice that our attention is getting caught up in our own thoughts about what's being said – for example, analysis, judgment, comparison, questions, or our own stories – simply notice, breathe, and return to presence with our Buddy. We will not offer any verbal response or confirmation of what we are hearing. We are allowing whatever rises as a response to our question to be given space to be heard.

Take a moment to check in with each other to be sure you both understood the guidance above for listening and responding. If needed, one of you can read the guidance out loud again.

Once both have understood, decide who will be "A" and who will be "B."

Then, bring your presence to the practice:

1. A asks B, "What is *respect*?"
2. B responds while A listens. When B is complete responding, B takes a breath and asks A, "What is *respect*?"
3. A responds while B listens. When A is complete responding, A takes a breath and asks B, "What is *safety*?"

4. B responds while A listens. When B is complete responding, B takes a breath and asks A, "What is *safety*?"

5. A responds while B listens. When A is complete responding, A takes a breath and asks B, "What is *trust*?"

6. B responds while A listens. When B is complete responding, B takes a breath and asks A, "What is *trust*?"

7. A responds while B listens. When A is complete responding, A takes a breath and says that they are complete.

8. Take three full breaths together.

Harvest

"Harvest" how this practice was for each of you. Harvesting is an opportunity to share anything that stands out about your experience, including what you enjoyed, what you found challenging, and what you learned or discovered.

Solo Practice Support

Discuss how you would like to support each other with doing the Solo Practices throughout the week. This could look different for each Buddy, based on what each finds most supportive. *For example, one Buddy might want to send a daily text message or email to the other after they've done their Solo Practice. Another might want to have a short, weekly phone call to share their experiences of doing the Solo Practices that week.*

Closing

Share any appreciations that you have for your time together.

WEEK 1 SOLO PRACTICES

A Place to Start

"An altar is a place where we can lay our wounds and our conflicts and our questions and our scars, giving them to God or the Great Spirit or to the little part of our pea brain that is our wisdom lobe and knows what to do but hasn't kicked in yet. An altar is a place where we lay down our swords and our shields and we ask for guidance. A visual installation dedicated to whatever we consider to be holy, an altar is a reminder to the mind to join with the heart."
– Nina Wise

Today…

Make a physical space that nurtures you. This can be a whole room, but it also can be just the corner of a room or even be outdoors. Choose and create a space that, as much as possible, contributes to a quality of being that is light and deep, alive and still. It's generally helpful if this space is quiet and free of visual clutter. We want to create a place that opens and warms the heart and offers support for the mind to settle down and not get pulled into engaging with anxious distractions. Take the time now to remove or creatively veil anything in this space that doesn't support you in this way.

If you already have such a space, take the time to freshen it up so that it's clean, alive, and speaks to your present-day heart. For example, you may want to dust and remove any items that are no longer relevant to your practice. Be creative – follow your intuition about what wants to be in this space and what doesn't at this moment in your life.

Add to this space anything that seems essential to supporting your Ongo practice. Minimally, you will want a chair or sitting cushion that supports you to sit comfortably and upright for meditation. You may also want favorite writing/drawing pens or pencils, blanket(s), soft lighting or a candle, water, incense, plants or flowers, a gentle alarm or timekeeping device, and photos or images that inspire you and remind you of your spiritual intention.

Write down your Ongo intention, if you haven't already, and place it in the space. What is calling you to Ongo at this moment in your life? What do you hope to walk away with at the end?

Take a few minutes (or more!) once you're done to simply enjoy being in the space. Smile and breathe.

A Place to Start
Remembering

"The sanctuary's physical existence as sacred space mirrors the earth with its smells, light, food, flowers, grass tatami mats, wood, and stone statues. Every person is a Zen temple ... When we take care of ourselves, we take care of the sanctuary. Simultaneously, when we take care of the earth, we take care of humanity, because we are the earth. So, when we enter the sanctuary, we enter ourselves, we bow to our lives, and we make offerings from the earth before we take a seat upon it."
– Zenju Earthlyn Manuel

Today is our first Remembering day. Remembering days invite us to deepen our understanding of the Solo Practice from the day before, in whatever ways we find most supportive. They are an opportunity to freely experiment with the practices that most call to us. For example, on Remembering days, you could:

- Take a few minutes to read the Remembering (the quote) and reflect on its meaning for you, in light of the Solo Practice from the day before. Use the space underneath the Remembering to write down your reflections (this is the only Remembering day in *The Ongo Book* where there is guidance written, rather than blank space).

- Go deeper with the Solo Practice from the day before by doing it again, possibly in a different way or in a different context. Perhaps there's an aspect you would like to explore further or take more time with.

- Do any other practices that you find supportive and heart-opening, like taking a walk outside, meditating, praying, doing yoga, or dancing.

However you choose to practice on Remembering days, minimally, we recommend always reading the quote and taking a moment to consciously connect with your Ongo practice.

Mindfulness of Breath

"Enlightenment is always there. If you breathe in and are aware that you are alive – that you can touch the miracle of being alive – then that is a kind of enlightenment. Many people are alive but don't touch the miracle of being alive."
– Thich Nhat Hanh

The simple meditation practice of paying attention to the breath, the inhalation and the exhalation, has deep and long-lasting benefits, not just as a moment of peace in our day but as a natural instinct that, when remembered, creates the freedom for us to respond to life as we choose instead of merely reacting to life from our conditioned habits of fight, flight, and freeze.

Today…

Sit in the practice space you created on Day 1. Whether you're on a chair, a blanket, or meditation cushion, take some time to find a sitting position that's both comfortable and supports being awake.

Feel your body supported by the Earth below. Rest into the place where your body meets the chair or cushion. Feel what that feels like. If your feet are on the ground, feel that connection and rest into it.

Set a timer for 12 minutes, or ask someone to let you know when 12 minutes has passed. During this time, simply be with the flow of the breath as if you were in the ocean, feeling the rise and fall of the waves. If possible, breathe only through the nose, instead of the mouth, to support the breath to quiet and soften.

Be with the inhalation until it reaches its peak, then the moment of pause, then the release of the exhalation, then the moment of silence, then the inhalation as it naturally picks up again. Continue being with the breath in this way until the time is up. If possible, let the sound of breathing grow ever quieter; let the amount of effort grow ever smaller.

When attention wanders to thoughts, as it often will, gently nudge it back to the in and out flow of the breath and the sense of the body resting on the earth. There's no need for blame or shame about the attention wandering – just return to the simple intention of being present to the flow of breath. There's no right or wrong to any of this – just return to simply being present with the breath.

At the end of the 12 minutes, take a moment to gently stretch your body from its sitting place. Close with an appreciation of yourself for taking this time to be with life's gift of breath and an appreciation of the earth for supporting you.

 Tip – If your focus on the breath is feeling emotionally overwhelming, or you notice that you are disassociating from your body, shift your focus to a place in the body that feels pleasant, calming, and grounding. For example, feeling where your body meets the earth. Or, perhaps a place of warmth on your skin. Then, as you feel re-sourced, expand your focus to include the breath again, and gradually return to mindfulness of the breath. Do this as needed to support yourself to stretch your learning but not be overwhelmed.

 Audio – There is a guided audio recording of this meditation available on The Ongo Companion Website at ongo.global. You can also make your own guided audio meditation by recording yourself reading the practice out loud. If you make your own, remember to speak slowly and allow lots of silence in between instructions so you can easily follow along when listening to it later.

 Instant – Stop, wherever you are. Whether you're standing, sitting, or lying down, take a moment to feel where the body is contacting the earth. Breathe and allow the body to rest into that support. If needed, adjust the body's position to support both comfort and awakeness. Feel the connection with the earth. Now, let your awareness expand to include breath. For the next minute or two, simply be with the flow of the breath, as described in the full practice, gently nudging your attention back to that flow anytime it gets lost in thoughts. Close with a moment of appreciation for yourself for practicing and for the earth for its ever-present support.

 Deepening – Practice mindfulness of the breath both at the beginning and end of your day. As you get more comfortable with it, gradually increase the length of the meditation to 30 minutes or an hour. Once a month, try taking a morning or even a whole day in silence. In that silence, practice maintaining an awareness of the breath and the body's connection to the earth while you go about doing other things, like preparing breakfast or washing dishes.

Mindfulness of Breath
Remembering

"[T]he purpose of meditation is to encourage you to be kind with yourself. Do not count your breaths just to avoid your thinking but to take the best care you can of your breathing. If you are very kind with your breathing, one breath after another, you will have a refreshed, warm feeling in your zazen [meditation]. When you have a warm feeling for your body and your breath, then you can take care of your practice, and you will be fully satisfied. When you are very kind with yourself, naturally you will feel like this."
– Zenkei Blanche Hartman

Mindfulness of Body

"If we are to fully know freedom, we must find that freedom not only in the mind but also in the body, the house of our being. The physical body is our medium for connecting the sacred and the profane, the transcendent and the ordinary, a medium for giving expression to our essential nature, which is unencumbered and open and zesty."
– Nina Wise

The body is a wise instrument, developed over the course of millions of years of adaptation. Practicing mindfulness of the body allows us to access that built-in wisdom, which in turn helps us to both deepen our basic sense of trust, belonging, and "okayness" in life, and to clarify what truly needs attention. As simple as this practice is, it has the power to profoundly affect how we relate to the world. When we are rooted and present within our own bodies, we are less easily swayed by the winds of our thinking or shaken by the words of others. Together with mindfulness of the breath, it is the basis of how *not* to take things personally while still remaining engaged with the world. **For today's practice, feel free to close your eyes anytime that it supports you to tune in more fully to what you're feeling in the body.**

Today…

Sit in your practice space. Whether you're on a chair, a blanket, or meditation cushion, take some time to find a position that's both comfortable and supports being awake.

Settle in. Take a few deep, unhurried, full breaths. Gently stretch out the spine and relax the shoulders, allowing more room for breath and life to come in.

Now, take a deep, full breath and bring attention to your toes. Wiggle your toes slightly. Take a breath and expand your attention to include the whole of your feet. Notice any sensations there. No need to move them or respond. Simply notice. What do these feet that have carried you this far in your life feel like right now? Breathe with whatever you feel.

Taking a full breath, slowly draw your attention up from your feet to your legs, resting it at your knees. Notice any sensations there. As you breathe into these knees that have supported you, what do they feel like? What emotions are carried here? Simply notice. And breathe.

Breathe and draw your awareness up through your upper legs to your hips. Be with your hips. Notice how your legs and torso meet here. Breathe for a moment and be with the whole support system of your legs and hips. Now, breathe into each hip. What sensations arise? What does it feel like here? Simply notice. Simply breathe.

Take a full breath into the abdomen and rest your attention on the belly. What sensations are here? What do you notice? Be with your belly. Breathe with whatever you feel.

Take a full breath into the lungs and bring your awareness into the chest. Let your lungs fill, front and back. Notice for a few breaths the full length of your spine. Take full breaths down and up the back, then rest your attention in the center of your rib cage. What sensations arise? What does it feel like here? Simply notice. And breathe.

Take a breath into your shoulders. Shrug them slightly. With your arms relaxed, gently rotate the shoulders in their sockets once or twice. Let them fill your awareness. What sensations do you feel here? What emotions do you notice? Simply notice. Simply breathe.

Take a long, full breath down each arm to your elbows. What sensations do you notice here? Take another full breath, breathing your way down the forearms into the wrists. Simply notice what's here. Breathe into your hands. Wiggle your fingers. Bring your attention to these hands that have been helping you your whole life. What sensations are here? What emotions do you notice? Be with these hands. Breathe.

Taking full breaths, travel your attention up the arms and into your neck. Gently tilt the head side to side, lightly stretching the neck. Notice the spine in the neck. Notice your throat. Breathe the full length of your neck and throat. What sensations do you feel? What emotions come alive here? Simply notice. Simply breathe.

Take a breath, drawing your attention to the face. Stretch the mouth open for a moment. Bring awareness and breath to all aspects of your face – forehead, eyes, nose, cheeks, chin – being with the sensations that arise. Simply notice, without judgment. Breathe.

Taking a full breath, arrive to the top of your head. Notice how attention here encourages the spine to lengthen.

Now, expand your awareness to include the whole body. Breathe a few long breaths, being with the whole body, then let your attention completely relax. Breathe for a few moments longer. Continue with your eyes closed until you feel ready to shift to mapping.

On the image of the body on page 38, create a map of your meditation today. Color, draw, and write the sensations and feelings that you noticed. Place them close to the area on the body where you experienced them. If you would like some suggestions for words to describe what you felt, see "Feelings" and "Body Sensations" in the Appendix. Also feel free to use only colors and images without words to map your experience.

Tip – If more than you expected arises during this practice, including emotions or memories you have not previously experienced, or you are working with specific trauma, take your time to slow it down. You can do a scan of just one or a few parts of the body at a time, creating breaks for integration with dance, a walk outside, or a phone call to a trusted support person about the experience. Remember, you always have the power to choose the depth that you'd like to explore with each of your meditations.

Audio – There is a guided audio recording of this meditation available on The Ongo Companion Website at <u>ongo.global</u>. You can also make your own guided audio meditation by recording yourself reading the practice out loud. If you make your own, remember to speak slowly and allow lots of silence in between instructions, so you can easily follow along when listening to it later.

Instant – Stop, wherever you are. Whether you're standing, sitting, or lying down, take a few deep, unhurried breaths – full inhale and full exhale. Bring your attention to the body. For the next minute or two, simply notice what sensations are present. As you notice sensations, place your hands where they are arising in the body. Breathe into those places. Close by expanding your awareness to include the whole body and breathing a few deep breaths.

Deepening – Practice mindfulness of the body both at the beginning and end of your day. Before you get out of bed in the morning, and before you fall asleep at night, do a full body scan from head to toe, breathing and gently being with whatever sensations you notice. Incorporate this awareness into other activities during your day, like being present to the sensations in your hand when you type, or breathing with sensations in your chest during an emotional conversation.

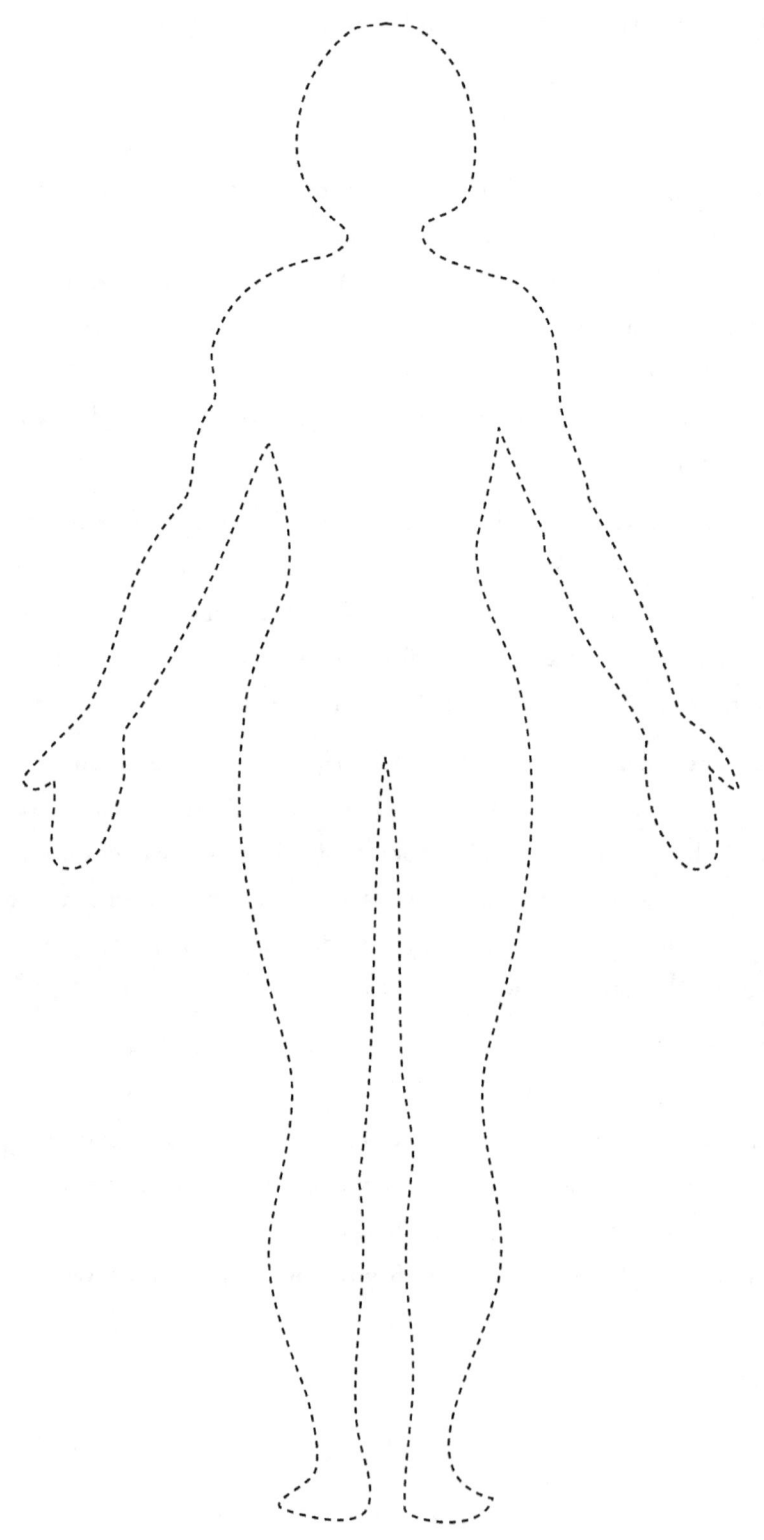

Week 2

The Empathy Circle

"When we listen for the truth of a moment, we know better what to do and what not to do, when to act and when not to act. We hear that we are all here together, and we are all we've got. In Gandhi's terms, we are letting the music of our voices make way for the music of life."
— Mirabai Bush

 Preparation – Group Guide:

- A day or two before the Group Gathering, remind everyone of the day, time, and place of the gathering.

- Read "Leading Group Practice" (page 13) and do the points listed under "Responsibilities of the Guide."

- Prepare one set of Needs cards (see "Needs Cards" on page 276 in the Appendix) for every eight people in the group (i.e., for groups of one to eight people, make one set of cards; for groups of nine to sixteen people, make two sets of cards; for groups greater than sixteen people, make three sets of cards).

 Opening Meditation

Invite everyone to take their seats in the circle.

Welcome everyone by inviting them to say their names into the circle, one at a time. Start with the person on your left and go around the circle from there, ending with you. Ask the group to bring their presence to each person by taking a full breath of silence between names.

Ring a bell to signal the beginning of the sitting meditation.

After a moment of silence, read the guidance below to the group. Read in a way that supports the group to relax into the guidance, allowing space and breaths of silence between sentences:

> Settle in to where you are sitting. Sit comfortably and at ease.
>
> Let your eyes soften or close. Allow yourself to feel the full support of the chair or cushion and the floor beneath you.

Allow yourself to take full breaths in, breathing in through your nose, filling your lungs fully.

Allow yourself to release full breaths out, breathing out through your nose, letting your belly soften as you let go.

Allow yourself to be still.

Allow your belly to soften a little bit more with each breath.

Soft belly allows a little more space for us to be mindfully present.

Each breath gives way to a little more compassionate listening – to ourselves and to the world around us.

Connecting with ourselves and others in this way is the beginning of empathy. Empathy enables us to openly receive what is being experienced, by ourselves and others, from a place of love rather than fear.

Sit in silence for three more minutes and then ring the bell three times to end the meditation.

Place your palms together and offer a bow of gratitude to the circle.

Introduction to Empathy

Read to the group:

Today we're going to explore a practice called "Empathy." Empathy turns the listening up in our hearts and quiets the mind by engaging our sense of curiosity about ourselves and others.

We consider Empathy to have five key components, in this order:

1. <u>Curiosity</u> – In English, the word *curiosity* comes from the Latin root *cura,* which means "care." When we begin with this caring energy, we invite exploration without an agenda. We're here to find out what's here. This child-like inquiry naturally inspires mindful presence.

2. <u>Mindful Presence</u> – Being mindful means to be aware, and being present means to exist. Mindful presence is nothing special; it is a newborn infant's state of being, being moment-to-moment with what is happening, without separation, concept, or judgment.

3. <u>Intention to Connect</u> – The intention to connect makes our listening active. It sets our sights on understanding and relating to that which is alive in each moment in ourselves and others, rather than reacting, analyzing, or fixing. We are using our power to choose curiosity and mindful presence over other forms of engagement.

4. <u>Focus on Universal Needs</u> – What is alive in each moment is the expression of universal needs, the current of life that runs through all thoughts, feelings, words, and actions. By focusing on universal needs, we are opening our listening to something that goes deeper than the words we use to describe it. We are validating the truth of our existence together.

5. <u>Confirmation</u> – This is the only component of Empathy that involves speaking or acting. Until this step, our understanding of what universal needs someone might be expressing is just our best guess. Confirmation offers an opportunity for us to check our understanding with the person we're listening to. It is the outward expression of all the other components of Empathy, letting the person we're listening to know that we are present with them, validate their experience, and show we are curious to explore further.

The first four components of Empathy – curiosity, presence, intention, and focus on universal needs – are completely silent. Only the fifth component, confirmation, involves any talking. Empathy is four parts listening and only one part talking.

Our next activity will give us an opportunity to put these concepts into practice.

Empathy Circles

For groups of more than eight people, divide the group (including yourself) evenly into smaller groups of no more than eight. For example, a group of eleven would divide into a group of five and a group of six. This gives everyone enough time to share.

Invite each group to sit in their own circle with a deck of Needs cards spread out face-up on the floor or a table in the middle. If possible, it's best if there is some space between groups so that everyone in each circle can easily hear one another without being distracted by the voices in another circle.

Read this guidance to everyone:

One person (in each group) will share for a few minutes about something that is happening in their life. This could be something either painful or joyful. The only request around what you share is that you share something that is alive and meaningful to you today, and something that allows you to practice being vulnerable, without being overwhelmed. In other words, choose to share what you would consider to be a medium weight, not a light weight or heavy weight.

While the speaker is sharing, everyone else in the group listens silently, bringing curiosity, mindful presence, and an intention to connect to the speaker.

After the speaker has finished sharing, the listeners focus on universal needs by looking at the Needs cards in the middle of the group and silently guessing which needs seem important to the speaker.

Each of the listeners then offers confirmation to the speaker by quietly picking up one or two Needs cards and placing them in front of the speaker.

The speaker then looks at the Needs cards that were placed in front of them and takes a minute to quietly receive these words by breathing and feeling whatever feelings are touched inside. When the speaker feels ready to move on from this connection, they put the cards back into the center of the circle.

Now, another person in the circle becomes the speaker and the Empathy Circle repeats until everyone in the circle has had a chance to share.

Throughout the Empathy Circle, the only person who ever speaks is the person sharing. Listeners are asked to respect the space by refraining from commenting or asking questions. We will have an opportunity after this practice as a whole group to share about our experiences of listening and speaking.

One last suggestion before we get started: if, at any point, as a listener or speaker, you find yourself getting caught up in your own thoughts, simply breathe and come back to presence with what's being shared. As a speaker, this means bringing your presence to whatever wants to be spoken through you without worrying about whether it makes sense or how it sounds to others. As a listener, this also means that, when choosing from the Needs cards, you simply select cards from a place of curiosity, mindful presence, and intention to connect without worrying about whether or not it's the "right" word or the "right" guess.

Check if anyone is unclear about the practice and would like to hear the instructions again. Once everyone is clear, invite everyone to take a breath together and to bring their presence to the Empathy Circle.

Invite everyone to begin. Participants can self-select who will be the first speaker in each group.

Keep track of time for the group. Allowing at least 10 minutes for "Harvest" and "Closing" below, let everyone know when they are halfway through their available time for the Empathy Circle. Ask that each group balances the remaining time so that everyone has the opportunity to share.

Give one more time reminder to everyone five minutes before the start of "Harvest." If participants seem to require more time than is available, suggest to the group that those who would like more support could ask their Ongo Buddies to meet with them after the Group Gathering.

Close by inviting everyone back into one circle (if in separate groups) and by gathering the Needs cards.

Harvest

Read to the group:

> Harvest is a time when we are all invited to share our experiences of the practice today. What touched you? What challenged you? How was it to receive the Needs cards? What did you learn about yourself and your understanding of empathy? What did you learn about your own mindful presence?

Invite anyone who feels moved, including you, to speak.

When Harvest is complete, read to the group:

> Our Empathy Circle practice is a way for us to support one another as a community on the path of Ongo. When we share our hearts in the circle, we place our trust in the group in a way that invites other hearts forward. It is a gift to all. Together, we can rewrite the story that many of us have been taught, the story that says no one wants to hear about our struggles or our triumphs, that they are too small to matter to others or that they are a burden rather than a gift. Empathy contributes a nourishing sense of connection to everyone, listeners and sharers alike.

Each week that we gather, we will always have the option to hold an Empathy Circle after the opening meditation if there is something on anyone's heart or mind that wants to be shared. Instead of hearing from everyone, we will simply make time for those who feel called to share – one, two, or three people. If someone calls for an Empathy Circle, it would happen after the opening meditation, and we would still allow at least one full hour for the other practices.

This practice is one of the many gifts of Ongo to support us as a community and to help each of us grow.

Close by offering gratitude to everyone for their sharing and listening.

Closing

Ask for a volunteer to guide the group next week. Give that person the deck(s) of Needs cards.

Remind that volunteer to read the pages on "Leading Group Practice" (page 13) and Week 3's Group Gathering before the next meeting. Everything they need to know will be in those pages.

Invite everyone to take a collective full breath together.

Invite everyone to each share their name and one word that describes what they are taking with them from this second Ongo Group Gathering. Start with the person on your left and go around the circle clockwise until everyone, including you, has shared.

Empathy

"With empathy we don't direct, we follow. Don't just do something, be there."
– Marshall B. Rosenberg, Ph.D.

Opening Meditation

Choose one of you to time a five-minute meditation.

Sit in silence together, being with the breath, the body, and the earth.

Whoever is keeping time signals the other when five minutes have passed.

Close with a bow of appreciation to your Buddy for sitting with you.

Sharing and Empathic Listening

Taking turns, slowly read the following guidance out loud to each other:

> Today, we are going to take turns sharing about something that is happening in our lives. While one is sharing, the other will listen with curiosity, mindful presence, intention to connect, and a focus on needs, all in silence. From time to time, the listener will also offer short, empathic guesses about the feelings and Needs that are being expressed, using the Needs Wheel on page 271 in the Appendix as a reference.

> For example, the listener might ask, "Are you feeling sad because you need connection?" or offer just a one-word guess about a Need, as in "Trust?". Other than those short, empathic guesses, the sharer will be the only one speaking. As listeners, we are following the sharer's lead and not trying to analyze the sharer's story or be "right" about our guesses. The guesses are simply reflections of our presence with the sharer. We will continue this way until the sharer arrives to a natural sense of completion for the moment. Then, we will switch roles.

> When sharing, we will each choose to share something that is alive and meaningful to us today and that allows us to practice being vulnerable without being overwhelmed. It is up to each of us to decide what we feel up for talking about today.

> When listening, if our mind jumps to advice, judgment, consoling, sympathy, or commiseration, we will simply breathe and return to listening silently with curiosity, mindful presence, intention to connect, and a focus on needs.

If at any point, either of us experiences a memory or emotion that feels overwhelming, we can ask to slow things down and decide whether or not to continue. If we decide not to continue, we can discuss what other form of support would be helpful in the moment. For example, we can do a short meditation together, then return to the practice. Or we can make a plan for the person experiencing overwhelm to get outside support, then meet again later to follow up and complete the practice.

Whatever is shared, let us hold ourselves and each other with wise care and compassion throughout this practice.

Decide who will share first and who will listen first. Have the Needs Wheel in the Appendix accessible.

1. <u>Sharer</u> shares about something happening in their life that's present on their heart and mind.

2. <u>Listener</u> listens with curiosity, mindful presence, intention to connect, and a focus on needs, all in silence.

3. When the sharer comes to a breathing place, a pause, the <u>listener</u> looks at the Needs Wheel and offers confirmation with a simple, empathic guess about the feelings and Needs that are being expressed. *For example, "Are you feeling sad because you're needing acceptance?" or "Am I hearing a need for trust?" or "Are you needing to be seen?" or "I'm connecting to needs of respect and consideration; how are these landing for you?" or just Needs words, as in "Love?" or "Compassion?"* Offer just one line – one Need – at a time. Let it be received, then take a breath.

4. Breathe together.

5. <u>Sharer</u> continues sharing whatever is still alive and present in their heart to say about the situation.

6. When there is another pause, the <u>listener</u> offers confirmation with simple, empathic guesses about the feelings and Needs that are being expressed.

7. Continue until <u>sharer</u> feels complete, often indicated by a relaxing of the energy.

8. Then switch roles.

Closing Harvest

After both have had an opportunity to share and to listen, harvest by sharing any learnings about yourselves and any appreciations from being listened to in this way.

WEEK 2 SOLO PRACTICES

Mindfulness of Needs

"If we contemplate desires and listen to them, we are actually no longer attaching to them; we are just allowing them to be the way they are. Then we come to the realization that the origin of suffering, desire, can be laid aside and let go of."
–Ven. Ajahn Sumedho

Today...

Sit in your practice space. Follow the guidance from the "Mindfulness of the Breath" practice (page 32), except this time, set your timer for 7 minutes instead of 12. We are suggesting a shorter meditation today to give more time for the rest of the practice, however feel free to sit for longer.

Afterwards, look at the Needs Wheel on page 271 in the Appendix. Turn the wheel and see which Need speaks to you most in this moment. Don't think about it too much – just let the word jump off the page.

Take another minute to feel what you feel when you say that Need word to yourself. Where do you feel it in your body? Touch that place. Breathe with the sensations. What does it feel like there? If you have trouble identifying body sensations, look at the "Body Sensations" page in the Appendix for suggestions.

Write or draw that Need in a place where you will be reminded of it throughout the day. *For example, you might make a card that sits on your desk or a picture that you set as the background on your phone or tablet.*

On that same reminder, write these questions:

- What do I feel when this Need is satisfied?
- What do I feel when this Need is not satisfied?
- What actions or words contribute to this Need's satisfaction?

Throughout the day, use this reminder to continue to listen to how the body communicates that Need, and feel what that Need feels like in different situations. Notice what fulfills that Need and what doesn't.

Write in your journal anything that you discover.

Instant – Right now, look at the Needs Wheel on page 271 in the Appendix and see which Need speaks to you most in this moment. Don't think about it too much – just let the word jump off the page. Say that Need word to yourself. Notice where you feel it in your body and what it feels like there. Take a moment to simply breathe with any feelings and sensations that are connected for you to that Need. As you continue on with the rest of your day, pay extra attention to what actions or words contribute to this Need feeling satisfied in you.

 Deepening – Make this an ongoing practice by choosing a different Need word to explore each week. Keep a regular journal of these Needs in which you record the feelings and body sensations that are connected to each Need when it's satisfied and when it's not satisfied. Record the specific actions or words that you notice contribute to a Need's satisfaction in you.

Mindfulness of Needs
Remembering

"In judging our progress as individuals, we tend to concentrate on external factors such as one's social position, influence and popularity, wealth and standard of education. These are, of course, important in measuring one's success in material matters, and it is perfectly understandable if many people exert themselves mainly to achieve all these. But internal factors may be even more crucial in assessing one's development as a human being. Honesty, sincerity, simplicity, humility, pure generosity, absence of vanity, readiness to serve others – qualities which are within easy reach of every soul – are the foundation of one's spiritual life."
– Nelson Mandela

Meeting Needs

"When any experience of body, heart, or mind keeps repeating in consciousness, it is a signal that this visitor is asking for a deeper and fuller attention. While the general rule in meditation is to stay open to the flow of whatever arises, when we encounter an insistent visitor, we must recognize that this is its way of asking us to give it more attention, to understand it more clearly."
– Jack Kornfield

Sometimes when we connect to a particular Need, we find that it stirs up pain or discomfort. This is often called an "unmet" Need. Rather than feel a sense of settling or peace when connecting to that Need, we touch impatience, frustration, or wounding. We may notice a restless seeking for fulfillment or a hopeless despair. These feelings let us know there is something alive in us that is wanting to be "met" with a deeper level of presence and curiosity. This is a different understanding of what it means to "meet" a Need. Our feelings are inviting us to meet our Need, like we would meet someone we are genuinely curious about getting to know. And when there is pain present, the first layer of meeting often involves becoming aware of the thoughts and beliefs that surround that Need in us.

Today…

Sit in your practice space, practicing mindfulness of the breath for a few minutes.

Now, choose a Need from the Needs Wheel (page 271) that brings up feelings of discomfort, frustration, or pain. If you are doing this for the first time, don't choose a heavy weight. Instead, choose a Need that only stirs up mild to medium discomfort for you. The aim is to practice, not to become overwhelmed.

In your journal, take 5 to 10 minutes to write down any thoughts and beliefs you have related to that Need. These might be thoughts or beliefs about yourself, about others, or about the Need. *For example, here are some typical kinds of thoughts:*

- Thoughts involving the verb **to be,** as in *"My partner **is** insensitive"* or *"I **am** lazy."*
- Thoughts involving the words **always** and **never,** as in *"I will **never** be free."*
- Thoughts involving predictions of the **future,** as in *"He **won't** understand."*
- **"Should"** and **"have to"** thinking, as in *"I **should** be more calm"* or *"I **have to** change."*

- **Beliefs** and **blanket statements,** as in *"I don't matter"* and *"They don't care about me."*
- **Right/wrong, good/bad evaluations,** as in *"I failed"* and *"I'm right."*
- **Interpretations,** as in *"rejected," "manipulated," "abandoned," "attacked"*

When it feels like a pretty complete list of your thoughts and beliefs around that Need (often, they just start repeating as variations on the same thoughts)**, take a deep breath and bring awareness to the body.**

Looking at your list of thoughts and beliefs, read the first one out loud to yourself. Notice what you feel in the body after you say that thought out loud. If it's hard to identify what you are feeling, take a look at the "Feelings" and "Body Sensations" pages in the Appendix and see which words jump out at you.

Breathe with the sensations that you feel. Be with these feelings and sensations as if they were a baby's cries, embracing them with a parent's love and compassion rather than avoiding or getting lost in them, or trying to hurry through the practice.

Continue in the same way with each of the thoughts on your list, one at a time. If at any point, a particular feeling or body sensation wants extra attention, take the time to be with that feeling, perhaps placing your hand on that part of your body while you breathe compassionately into it.

At the end of the list, take a few long, deep breaths, letting go of these thoughts for now and breathing ease into the body. Feel the support of the earth.

Close by writing or drawing the Need that you started with, however you'd like to depict it, in your journal or on a separate piece of paper. Be creative – for example, in your depiction, you may want to include some of the stronger thoughts surrounding that Need.

Breathe and take one last moment to honor and appreciate this Need that you're re-meeting today.

Meeting Needs
Remembering

"Ultimately, we can consider meditation a practice that constitutes resistance to the myriad ways that we are discouraged in our society from tuning out the noise and tuning into ourselves, from developing both the clarity of mind and the softness of heart that are sorely needed in order for us to address injustice effectively and create the conditions for peace."

– Alycee J. Lane

Being Needs

"The intimacy that arises in listening and speaking truth is only possible if we can open to the vulnerability of our own hearts. Breathing in, contacting the life that is right here, is our first step."
– Tara Brach

Most of us have been conditioned to think of Needs in a very dualistic way – we either have them or we don't, they are either met or they are unmet. They become objects outside of us that we can possess or lose, or act as external gods that we must somehow satisfy. To think this way is to lose a part of ourselves and miss an opportunity to connect with life.

Needs are likes notes on a scale. When we connect with a Need, it's as if we play that note. Through listening to each note's sound and how it resonates through our whole being, we are becoming more intimate with those aspects of life. The entire musical scale of Needs *is* life. We are deepening our intimacy with all of life. Today, we'll explore what it is to *be* Needs rather than to *have* them or to get them *met*. To be Needs is to be in touch with the qualities of life. To be Needs is, in fact, to be exactly who we are

Today…

Sit in your practice space and take a few minutes to settle into present, mindful awareness of the body and the breath. Without forcing it, allow your mind and body to relax into the support of the earth and the rhythm of the breath.

Choose a Need from the Needs Wheel that feels heart-opening to you in this moment. Don't think about it too much – just let the word jump off the page.

Now, say that Need word to yourself a few times. Each time you say the word, breathe and give space, continuing to be mindful of the body and the breath. No need to rush.

Notice where you feel the energy of that Need, even subtly. Where does it express itself in the body? For example, is it in the chest, or the belly, or the arms, or all over?

Say that Need word to yourself again, and notice how the body responds. What are the sensations like? For example, are they tingly, or flowy, or calm, or expansive?

Breathe and allow those feelings and sensations to expand throughout your whole body. What does that Need feel like when it's really full, really deeply satisfied? Don't just register the feelings intellectually as words. Allow yourself to have a felt experience. If it helps, say the Need word to yourself a few more times, breathing and giving room for it to express itself through the body.

To close:

- **If you have been able to follow this guidance so far and feel a living, breathing experience of the energy of that Need in your body, then take a couple more minutes to savor and be with it.** Breathe and rest into that energy.

- **If you have not yet been able to feel the energy of the Need in your body, try one of the following:**

  - **Remember a moment in your life when that Need was deeply satisfied, deeply met.** Where were you? Who was there? Take some time to bring back that memory. What contributed to that Need being so fulfilled? Perhaps it was something someone said or did, or something you said or did. Once you have a connection to that memory, notice what you feel in the body. What does it feel like when that Need is fulfilled in you? Where do you feel it? As your attention shifts more to those present-moment feelings and sensations in the body, you can let go of the memory and simply rest into that living, breathing experience of the energy of the Need.

  - **Imagine what would have to happen in your life for that Need to feel deeply fulfilled, even if it seems like an impossible wish.** Now, imagine that actually happening. Visualize it. Take some time to see yourself there, in that reality. Feel it. Experience the actual happening of it. Once there's a connection to that experience, notice what you feel in the body. What does it feel like when that Need is fulfilled in you? Where do you feel it? As your attention shifts more to those present-moment feelings and sensations in the body, you can let the imagination fade and rest into that living, breathing experience of the energy of the Need.

Tip – It's possible that this practice could also touch grief or mourning around a Need. If that happens, allow yourself to open to that experience, and feel it in the body. Let the feeling of the earth supporting your body hold you, as you feel the grief and allow it to express itself. As you do this, feel the sweet longing that is expressing itself through the mourning. As that longing becomes clearer, breathe and rest into that energy.

 Audio – There is a guided audio recording of this meditation available on The Ongo Companion Website at <u>ongo.global</u>. You can also make your own guided audio meditation by recording yourself reading the practice out loud. If you make your own, remember to speak slowly and allow lots of silence in between instructions so you can easily follow along when listening to it later.

 Instant – Right now, look at the Needs Wheel and choose a Need that feels heart-opening to you in this moment. Don't think about it too much – just let the word jump off the page. Now take a moment to imagine that Need really fulfilled. Notice where you feel it in your body and what it feels like there. Breathe with those feelings and sensations. Savor it, then bring that energy into your day.

 Deepening – Practice this as a daily meditation. Choose a different Need to connect to each day, or choose the same Need and practice connecting to it freshly each time. Experiment with choosing Needs that don't feel as easy to connect to. In your daily life, start shifting your focus from the "met-ness" or "unmet-ness" of Needs to noticing how, in any given moment, a Need is living and breathing inside of you – where it is in the body and what it feels like there.

Week 3

WEEK 3 GROUP

Self-Empathy

Don't go outside your house to see flowers.
My friend, don't bother with that excursion.
Inside your body there are flowers.
One flower has a thousand petals.
That will do for a place to sit.
Sitting there you will have a glimpse of beauty
inside the void and out of it,
before the gardens and after gardens.
– Kabir,
translated by Robert Bly

Preparation – All participants:

- Bring your copy of *The Ongo Book* and your journal to this Group Gathering.

Preparation – Group Guide:

- A day or two before the Group Gathering, remind everyone of the day, time, and place of the Gathering.
- Read "Leading Group Practice" (page 13) and do the points listed under "Responsibilities of the Guide."
- Lay the Needs cards out in an attractive mandala or spiral in the center of the circle.

Opening Meditation

Invite everyone to take their seats in the circle.

Welcome everyone by inviting them to say their names into the circle, one at a time. Start with the person on your left and go around the circle from there, ending with you. Ask the group to bring their presence to each person by taking a full breath of silence between names.

Ring a bell to signal the beginning of the sitting meditation.

After a moment of silence, read the guidance below to the group. Read in a way that supports the group to relax into the guidance, allowing generous space and full breaths of silence between sentences:

Settle in to a relaxed and awake sitting position, letting your eyes soften or close.

Feel the chair, the cushion, even the ground beneath you and its support. Feel the heart beating in your chest.

Take a full breath in, filling the body with life.

Release the breath completely, letting go of any unnecessary tension or holding.

Let your senses be open wide, taking in any sounds, loud or soft. Taking in any sensations, strong or gentle. Feeling any emotions, uncomfortable or comfortable.

Allow yourself to be gently curious about it all. Curious about what's there, without needing to change any of it.

Let the breath be your support in this, the inhalation and exhalation like gentle waves under your boat as you ride the sea of whatever arises.

Sit in silence for a couple minutes, then read:

Let yourself be curious about the mind. Sometimes we have thoughts and they simply drift in and out like our breath. Sometimes we have thoughts and our attention becomes engaged. We can lose connection to our sense of body, our sense of breath, our sense of place.

If that happens, gently return to body, breath, earth. There's nothing wrong with having gone on a ride with thinking. Just gently come back to presence with everything else that's here. Sensation, sound, feeling, breath.

Sit in a silence for a few more minutes, then read, slowly:

Pema Chödrön says it this way, "[B]y beginning to look so clearly and so honestly at ourselves – at our emotions, at our thoughts, at who we really are – we begin to dissolve the walls that separate us from others. Somehow all of these walls, these ways of feeling separate from everything else and everyone else, are made up of opinions. They are made up of dogma; they are made of prejudice. These walls come from our fear of knowing parts of ourselves."

Sit in silence for a couple more minutes, and then ring the bell three times to end the meditation.

Place your palms together and offer a bow of gratitude to the circle.

Introduction to Self-Empathy

Invite everyone to take out their copies of *The Ongo Book* and open to the "Communication Flow Chart" on page 275 in the Appendix.

Read to the group:

> Notice at the top of the Communication Flow Chart that it begins with Self-Empathy. To be wise and compassionate in our communication, we begin by being present to what is happening within.

Invite everyone to look at "Self-Empathy" on page 274 in the Appendix.

Continue to read:

> Notice on the Self-Empathy page that we also title it "What We're Bringing into the Room." With Self-Empathy, we are taking responsibility for what we bring to our connections with the world around us, including what triggers us, whether it is from our past or what is happening in the present moment.
>
> When we put together the practices we have been learning over the last two weeks, we have the beginning of a clear roadmap for navigating our inner terrain, terrain that can include judgmental thinking and feelings like anger, fear, guilt, shame, depression, and anxiety. This roadmap is what we call "Self-Empathy."
>
> Self-Empathy is an alternative to the belief that we need to get rid of our judgmental thinking or the emotions that challenge us. Rather than avoid what we experience, Self-Empathy invites us to turn toward it with clarity, compassion, and a grounded presence by engaging practices we have already been working with, practices like mindfulness of the body and the breath, awareness of thoughts, and connecting to the energy of Needs. When we practice, we are shifting our relationship to ourselves. We are opening to the possibility of change in moments that we feel stuck and allowing creative solutions to emerge in situations that seem hopeless. We are bringing connection to the experiences of disconnection in our lives, whether it's a conflict with someone else or a struggle within ourselves. To borrow a popular phrase, we are "being the change we want to see."

Take a few minutes for a group Harvest of the meditation and the introduction to Self-Empathy. Invite anyone who feels moved to share with the group about what the meditation or listening to the introduction to Self-Empathy inspired or touched in them.

Practicing Self-Empathy

Invite everyone to take out their journal, a piece of paper, and something to write with.

Read the guidance for the practice to the group, pausing after each numbered or lettered step long enough for everyone, including you, to follow the instructions:

1. Write down in your journal a situation you recently experienced with one other person that did not go the way you liked. What did you say or do? What did the other person say or do? Focus for a moment simply on what actually happened.

2. Now write down any thoughts you have about the situation. What are your judgments, beliefs, interpretations, or "shoulds" about yourself in this situation? What are your judgments, beliefs, interpretations, or "shoulds" about the other person in the situation? Give yourself the freedom to name these thoughts honestly, without trying to change them.

3. For this next step, look at "Self-Empathy" in the Appendix as a visual reference. We're going to take each thought we wrote down and practice the first three steps of Self-Empathy with them. Choosing one of your thoughts:

    a. Place one hand on your forehead and clearly name the thought as a thought, saying silently or out loud, "When I tell myself _____," inserting the thought. *For example, "When I tell myself I was being judged ... "*

    b. Taking a breath, bring your hand to your heart. Feel what emotions or body sensations you feel in your body and name them. Say silently or out loud, "I feel _____," inserting the feeling. *For example, "I feel tense and sad ... "*

    c. Taking a breath, bring your hand to your belly. Sense whatever Needs are there and name them. Say silently or out loud, "Because I need _____," inserting the Needs. *For example, "Because I need acceptance and belonging."* Write down the Needs you discover on a separate piece of paper.

4. Repeat these three steps of Self-Empathy with each of the other thoughts that you wrote down earlier. Start again by placing a hand on your forehead, saying, "When I tell myself ...," followed by the next thought that you wrote down. Continue by feeling and naming the feelings that are present, then sensing and naming the Needs. Write down any Needs you discover. Remember to breathe and let your hand help guide your attention in the process.

When it seems like almost everyone has finished practicing Self-Empathy with the thoughts they wrote down, ask the remainder of the group to complete whichever thought they are currently practicing with.

Once everyone has finished, invite everyone, including yourself, to form into pairs.

Read this guidance to the group:

> Give your partner the paper on which you wrote the Needs that you discovered. In a moment, you will each take a turn reflecting your partner's Needs back to them. As you read the Needs aloud, offer them one at a time with full breaths in between so that your partner can really take them in.
>
> Partners, when it is your turn to hear your Needs reflected back to you, simply receive and breathe. Let your hands rest on your belly and feel the body's response to hearing each Need. Breathe and allow those feelings and sensations to expand throughout your whole body. Without any effort, notice if your hands stay on your belly or if they want to open and rest on your lap.

Invite everyone to begin.

Once everyone has finished receiving their Needs, invite the group to take three breaths together.

Read to the group:

> The significance of the hands on the belly or open on the lap can sometimes be an indicator of what is happening within us. When the hands stay closed on the belly, there may be a Need that wants to be mourned or celebrated. It may be asking us to go deeper into learning what else surrounds that Need, which we will do in later practices on Core Beliefs and Forgiveness.
>
> At other times, when the hands open and relax into our laps, we may be ready to take action in the world. With hands open to give and receive, we name whatever request for action arises out of our connection to the Needs.
>
> Take a moment now to write down what the placement of your hands indicated to you. Write down any insights you have discovered about your situation, and any clear, doable requests for action that have arisen for yourself or the other person in this situation.

Harvest

Invite anyone who feels moved to share their insights, learnings, or discoveries from this practice with the group.

Close by offering gratitude to everyone for their sharing and practice.

Closing

Ask for a volunteer to guide the group next week. Give that person the deck(s) of Needs cards.

Remind that volunteer to read the pages on "Leading Group Practice" (page 13) and Week 4's Group Gathering before the next meeting. Everything they need to know will be in those pages.

Invite everyone to take a collective full breath together.

Invite everyone to each choose a Need card from the center that describes what they are taking with them from this third Ongo Group Gathering.

Starting with the person on your left, invite each person to share their Need with the group by holding their card face-out so everyone can see it. Go around the circle clockwise until everyone, including you, has shared.

Joining Alliances with Comparing Mind

*"A mind that is always comparing, always measuring, will always engender illusion.
If I am measuring myself against you, who are clever, more intelligent,
I am struggling to be like you and I am denying myself as I am.
I am creating an illusion."*
– Jiddu Krishnamurti

As we deepen our practice of empathy, we become more acutely aware of our thoughts, judgments (positive and negative), and labeling of our experiences, ourselves, and the people around us. We can, at times, be at odds with our mind as it tries to convince us that our comparisons are true. We call this "Comparing Mind."

Anything can awaken comparing mind: a social media post, a co-worker's comment, the presence of a teacher, even a neighbor's home improvement project. Once awakened, it can keep us up long into the night. We see what someone has posted on social media and compare that image against one of our internal images of self. We hear a co-worker gossip about another co-worker and compare that negatively against our angelized inner story about our self. We see how a teacher of ours places themselves out in the world to share their wisdom, and we compare that to our self-doubt. We see a neighbor make an improvement to their house that we wish we had done, and comparing mind places us at odds by thinking something negative about either that other person or ourselves.

Comparing mind places us in diametrically opposed positions. It is that thinking that constantly compares ourselves to others and others to ourselves. It is the dense fusion of judgments, fear, and separation that maintains protection over our hearts and drowns out our ability to listen and connect to ourselves or others. As Stephen and Ondrea Levine put it, "Comparing mind never lets us be. Comparing mind is complaining mind. It's too big! It's too small!" Truly, comparing mind places us at odds with everyone around us and, ultimately, ourselves.

One of the principles of nonviolence is to join alliances, even with those we would call our enemies. In nonviolent practice we understand that it is an illusion to think we can rid the world of our enemies, even when our enemies are our own unwanted thoughts or feelings, so it is a better use of effort and energy to make them into allies.

When we join alliances with our own comparing mind, we accept that there is nothing to get rid of. We become allies to our self. Even our most judgmental thoughts can become guideposts for connection. As we deepen our understanding and acceptance of comparing mind, we return to seeing ourselves and others as simply human. We return to seeing that we are just walking each other home.

Preparation – Before you meet:

- **Take a few minutes to free-write on how you define yourself in relation to a group you interact with (i.e., friends online, co-workers, neighbors, etc.).** We suggest you choose a group other than your Ongo group. *Here's an example of how that might look, using "family" as the group: "I define myself as willing to heal, talk, and try to forgive. I am the one who tracks every birthday. I am the one who calls. If I did not call my family, then there would be no relationship. I give everything and get nothing. I am completely different from anyone in my family."*

- **Below your definition of yourself, write down three clear observations that have supported this definition.** An observation is like a video camera's view of what happened, not your evaluation. *For example: "I take Nonviolent Communication trainings. I called each family member this year on their birthday. I eat organic vegetarian food."*

- **Name and define the group.** Be as elaborate as you like. *For example: "My family of origin: I define this group as hostile and unwilling to heal. They do not call or reach out. They do not speak the same language as me. They are only interested in themselves. They do not give unless they will get something in return."*

- **Below your definition of the group, write three clear observations that have supported this definition.** *For example: "No one in my family takes NVC trainings or goes to therapy. No one in my family came to my wedding. All members of my family eat meat."*

- **Bring these writings to your Buddy Practice.**

Opening Meditation

Choose one of you to time a three-minute meditation.

Sit in silence together, inviting presence into this moment of being together.

Whoever is keeping time signals the other when three minutes have passed.

Close with a bow of appreciation to your Buddy for sitting with you.

Joining Alliances with Comparing Mind

Choose who will be A and who will be B. Buddy A will follow the guidance below marked "A," and Buddy B will follow the guidance below marked "B."

A: Share what you wrote before the call.
B: Tune into curiosity, mindful presence, intention to connect, and a focus on needs – this is all in silence.

A: Read again – just the part about how you define the group and the related actual observations.
B: Using the Needs Wheel in the Appendix, guess aloud the Needs you are sensing spoken inside what is shared by Buddy A. Let the Needs words sprinkle like spring rain, anywhere from five to eight Needs words.

A: Take in each word. If the belly softens, let it land; if there is a questioning or the mind enters, let it go. Reflect back which Needs words landed.
B: Simply take note, writing the Needs words that landed for Buddy A.

A: Now read the part about how you define yourself in relation to this group and the related actual observations.
B: Listen in silence. When Buddy A is complete, guess aloud the Needs you are sensing spoken inside what is shared, anywhere from five to eight Needs words.

A: Take in each word. If the belly softens, let it land; if there is a questioning or the mind enters, let it go. Reflect back which Needs words landed.
B: Simply take note, writing the Needs words that landed for Buddy A.

A: Now settle in and receive the following guided meditation and see what happens.
B: Read the following to give guidance to Buddy A. Allow pauses so Buddy A can fully engage the guidance. Sense the pacing. Breathe.

> I invite you to take a few deep breaths into your body.
>
> Noticing that the mind has many voices, let its words just float.
>
> Let the even flow of your breath soften the belly.

B: Read one or two Needs words from the list you made from Buddy A. Read:

> Notice what voices of the mind arise when you hear these Needs.

B: Say another one or two Needs words from the list. Read:

Notice what words begin to form as you relate to these Needs.

Explore the sensations in the body. Is there tension? Resistance?

B: Say another one or two Needs words from the list. Read:

Let your attention be drawn to whatever sensations are there. Explore the body patterns that arise in relation to these Needs.

What has the mind labeled these Needs? Does it call them "selfish"? Does it call them "impossible"? Does it call them "joy"?

B: Say a few more Needs words from the list. Read:

Simply notice the voice of the mind. Simply listen.

Is it an angry voice? A frightened voice? A confused voice?

Listen to the tone. Does it accept you as you are?

B: Say the Needs words again. Say each one, with a breath or two before the next. **Read:**

Just observe the voices that respond to these Needs.

Watch how naturally each thought ends. Watch how spontaneously the next thought begins.

Notice the constant unfolding.

Let it unfold moment to moment.

Watch how each thought, each emotion arises.

Constantly coming, constantly going.

Give these constantly changing sensations and thoughts a little more space, a little more room to unfold in a soft body, an open heart.

B: Say the Needs words again. Pause for a breath or two between saying each one. **Read:**

Simply receive these Needs in this moment, without clinging or condemning.

Nothing to change. No one to be. Nothing to do.

B: Say the Needs words again. Pause for a breath or two between saying each one. **Read:**

Letting sensations arise and dissolve in soft belly.

Allowing. Receiving. Observing. Resting into being.

This unfolding, life itself, so precious, so fully lived.

> All Needs matter.
>
> All Needs fully alive.

B: Allow a moment of silence to end the guided meditation.

A: Share how you are now. Take a moment to write down any insights and share what you are discovering about yourself and your comparing mind. Share what you are learning about universal needs.

Then switch roles.

Closing Harvest

Harvest by sharing any insights, learnings, or discoveries and any appreciations from your time together.

WEEK 3 SOLO PRACTICES

To-Be List

"Nonviolent Communication requires that we take our time to come from our divine energy rather than our cultural programming."
– Marshall B. Rosenberg, Ph.D

Many of us lead daily lives that emphasize *do*-ing and "getting things done" and not as much on *be*-ing and what we want the spirit behind our actions to be. This way of living can feel mechanical and lifeless because we are disconnecting from who we are. By contrast, when we "do" from a place of being connected to the energy of our Needs, our words and actions come alive with a sense of depth and meaning and our lives can feel richer and fuller.

Today…

Settle into present awareness of the body and the breath. Rest there for a few minutes.

Now, look at your "To-Do" list for the day or week. If you don't have one, take a moment to jot down what feels important to take care of today.

Consider what energy you would like to come from, what you would like "To Be" as you do these "To Do's." What Needs would you like to be in touch with and have expressed through your actions and words today or this week? **Looking at the Needs Wheel, write down the Needs you would like "To Be" next to your "To Do's."**

For example, our list might look like this:

To Do	To Be
Clean the house	Play, Beauty
Respond to client messages	Connection, Presence, Empathy
Pay bills	Ease, Trust, Order

Treat this To-Be list the same way you would treat an important To-Do list, carrying it with you and/or posting it in a place where you're sure to see it.

Check off a To-Be item whenever you notice that you're being that quality. Unlike a To-Do item, you can check off a To-Be item multiple times!

To-Be List
Remembering

"We often think that to be spiritual or enlightened we need to have some special experiences, just as we think that in order to make a great meal or become a master chef we need special ingredients and a fancy kitchen. But all we have to do to make a meal is put all the pots and pans and ingredients in their proper places. And all we have to do to be in touch with our spirituality is to let the mind settle itself, like a cloudy glass of city tap water."

– Bernie Glassman

Self-Empathy Journal

"If you have some experience of how the weeds in your mind change into mental nourishment, your practice will make remarkable progress."
– Shunryu Suzuki

Self-Empathy is a practice of bringing awareness and compassion to the thoughts, feelings, needs, and requests that arise within us in everyday life. Although Self-Empathy can be practiced anytime, it can feel easier when first building our Self-Empathy muscles to practice in a nurturing environment, like our practice space, rather than in a social situation. The Self-Empathy Journal is a way to do that. It's both a tool for self-reflection and a practice of connecting to life. It supports growth and clarity after difficult interactions and channels energy toward life-enriching actions. Over time, when used regularly, it develops and accelerates our ability to access the consciousness and language of Nonviolent Communication in "live" interactions as well.

(An example of today's practice can be found on the page following the practice.)

Today…

Sit for a few minutes, present with the body, the breath, and the support of the earth.

Bring to mind a current, unresolved interaction you had with yourself or another person that you'd like to explore more deeply – a situation in which you or the other person said or did something that stimulated a reaction in you. Choose a specific interaction you had, even if you have experienced that same pattern in multiple situations with that person or with yourself. If this is your first time doing this practice, choose a medium-weight situation rather than one that is heavy with history.

1. **Start a new page in your journal and write "Situation:" at the top. Next to that, free-write about what happened in whatever way helps you to recall that interaction.**

2. **Below that write "Stimulus:" and, next to that, whatever specifically was said or done by you or the other person that triggered you.** This is a clear observation, not your evaluation of what happened. You can think of it as a video camera's point-of-view. *For example, "She criticized me" is an evaluation; a video camera doesn't interpret words as criticism. An observation in that case might be, "She said to me, 'Why are you always so late?'" – just the words that were said.* The same principle applies if what happened

was an action. *For example, "He ignored me" is an evaluation. An observation of that same situation might be, "He walked past me without looking at me" – just the action that occurred.*

3. Now, divide your page into three columns: "Thoughts," "Feelings," and "Needs."

4. **Place one hand on your head. In the "Thoughts" column, one-by-one, write down all the charged stories, judgments, interpretations, and beliefs you have around the situation, each on its own line.** If you have trouble identifying any, look at the example bullets from last week's Solo Practice "Meeting Needs" (page 53).

5. **When it feels like a pretty complete list of your thoughts around this particular stimulus** (often, they just start repeating as variations on the same thoughts), **or if your attention starts to shift to what you're feeling, take a deep breath and bring awareness to the body.**

6. **Move your hand to your heart. Reread the first thought on your page out loud to yourself, noticing what you feel in your body when you hear it. Breathe and allow yourself to truly feel those feelings. Write those feelings or body sensations down next to the thought in the "Feelings" column.** If you have trouble identifying any feelings or sensations, look at "Feelings" and "Body Sensations" on pages 272-273 in the Appendix and write down any words from there that match what you're feeling.

7. **Now, take a deep breath and move your hand to your belly. Look at the Needs Wheel on page 271 in the Appendix. Which Needs are being expressed by that thought and its related feelings?** Without thinking about it too much, write down whichever Needs words jump out at you in the "Needs" column. If new thoughts emerge, add them to the "Thoughts" column.

8. Repeat steps 6 and 7 with the other thoughts on your list, writing down the feelings and Needs connected to each one. Be present to what you feel in the body and the breath throughout this process.

9. Reread all the Needs in your "Needs" column out loud to yourself, feeling what you feel in your body as you hear each one.

10. Below the columns, write "Sitting with the Needs:" and, next to that, just the Needs that spoke to you most strongly. Take some time to simply be with those Needs – noticing where you feel them in your body and what they feel like there. Notice what they mean to you. Don't rush this step – give yourself permission to go out for a walk with these Needs or even take the day to reflect on them. Also, pay attention to any lingering unseen thoughts that still want attention.

11. Write "Insight:" and, next to that, any insights that you have into this situation after reflecting on it from the perspective of "Sitting with the Needs."

12. Finally, write "Action Request:" at bottom of the page. When you revisit the original "Stimulus" from the perspective of "Sitting with the Needs," is there any request you have of yourself or others? Are there any *small* steps you want to take to respond to the situation? **Write down any action requests you would like yourself to act on.** We suggest small steps because they are more likely to be acted on than big, ambitious ones. Also, the clearer and more specifically defined the action, the easier it will be to act on.

Close with a moment of appreciation for anything that today's practice offered to you. Include an acknowledgment of your own effort in making this happen.

Instant – In a moment of noticing that something is "on your mind," stop and breathe. On a piece of paper, jot down whatever thought or thoughts you notice keep arising. Take a deep breath and feel what's going on in your body. Write down those feelings or sensations. Take a deep breath and look at the Needs Wheel. What Needs are being expressed by the thoughts and feelings you're experiencing? Write down those needs. Take another full breath and connect to the clarity of those Needs. Do whatever calls to you now.

Deepening – Take up the Self-Empathy Journal as a weekly practice. Journal a variety of situations, lightweight and heavyweight – whatever situation is most alive for you when you sit down to journal. Journal enjoyable situations, too, recording the pleasant thoughts and feelings you're experiencing and the Needs that they're expressing. As you journal, pay special attention to "evolved" thinking, like, "This process won't work on me." As you become familiar with Ongo, combine this practice with the Unpacking Core Beliefs practice in Week 5.

Example: Self-Empathy Journal

Situation: I was so exhausted after working all day, and I came home wanting some ease and rest. Lee was acting really weird, and I didn't want to deal with it. Finally he started going into how I never spend time with him anymore, and I just about lost it.

Stimulus: Lee saying to me, "You never spend any time with me."

Thoughts:	Feelings:	Needs:
Lee doesn't have any idea how hard I work to support us!	Tension in shoulders, annoyed	Appreciation, understanding
I should've never moved in with him.	Hot in face, deflated, exasperated	Peace of mind
He's so irresponsible.	Angry, tight chest	Support
We wouldn't survive if I lived like him.	Tight in belly, hurt back, worry	Security, well-being
I have to work hard for us to survive.	Frustrated, tired	Ease, security

Sitting with the Needs: Ease and security

Insight: I realize that I'm putting a lot of pressure on myself by believing that our basic survival depends on me working really hard. That pressure is really what's triggering my anger. By acknowledging that I also have a need for ease, I feel more wholeness in myself and more willingness to connect with Lee.

Action Request: I'll ask Lee if he'd be willing to hand me my journal (with a kiss!) next time I look stressed. I'd also like to spend 10 minutes at lunch tomorrow sitting with the need for ease so I can connect to the quality of that life energy more readily in my work day.

Self-Empathy Journal
Remembering

"Many people try to find a spiritual path where they do not have to face themselves but where they can still liberate themselves – liberate themselves from themselves, in fact. In truth, this is impossible. We cannot do that. We have to be honest with ourselves. We have to see our gut, our real shit, our most undesirable parts. We have to see that. That is the foundation of warriorship and the basis of conquering fear. We have to face our fear; we have to look at it, study it, work with it, and practice meditation with it."
– Chögyam Trungpa

Self-Empathy Meditation

"It is a radical shift to embrace any reactivity we experience and not make an enemy of it. Rather than saying, 'I must get over this, get rid of this' or 'I must heal this,' we go toward our reactivity and see it as our life force expressing in us, saying, 'See me, allow me.' Our liberation, our freedom is in attending to our greatest fears with an allowing presence. The action of turning toward that which we perceive as the block in our lives is the act of self-compassion."
— Robert Gonzales

We all have moments when we need immediate empathy and have neither access to a friend who can offer it nor time to self-empathize through journaling. In those moments, we can practice this Self-Empathy Meditation. This practice is most effective when we are present to the body and the breath throughout the process. Without that presence, this practice loses its power, and we can easily get lost in our reactive thinking and emotions. The hand movements that are offered as part of the guidance below, as well as the reminders to breathe, are designed to support us in staying present to our body and breath even in the middle of strong thoughts and emotions. Although we might not use the hand movements in a social situation, we strongly recommend using them when learning this practice in private.

For today's practice, use "Self-Empathy" (Appendix, page 274) as a visual reference.

Today…

In a moment of noticing something on your mind or heart that is wanting compassionate attention, stop whatever else you're doing and do this practice. *For example, you can't stop thinking about something, or a particular emotion keeps arising in your chest, or you keep reacting to situations in a way that you don't enjoy.*

Take a moment to breathe and feel your body on the earth.

Bring to mind the situation that's wanting your attention.

1. **Touch your hand to your head. As thoughts – the charged stories, judgments, interpretations, and beliefs about the situation – come to mind, name them out loud, one at a time, prefaced by the words, "I'm telling myself …" Pause between each thought to breathe and connect to the support of the earth.** *For example, "I'm telling myself that I will never be happy," then pause, take a breath, connect to the earth.*

Then, "I'm telling myself that everyone else has their life figured out," then pause, take a breath, connect to the earth. Then, "I'm telling myself that I'm a burden to others," etc. **Allow yourself to really hear and experience each thought without trying to get rid of it. When thoughts start to quiet down and your attention naturally starts to shift away from them, take a deep breath and touch your hand to your heart.**

2. **Bring awareness to body sensations and feelings. As you notice different sensations and emotions, say them out loud. Pause between each feeling to breathe, feel it without trying to change it, and connect to the support of the earth.** *For example, "Frustration," then pause to breathe, feel the frustration, connect to the earth. Then, "Tension in shoulders," then pause to breathe, feel the tension in the shoulders, connect to the earth. Then, "Sadness," etc.* **At a certain point, you'll feel the body quieting and softening and your attention naturally starting to shift. At that point, take a deep breath and touch your hand to your belly.**

3. **Look at the Needs Wheel. Listen inside: which Needs are all those thoughts and feelings expressing?** Look for which Needs jump up off the page at you rather than trying to "figure it out" or thinking too much. **Say out loud each Need word that resonates with you. Pause between each word to breathe and feel what that Need feels like in the body.** *For example, "Trust," then breathe and feel trust in your body. Then "Support," then breathe and feel support in your body. Then, "Ease," etc.* Notice whenever a new thought starts to pull your attention away from your Needs. If that happens, repeat steps 1 through 3 with that thought. Or, if a new feeling starts to pull on your attention, then repeat steps 2 and 3 with that feeling.

4. **With your hand on your belly, take a minute simply to be with the Needs you've named, resting into what you feel when you connect to them.** It's common at this point to feel a deep quality of peace and lightness in your connection to the Needs. If you don't feel this, then it's possible there is a thought or feeling that wants attention, in which case you would go back to either step 1 (thoughts that want attention) or step 2 (feelings that want attention).

5. **Now, with your hand on your belly as an anchor to this deep, felt connection with the Needs, bring back to mind the original situation. Looking at the situation from this perspective of being connected to the Needs, is there an action that you would like to take in response to the situation? If so, open your hands and take the action, or write it down as a reminder for later.**

6. **Breathe. Connect to the earth. Give thanks.**

Tip – This practice is nonlinear even though it's written in sequential order. In other words, it's quite possible that you will become aware of new thoughts, feelings, or Needs at any time during the meditation. If that happens, the practice is to attend to that new thought, feeling, or Need as the next step in the meditation. Let your body guide you – stay compassionately present with whatever is tugging at your attention.

 Video – There is a video demonstration of this practice available on The Ongo Companion Website at ongo.global.

 Instant – When you notice that something inside is calling for attention, stop and breathe. If it's a thought, bring one hand to your head and name the thought out loud to yourself. Allow yourself to experience that thought without trying to change it. If it's a feeling calling for attention, bring one hand to your heart and feel what you feel in your body without trying to change it. After you've taken a moment to experience the thought or feeling that was there, take a deep breath and place one hand on your belly. Look at the Needs Wheel and name whatever Needs are being expressed by the thoughts and feelings you're experiencing. Take another full breath and connect to the clarity of those Needs. Do whatever calls to you now.

 Deepening – Practice the Self-Empathy Meditation anytime you notice something on your mind or heart that wants compassionate attention. As the practice becomes more familiar, let the body guide you more and more to whatever wants attention without concern for whether or not you're doing all the steps of the process. Perhaps simply bringing a moment of awareness to a thought or a Need will be enough for that moment. Give special attention to any subtle desire to use this practice as a way to change or fix what's happening rather than as a practice of moment-to-moment compassionate presence. Practice this meditation with those thoughts too. *For example, "I'm telling myself this practice isn't working ..." or "I'm telling myself that I should be feeling something different now ...," etc.*

Week 4

Turning Toward Suffering and a Power Greater Than Ourselves

*"I suppose some would be shocked at our seeming worldliness and levity.
But just underneath there is deadly seriousness.
Faith has to work twenty-four hours a day in and through us, or we perish."*
– Bill W.

Preparation – All participants:

- Bring your copy of *The Ongo Book*, your journal, and any writing utensils you enjoy.

Preparation – Group Guide:

- A day or two before the Group Gathering, remind everyone of the day, time, and place of the Gathering.

- Read "Leading Group Practice" (page 13) and do the points listed under "Responsibilities of the Guide."

- Bring a "talking stick" (a stick, stone, or object that can easily be held in one hand for Council). Read the "Council Rounds" practice (page 87) to see how it will be used.

- Lay one deck of Needs cards out in an attractive mandala or spiral in the center of the circle. Place the talking stick in the center.

Opening Meditation

Invite everyone to take their seats in the circle.

Ring a bell to signal the beginning of the sitting meditation.

After a moment of silence, read the guidance below to the group. Read in a way that supports the group to relax into the guidance, allowing generous space and full breaths of silence between passages:

> Let the breath settle you as you arrive here to the Ongo group. Just letting yourself breathe. Just noticing how your being breathes. No effort.

> As we breathe, just let the belly soften a little bit more. Acknowledging any tension that may be there. Acknowledging any holding from the day or the week.

Just letting yourself breathe. Letting the belly soften.

Simply return to the breath when the mind wanders from its seat. Whatever's there, just breathe with those thoughts. Just soften the belly.

This is your moment to arrive. There isn't one more thing that needs to be figured out. Nothing needing to be done.

This is the practice. Being with the breath. Something bigger than us. Our breath breathes all the time without effort. Now we get to receive that precious gift. Letting the belly soften.

Sit in silence for a couple more minutes and then ring the bell three times to end the meditation.

Turning Toward a Power Greater Than Ourselves

Read to the group:

> When we open ourselves to the support of community in our practices, when we offer our vulnerability to be held by others, we are surrendering to something greater than "me." We are acknowledging that, perhaps, we can't do it all on our own.
>
> The more we sit – the more we become aware of our thoughts, feelings, and Needs – the more we realize how impossible it is for us to will ourselves to be peaceful or compassionate. Too often, we seem to be powerless over our reactions. We need help – yet we're often afraid to reach out for support.
>
> At some point, perhaps because we've suffered enough or because we're ready for a change, we will decide that the risk is worth it. Better to humbly admit our limitations than to become exhausted by trying to manage it all on our own! At some point, we will look up out of the hole we've dug for ourselves and discover we're not alone.
>
> What we call that "not alone–ness" is personal. Throughout time, it has been called many names: God, Buddha-nature, Higher Power, Love, the Living Energy of Needs. No matter its name, it boils down to whatever you experience as something greater than your conception of "me."

Invite everyone to take out their journals or a piece of paper. Set out the crayons, colored pencils, and/or markers. Then read:

> Take some time now to consider what the idea of "turning toward a power greater than yourself" means to you. Freely draw, color, and write whatever comes, without censoring yourself or worrying about how your depiction of it "looks." I will also offer a reading during this time, which you can receive like rainfall in the background, while you continue to draw, color, and write.

Allow a minute or two for everyone to settle into their drawings and writings, then read, clearly yet gently, at a meditative pace:

> When we practice any spiritual discipline, part of what we do – some would say, most of what we do – is to recognize our limitations and give over to a power greater than ourselves. In Ongo, we give over to the structure of Ongo, we give over to the Ongo group, we give over to our Buddies, we give over to the Solo Practices. These are all mirrors for life.
>
> At this point in Ongo, we're starting to seriously turn toward suffering rather than run away from it. Through our Empathy and Self-Empathy practices, we are actively looking at suffering with our whole being. Instead of trying to fix it or change it, we are flowing with it, holding it with love and compassion.
>
> Our ability to lean into a force more powerful than ourselves is what makes it possible for us to turn toward suffering without getting overwhelmed or burnt out. Gandhi called this force "Satyagraha," or "soul-force." It is a force born out of unconditional love, the same love that we find when we give up all the conditions we place on love for the possibility of still being loved in all our unlovableness. It is the *agape* that Dr. Martin Luther King Jr. spoke of when searching for the strength to confront intolerable hate and violence.
>
> In our own life, we too can find this strength. It begins with leaning into our spiritual community, our Ongo group, and the teachings of those who walked before us, our Ongo practices.

Give another few minutes for everyone to continue their drawing and writing. During this time, you can do your own drawing and writing on the topic.

When you sense that most people are complete or close to completion, wait one minute longer, then ring a bell.

Council Rounds

Invite everyone to put their journals and papers aside. If people are spread out, invite the circle to re-form for this practice.

With the talking stick that you brought in your hand, read this guidance to the group:

> Now we will share in Council Rounds. During the Council Rounds we will pass this talking stick around the circle to signal who has our attention.

Show the talking stick that you brought to the group, then continue reading:

> The person speaking will have our full, silent presence. While they are speaking, we will not comment on or respond to their words, nor will we be thinking about what we will say when it is our turn to speak. We will hold the space of empathy for each speaker. When it is our turn to speak, we will not refer to anyone else's sharing. Instead, we will speak from our own experiences and ideas.
>
> We will have three rounds of sharing. For the first round, each person will share on the topic: "Tell us about the suffering you witness in yourself and in the world." We will start with whoever first feels called to speak on the topic, then the talking stick will pass to the person on their left, and that person will share. We will continue around the circle until the talking stick comes back to the person who first spoke, at which point I will introduce the next topic to share on. Given that there will be three rounds of sharing and a number of us here, let us all be mindful about the length of our speaking so that there is time for everyone's voice to be heard. At the same time, honor your own voice by giving it the space it needs to be expressed.

Check if anyone is unclear about the practice and needs to hear the instructions again. Once everyone is clear, invite everyone to take a breath together and to bring their presence to the circle. Read:

> Tell us about the suffering you witness in yourself and in the world. Who feels called to speak now on this topic?

Pass the talking stick to that person to begin the first round of sharing.

Once the talking stick has made its way around the circle back to the person who first shared, take the talking stick and invite everyone to take a breath together. Then read:

> For the second round, tell us about what turning toward a power greater than yourself means to you. Who feels called to speak now on this topic?

Pass the talking stick to that person to begin the second round of sharing.

Once the talking stick has made its way around the circle back to the person who first shared, take the talking stick and invite everyone to take a breath together. Then read:

> Before the third round, in silence, let us each look at our Needs Wheel or the Needs cards in front of us in order to connect to the Needs that our sharing has brought alive. Breathe as you look over these Needs and see which ones speak to you in this moment.

Allow a minute of silence for everyone to look at the Needs before continuing to read:

> For the third round, tell us about the Needs that you notice have come alive during this sharing. How do these Needs relate to your ideas of suffering and/or the idea of a power greater than yourself?
>
> Who feels called to speak now on this topic?

Pass the talking stick to that person to begin the third round of sharing.

Once the talking stick has made its way around the circle back to the person who first shared, take the talking stick and invite everyone to take a breath together.

Place the talking stick in the center of the circle.

Harvest

Invite anyone who feels moved to share what touched them, what challenged them, what they learned, or what they discovered from today's practice with the group.

Close by offering gratitude to everyone for their sharing and presence today.

 **Closing**

Ask for a volunteer to guide the group next week. Give that person the deck(s) of Needs cards.

Remind that volunteer to read the pages on "Leading Group Practice" (page 13) and Week 5's Group Gathering before the next meeting. Everything they need to know will be in those pages.

Invite everyone to take a collective full breath together.

Invite everyone to each share one word that describes what they are taking with them from this fourth Ongo Group Gathering. Start with the person on your left and go around the circle clockwise until everyone, including you, has shared.

Facing Suffering, Finding Serenity

*"God grant me the serenity to accept the things I cannot change,
the courage to change the things I can,
and the wisdom to know the difference."*
– The Serenity Prayer

When we turn toward suffering and lean into a power greater than ourselves, we find serenity by knowing what is in our control and what is not. We learn the difference between what requests are doable for ourselves or others and what requests are not within our power to actually do. We often create more suffering than is necessary when we try to control what is not within our control.

Preparation – Before you meet:

- **Write down three areas in your life that you cannot control and describe any frustrations that result when you try to control them.**

    For example:

    <u>My spouse:</u> *I get really frustrated if there is something in his behavior that has not changed even though I really think it needs changing. When he does the behavior again and I try to let him know it's "wrong," we just fight and feel even more disconnected.*

    <u>My mother's "prejudices":</u> *I get frustrated that after years of telling her that saying some of her beliefs in public is not appropriate, she still says things I would never want my children to hear or imitate. When I try to get her to change, it simply adds to our disconnection and distance.*

    <u>Decisions the U.S. president makes:</u> *Although I believe I can influence decisions, ultimately I know the president will do whatever he himself chooses. I get frustrated because I still tell myself "I know what's right and what he should do." When I try to do more to influence his choices than what is really within my power, I make myself physically ill and emotionally depressed.*

- **Write down three areas in your life that you can control and describe how you take responsibility for them.**

For example:

My career choice: I can choose what I do for work. I have taken responsibility for that by not staying at a job longer than actually contributes to my happiness.

The food I eat: I have the power to choose the food I eat. I take responsibility for that by noticing when my body does not respond well to something I am eating and then choosing to no longer eat that particular thing.

What I say: I have the power to choose what words I speak. I take responsibility for that by expressing regret when what I say has not contributed to connection in a way I enjoy or by practicing mindfulness to become more aware of what I'm saying.

- **Bring what you wrote to your meeting with your Buddy (or, if you are meeting by phone, email what you wrote to your Buddy beforehand).**

Opening Meditation

Greet your Buddy.

Choose one of you to time a 5-minute meditation.

Sit in silence together, resting attention on the breath, allowing the body and mind to settle.

Whoever is keeping time signals the other when 5 minutes have passed.

Close with a bow of appreciation to your Buddy for sitting with you.

Facing Suffering, Finding Serenity

Hand or email your Buddy the writing that you prepared earlier. Also, have the "Needs Wheel" on page 271 in the Appendix nearby.

Decide who will be Buddy A and who will be Buddy B.

1. Buddy A reads out loud the first item on Buddy B's list of areas in their life that they cannot control. Buddy B listens silently, with curiosity, presence, and an intention to connect.

2. When Buddy A finishes reading, Buddy B looks at the Needs Wheel and names out loud one or two Needs that they heard being expressed.

3. Buddy A writes down the Needs that Buddy B has offered.

4. Repeat steps 1 to 3 for the remaining two items on Buddy B's list of areas in their life that they cannot control, and then the three items on Buddy B's list of areas in their life that they can control.

5. Once Buddy A has read aloud all the items on both of Buddy B's lists and written down all the needs that Buddy B has named, Buddy A offers all the Needs words back to Buddy B one by one, slowly, with a full breath in between each word. Buddy B, with their hand on their belly, simply receives all these Needs, breathing and being with whatever arises.

6. Take a few breaths in silence and share any insights that arose.

7. Switch roles.

Closing Harvest

Harvest by sharing any insights, learnings, or discoveries and any appreciations from your experiences of the practice.

Also, take some time to share any appreciations you have for your time together as Ongo Buddies, for welcoming yourselves and each other into the group this way. Next week, you will begin with new Buddies for your second month of Ongo Buddy Practice.

WEEK 4 SOLO PRACTICES

Life's Inbox

"[T]he hard thing about devotional practice is suspending 'intelligence' and just entrusting our heart-minds to the grace of the uncontrollable forces which support us. ... [It] is a love letter and a request.... And when you conjure up from within your own heart, love for mountains and rivers and sidewalks and park benches, you get to experience and be supported by that very love you're conjuring up.... [F]ostering that mind of "true entrusting" creates a stability of heart which is as good as enlightenment itself. And it's a heck of a lot easier and humble. It just requires the suspension of sophistication.... So it's just ... 'Bless this mess.'"
– Koji Acquaviva

As we develop in our practice, we may find ourselves upgrading our "shoulds." What may have once sounded in our heads like an endless list of tasks that "I should" do now sounds like a litany of bad spiritual advice, like "I should be more calm" or "I should be more empathetic." In fact, as we become more present to our inner workings, it seems that the same mind that readily dispenses advice is also creating the problems.

This being the case, one of the most sane things we can do in daily life is to admit our own limitations and the need for support beyond our "stinking thinking." Whether or not one believes in a higher power, we all need a place to rest our concerns that both honors their importance and gives our minds and bodies a real break.

Today...

Create a "Life's inbox" and place it in your practice space. Life's inbox is a container where you place your mind's preoccupations and concerns, giving them up and asking Life to resolve them, in Life's way, on Life's time frame. "Life" here is shorthand for all that is greater and beyond our mind's grasp of life. Use whatever equivalent works for you.

For example, create a Buddha box, or a God box, or a Universe box, or a That-which-is-bigger-than-my-mind-can-conceive box.

Write down something specific that your mind and heart has been wanting resolved and place it in Life's inbox.

Throughout your day, if that concern arises again, remember that it's in Life's inbox and will be resolved on Life's time – it's out of your hands now. If you like, direct any energy that wants to "do something" into one of the Self-Empathy practices from last week, or simply be with the breath. This is not an instruction to ignore any particular actions you feel called to take. As with our Self-Empathy practices, once you're connected to your Needs, if you feel called to act in a particular way, then act. What we are letting go of is any expectation that these actions will produce a particular outcome. That outcome is now in the hands of Life.

For the rest of Ongo, continue to make use of Life's inbox whenever you find that a particular concern is becoming an all-consuming preoccupation of the mind. Notice when those issues do actually resolve and take those moments to thank Life for finishing the job!

 Instant – Right now, if you are preoccupied with a concern that is beginning to feel heavy or overwhelming, take a deep breath and visualize yourself taking that concern off your shoulders and placing it in Life's inbox, along with any hopes you have of how you'd like it resolved. If you sense that there is a specific action for you to take, then take that action. Otherwise, exhale and release the concern completely, knowing that it's in Life's hands now.

 Deepening – As an ongoing practice, whenever you find yourself faced with a difficult situation, start by admitting, silently or out loud, that this challenge is beyond your ability to manage on your own. In your own words, ask Life for its support to resolve the situation in a way that causes the least harm and contributes to the greatest good for all. Take a moment to breathe and rest into the awareness that you are not alone in facing this challenge. At the end of the day, take some time to review your day and acknowledge and appreciate any moments in which you received the help of a power greater than yourself.

Life's Inbox
Remembering

"[L]eft to our own devices, we – as a species – tend to lug these big rocks around. They are the rocks of our concerns. Every time we get up, we reach down for our big rock and then we lug it out the door, down the stairs, and roll it into the back seats of our cars. Then after we drive someplace, we open the back door, get out our rock, and carry it with us wherever we go. Because it's our rock. It is very important to us and we need to keep it in sight. Also, someone could steal it. So these [sober] drunks suggest that you practice dropping the rock. That you put it down, on the ground at your feet. And that you say to God, to Mary, to Pele, Jehovah, Jesus, or Howard: 'Here. I'm giving you the rock. YOU deal with it.'"

– Anne Lamott

Daily Miracles

Instructions for living a life.
Pay attention.
Be astonished.
Tell about it.
– Mary Oliver

In everyday life, most of us tend to place the majority of our attention on the most minor events. We preoccupy ourselves with the minutiae of human relationships, jobs, material possessions, money, and politics, while in the background, unseen and unacknowledged, are all the events and forces that make it possible for us to live the way we do. We act as if human intelligence and design are what create the world we live in, and we forget how much is unconditionally given to us – like the very ground under our feet. In every waking and sleeping moment of our lives, that ground supports the weight of our bodies. Earth and gravity enable us to rest, standing, sitting, or lying down. It is a gift that is freely given, without expectation or charge. From the moment we are born until the moment we die, we receive its support. We don't have to be enlightened or spiritually evolved. We don't have to believe in a god or do good deeds. We don't have to have money, privilege, or fame. Earth cradles us unconditionally. Whether we see this as a miracle of life or as part of the interdependent fabric of causes and conditions that make up our life as we know it, the important thing is that we see. To see the miracle of life is to be free from our self-centered stories of life and to be open to the support that may be right under our feet.

Today…

Sit for a few minutes, present with the body, the breath, and the support of the earth. Notice anything that impresses upon you the idea that there is something much greater than you at work in your life. It can be anything from witnessing a nearby butterfly take flight to realizing that a problem you had has seemingly resolved itself.

Continue this awareness throughout your day.

Make a list of these "miracles" that you notice. Write down at least 10 of them.

Daily Miracles
Remembering

"There is the wind, the sound of rustling leaves, the brightness of the room, the breathing, the color of the wooden floor, the hands resting, the heart beating. There is saliva gathering in the mouth, and the swallowing of it. What's so hard about being in touch with what is real, with what is actually here this moment, unspectacular though it may be? Is this one of our problems? That to be in touch with reality we expect something spectacular, something out of the ordinary? So we fail to be with our feet on the most ordinary of grounds, a soggy path or a wooden floor, a rug…. The entire universe is there – the wonder of it, not the concept."

– Toni Packer

Calling on Our Ancestors

"Can you sense the love that burns in your ancestors, their devotion to their families, their land? Receive that love as their gift to you.... Your ancestors have gifts from their suffering, too: courage, endurance, resilience, stubborn perseverance. Receive these as their gifts to you."
– Joanna Macy

In modern times, the idea of seeking help from our ancestors – those whose footsteps we're following in – can seem strange, superstitious, or foreign. Yet when we look at the lives of great spiritual leaders like Dr. Martin Luther King Jr., Gandhi, and H. H. the 14th Dalai Lama, we find that each of them studied, prayed to, and drew strength from others who came before them. Our own ancestors – those teachers, friends, and family members who are no longer with us but whose lives and actions have deeply inspired us – can be a source of strength and wisdom in our spiritual practice. By recognizing that our own accomplishments rest in part on all that they did, and by connecting to the force of their combined presence, a force greater than our personal limitations, we are able to remain both humble and empowered in our practice. Each of us is a part of that long lineage of nonviolence, a lineage that extends infinitely into the past and into the future. When we call on our ancestors, we are taking our place in that lineage.

Today...

In your practice place, if you haven't already, add some pictures of those who have gone before you in this work: teachers, friends, and family members who have taught you and inspired you through their example.

Make an offering to them, as if you were welcoming honored guests. *For example, place some flowers, a cup of water, or a small plate of their favorite foods in front of them.*

After, take a few minutes to look at each of these ancestors' images. If you are facing any challenges in your life today, internally or externally, name those challenges to your ancestors and ask for their help and guidance.

Either way, whether you're facing any challenges or not, consider what wisdom your ancestors are offering you in the moment. Breathe in their support and teaching.

Close by expressing gratitude to them for their presence and guidance in your life.

 Tip – Consider this as an ongoing relationship, rather than a one-time practice. How might you incorporate both giving and receiving to your ancestors into your daily life? This could look like making regular offerings to them of things that they would enjoy, and taking time to sit with them and listen each day.

 Instant – Take a moment now to bring to mind one of the teachers, friends, or family members who have deeply influenced and inspired you in your life. Greet them in your heart. If you have a question or challenge that you're facing in this moment, ask for their help and guidance. Breathe and receive whatever response comes. If you have no questions or challenges in the moment, simply breathe and appreciate that person's presence in your life. Acknowledge one thing that they contributed to you through their words or actions.

 Deepening – Wherever you go, consider whose ancestors may have lived on the land that you walk on. Greet them in your heart, acknowledge their presence, and offer an appreciation for their life's contributions. Before you make a big decision or enter into an important interaction that requires your leadership or participation (i.e., before a class you're teaching, a meeting you're a part of, or a difficult conversation with someone), always take a few minutes to ask for the support of your ancestors and invite them to help guide your actions. Afterwards, if you are offered compliments or praise, take a moment either silently or verbally to appreciate the contributions of your ancestors to who you are today (i.e., "I'd like to extend your gratitude to my teachers as well, because it's their teaching that helped me to be who I am now, and I'm grateful that I am now able to share something of what they taught me.").

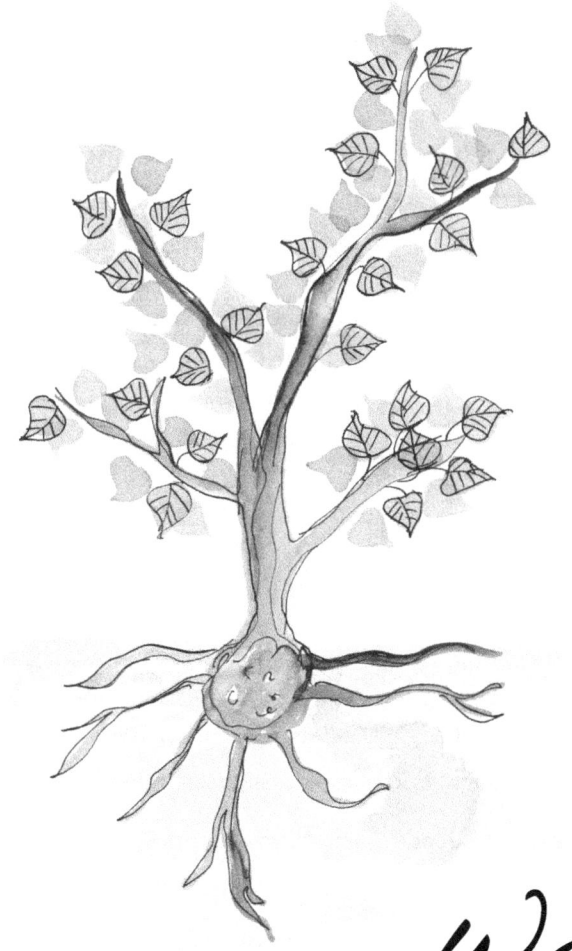

Week 5

Core Beliefs

"Becoming 'awake' involves seeing our confusion more clearly."
– Chögyam Trungpa

Preparation – All participants:

- Bring your copy of *The Ongo Book* and your journal.

Preparation – Group Guide:

- A day or two before the Group Gathering, remind everyone of the day, time, and place of the Gathering.

- Read "Leading Group Practice" (page 13) and do the points listed under "Responsibilities of the Guide."

- Lay the Needs cards out in an attractive mandala or spiral in the center of the circle.

Opening Meditation

Invite everyone to take their seats in the circle.

Ring a bell to signal the beginning of the sitting meditation.

After a moment of silence, read the guidance below to the group. Read in a way that supports the group to relax into the guidance, allowing generous space and a few breaths of silence between passages:

> Take a moment to find a position in your seat that supports you to be both relaxed and awake.
>
> Take a deep breath. On the exhale, release any tension that wants to be released, and settle in.
>
> Let your eyes soften or close. Allow yourself to feel the support of the earth beneath you.
>
> Take a deep breath. On the exhale, release any tension that wants to be released in the mind, letting your thoughts settle into the support of the earth.
>
> Feel the gentle rise and fall of the belly as you continue to breathe. Let your attention rest there.

Allow a few minutes of silence, then read:

> If at any point, you notice your attention getting lost in thoughts, simply take a deep breath. Let the exhale gently guide your attention back to resting on the belly and the breath.

Allow a few more minutes of silence, then read:

> Just sitting.
>
> Like holding a newborn just out of the womb. Presence that calls in more presence.
>
> Like sitting with someone who knows that death is coming to meet them. That presence that calls in presence. Giving ourselves that space right now.
>
> A space we knew at birth and when we witness birth.
>
> A space we'll know at death and when we witness death. Just breath. Just presence.
>
> Just breath.

Sit in silence for a couple more minutes and then ring the bell three times to end the meditation.

Place your palms together and offer a bow of gratitude to the circle.

Introduction to Core Beliefs

Read to the group, or invite others to take turns reading one or more of the paragraphs to the group:

> Between birth and death, we know life, and in that life, we have experiences that shape the rest of our existence, particularly when we're young. We may have noticed this in our practice: certain thoughts and feelings that feel familiar and repetitive. We may have seen the same old story about ourselves or others show up in multiple situations. Looking deeply, we may even see that most of our thinking revolves around a fairly limited set of core beliefs about who we are and how the world is. Today, we will begin to explore some of those core beliefs and how they show up in our consciousness.
>
> Our core beliefs began simply as a momentary expression of Needs from ourselves, our parents, our teachers, or the society we grew up in. At the time, these expressions may have been our own best attempt to make sense of the world around us or to find safety, love, or acceptance. For example, the belief that "you can't trust people" may have been a useful way for us to stay safe. These expressions may also have been our parents' best attempt to contribute to us, or to find security, love, or belonging, based on what

they had learned from their own parents, teachers, or the society they grew up in. An expression like "you're irresponsible" may have been the only way our parents knew how to share their concern for our survival.

Over time, as these expressions "proved" themselves by helping us to survive and belong in our world, they became part of our fundamental worldview, shaping the way we understood and responded to life experiences. This is why we call them "core beliefs." The reason we are looking at them today is because we have arrived at a moment in our lives where we have outgrown some of these core beliefs in many of our relationships. For example, perhaps the belief that "you can't trust people" has kept us safe and can still offer moments of safety with certain places in our society, but we can see now how it's creating pain in our connection with someone in our lives.

There's nothing wrong with having core beliefs. It's possible that we are ready to grow beyond these beliefs, but the society or family system that helped shape them is not. Being able to recognize our core beliefs and how they have protected us can help us discern when to keep ourselves safe from current harm and when we are responding from a core belief out of habit or post-traumatic reaction. This knowledge supports us to make life-serving boundaries that contribute to all Needs, which we'll explore more later in Ongo.

Today, we'll identify some of our own core beliefs and the Needs behind them so that we can begin to understand how they affect our responses to the immediate world around us.

Exploring Core Beliefs

Invite everyone to take out their journal or a piece of paper and something to write with.

Read the guidance for the practice to the group:

> Core beliefs tend to show up as variations on five basic themes. We're going to take some time now to explore how each of those themes shows up in our lives. Let this be a kind of meditation, sometimes writing, sometimes just sitting and being with the process, feeling whatever is touched in you. After, we'll open it up for sharing and discussion.
>
> The first theme we'll explore is that of deficiency or scarcity. This is the voice that tells us, "I'm not enough," "I'm alone," "I'm unloved." It also might sound like this: "I'm too intense," or "I'm too much for other people." For each of us, the specific words may sound different, but the feeling inside still carries that same sense of deficiency or scarcity.

> In our journals, we'll start a list of anything that we tell ourselves that feeds this sense of deficiency, this idea of "not-enough-ness." Include any judgments about others that also feed this core belief of not-enough-ness or too-much-ness or deficiency. We'll take a few minutes in silence now to do just that much, listing a few of these thoughts. Just to explore.

Allow a few minutes for the group, including you, to journal in silence. Once everyone has a few thoughts on their lists, continue to read:

> Now we'll explore the theme of struggle. How do you tell yourself that life is a struggle? How does comparing mind tell you that others have it easier than you? What do you judge in yourself or others that feeds this idea that life is a struggle, that fundamentally, it will always be a struggle?
>
> Notice any resistance to turn toward these thoughts or judgments. Then, just take a breath and go gently. Allow them to surface.
>
> We'll take a few minutes in silence now to list the thoughts we have around struggle.

Allow a few minutes for the group, including you, to journal in silence. Once everyone has a few thoughts on their lists, continue to read:

> Now we'll explore the theme of suffering, the core belief that life is fundamentally suffering, that no matter what we do, we have to suffer. However this idea expresses itself in you: "the earth is suffering," "relationships are suffering," "work is suffering." What judgments do you hold about yourself or others that feed this idea that life is fundamentally about suffering?
>
> Take a few minutes now to list how the theme of suffering shows up in your thoughts.

Allow a few minutes for the group, including you, to journal in silence. Once everyone has a few thoughts on their lists, continue to read:

> Now we'll explore the theme of danger, the core belief that life is fundamentally dangerous. For example, the belief that you always have to watch your back, that you can't trust people, or that the world isn't safe. What ideas do you hold about yourself or others that feed this sense of life as always being dangerous?
>
> Take a few minutes now to list how the theme of danger shows up in your thoughts.

Allow a few minutes for the group, including you, to journal in silence. Once everyone has a few thoughts on their lists, continue to read:

> Now we'll explore the theme of dichotomy, the idea that, fundamentally, life is black and white. What are the things you tell yourself that feed this sense of dichotomy, that

people are either good or bad, choices are either right or wrong, situations are either win or lose, everything is either this or that? What judgments do you hold of yourself or others that feed a sense of dichotomy?

Take a few minutes now to list those thoughts that you tell yourself and the judgments you are holding of others that feed this sense of life as a dichotomy.

Allow a few minutes for the group, including you, to journal in silence. Once everyone has a few thoughts on their lists, continue to read:

Now, take a breath. Take a look at your lists and read them to yourself for a moment.

Pause a moment for everyone to look at their lists, then continue:

Notice and feel what happens in your body, in your being, as you read these lists to yourself. Remember to breathe.

Feel what you feel as you turn toward your core beliefs and the thoughts and judgments that feed them.

Pause a minute for everyone to continue to read their lists, then continue:

There may be some discomfort in being with these thoughts, the inhale of feeling all the history that's there. And there may be some relief, the exhale of "Ah, finally, we're taking a look at this."

Let's work in pairs to continue our exploration so that we can support each other in practicing mindful awareness and Self-Empathy with these thoughts. For this practice, you will sit facing a partner. If you want, you can open to "Self-Empathy" on page 274 in the Appendix as a visual reference for this practice.

Once everyone has settled into pairs, facing each other, read the guidance slowly, for clarity:

In this practice, your partner will be the voice of your mind, creating some space for you to experience your thoughts as a witness. Choose three thoughts from your lists that you would most like to practice with and give them to your partner, either written on a separate piece of paper or highlighted in your journal.

Your partner will say these thoughts out loud to you, one at a time, with feeling – not like a robot reading a script.

As your partner reads each of your thoughts to you, place your hand on your head and breathe, receiving the expression.

After each thought is read, your partner will offer their silent, empathic presence while you continue with the Self-Empathy practice. Take a breath and bring your hand to your heart, feeling any emotions or sensations in your body. Say any emotions or body sensations you notice out loud.

Breathe and bring your hand to your belly. Sense what Needs are there. What quality of life is the thought expressing? Say the Needs out loud, and your partner will record them on a piece of paper.

When you feel ready to self-empathize with another thought, simply open your hands on your lap, expressing your willingness for your partner to read the next thought on your list to you. Then, as your partner reads that thought out loud to you, you will bring your hand back to your head and repeat the Self-Empathy practice with that thought.

Once you have self-empathized with all three thoughts, take a deep breath and rest one hand on your belly. Yout partner will read back to you just the Needs that you had identified, slowly, one by one. Take this time to deeply connect to what each of these Needs means to you and how they feel in your body.

From this connection to the Needs, sense if there are any requests you would like to make of yourself to honor what you're in touch with now. Your partner will record any requests that come. Then you will switch roles.

Check if anyone is unclear about the practice and needs to hear the instructions again. Once everyone is clear, invite everyone to take a breath together and to bring their presence to the practice.

Keep track of time. Allowing 10 minutes for "Harvest" and "Closing," let the group know when there's just five minutes left in this practice.

Ring a bell when it's time to shift to "Harvest," and invite everyone to thank their partners, then re-form the circle.

Harvest

Invite anyone who feels moved to share what touched them, what challenged them, what they learned, or what they discovered from today's practice with the group.

Close by offering gratitude to everyone for their sharing and practice.

Setting up Ongo Buddy Practices

Invite everyone to sit next to their Ongo Buddies. Then, read to the group:

> Today, we will select new Ongo Buddies for the second month of Ongo. As before, our only recommendation is that family members and life partners wait until the third month to be partnered together in order to care for the vulnerability at the beginning of the learning process and the deep bond of those relationships. Beyond that, the goal is not to find "perfect pairings" but rather to let an intuitive process unfold. Let's each take a minute now in silence to breathe and imagine, from where we sit with our current Ongo Buddy, two other people in this circle we feel called to continue our one-on-one practice with.

After a minute of silence, read:

> Now, breathing into any vulnerability that you may feel, turn toward one of those two people. With this as our beginning, let's discuss who the pairings will be for this second month. We'll take five minutes for this discussion.

Keep track of time. Let the group know when there's just one minute left for the discussion.

After everyone has a Buddy, read:

> After this meeting, please take a moment to connect with your Buddy to schedule your first meeting together. Also, remember, if you or your Buddy aren't showing up consistently for your Buddy Practice together, please reach out to the group and ask if someone else might be willing to be your backup Buddy for the month.

 Closing

Ask for a volunteer to guide the group next week. Give that person the deck(s) of Needs Cards.

Remind that volunteer to read the pages on "Leading Group Practice" (page 13) and Week 6's Group Gathering before the next meeting. Everything they need to know will be in those pages.

Invite everyone to take a collective full breath together.

Invite everyone to each choose a Need card from the center that describes what they are taking with them from this fifth Ongo Group Gathering.

Starting with the person on your left, invite each person to share their Need with the group by holding their card face-out so everyone can see it. Go around the circle clockwise until everyone, including you, has shared.

Empathy

"Deep listening is the kind of listening that can help relieve the suffering of another person. You listen with only one purpose: to help him or her to empty his heart."
– Thich Nhat Hanh

Opening Meditation

Take a few minutes to meet your new Buddy, perhaps sharing something with them that they might not know about you yet.

After, decide who will time a five-minute silent sitting meditation.

Sit in silence together, being with the breath, the body, and the earth.

Whoever is keeping time signals the other when five minutes have passed.

Close with a bow of appreciation to your Buddy for sitting with you.

Sharing and Empathic Listening

Check if either of you would like a refresher on the Empathy Buddy Practice. If so, you can take turns reading out loud just the reading part under "Sharing and Empathic Listening" from the Week 2 Buddy Practice on page 46.

Then, decide who will share first and who will listen first. Have the "Needs Wheel" in the Appendix accessible.

1. **Sharer shares about something happening in their life that's present on their heart and mind.** This could be something small or big, painful or joyful. The only request is that it be something that is alive and meaningful to the sharer.

2. **Listener listens with curiosity, mindful presence, intention to connect, and a focus on Needs, all in silence.** If the mind jumps to advice, judgment, consoling, sympathy, or commiseration, breathe and return to curiosity, mindful presence, intention to connect, and a focus on Needs.

3. **When the sharer comes to a breathing place, a pause, the listener looks at the Needs Wheel and offers confirmation with a simple, empathic guess about the feelings and needs that are being expressed.** *For example, "Are you feeling sad because you're needing acceptance?" or "Am I hearing a need for trust?" or "Are you needing to be seen?" or "I'm

connecting to needs of respect and consideration; how are these landing for you?" or just Needs words, as in *"Love?"* or *"Compassion?"* Offer just one line – one Need – at a time. Let it be received, then take a breath.

4. **Breathe together.**

5. **Sharer continues sharing whatever is still alive and present in their heart to say about the situation. When there is a pause, the listener offers confirmation with simple, empathic guesses about the feelings and Needs that are being expressed.**

6. **Continue until sharer feels complete, often indicated by a relaxing of the energy.** It's important in this process that the listener follow the sharer's lead and does not try to be "right" about their guesses or analyze the sharer's story. Let the guesses simply be reflections of your presence with the sharer rather than an anxious exercise in trying to reflect every word you hear.

7. **Then switch roles.**

Closing Harvest

After both have had an opportunity to share and to listen, harvest by sharing any learnings about yourselves and any appreciations from being listened to in this way.

Buddy Support

Discuss how you would like to support each other this month with doing the daily Solo Practices. This could look different for each Buddy, based on what each finds most supportive. *For example, one Buddy might want to send a daily text message or email to the other after they've done their Solo Practice. Another might want to have a short, weekly phone call to share their experiences of doing the Solo Practices that week.*

Also, discuss whether there is any mutual interest or openness to having empathy calls with each other outside of the regular Buddy Practice. *For example, scheduling a second weekly call just for empathy, or agreeing to be available to each other for "on-call" empathy.*

WEEK 5 SOLO PRACTICES

Unpacking Core Beliefs

"[W]e tend to operate from assumptions we make about ourselves without even knowing what we are doing. Sometimes it is not until we start meditating that we begin to realize how in our lives so much fear and lack of confidence come from childhood experiences. The rational mind knows that it is ridiculous to go around thinking about the tragedies of childhood. But if they keep coming up into consciousness when you are middle-aged, maybe they are trying to tell you something about assumptions that were formed when you were a child."
–Ven. Ajahn Sumedho

Core beliefs are our fundamental conceptions about ourselves and about life. They reflect our history – the life experiences that helped shape who we are today. Core beliefs tend to fall into five basic categories:

- Deficiency: *i.e., I'm not ___ enough, I'm alone and unloved (i.e., not enough love), there's not enough of ___ in life*
- Struggle: *i.e., life is fundamentally a struggle, I always have to work*
- Suffering: *i.e., life is fundamentally suffering, I'll never be free*
- Danger: *i.e., life is fundamentally dangerous, I always have to watch my back*
- Dichotomies: *i.e., I'm a good/bad person, right/wrong, win/lose*

Each of our individual core beliefs will be worded differently according to the conditions in our lives that shaped them. A core belief is defined more by the primal sense of discontent it provokes in us than the words used to describe it. Core beliefs filter our reality, affecting how we think, feel, and react to situations in our lives. When we cling to them as truth, we tend to act in ways that disconnect us from ourselves and others. On the other hand, when we recognize our core beliefs for what they are – expressions of past attempts to meet Needs, that may or may not meet our Needs today – we can bring compassion to their expression when they arise.

Today…

Settle into a conscious, present connection with the earth and the breath.

Bring to mind an unresolved moment with yourself or another person that you would like to explore more deeply – you or the other person said or did something that stimulated a reaction in you. This situation doesn't have to be one that involves another person – for example, it could be a moment in which you did something that harmed only you. In either case, choose a situation that you feel safe to explore today, on your own.

Bring to awareness the thoughts you have around this situation. If it helps your focus, write these down.

Which of these thoughts are familiar old stories about yourself, others, or the nature of life? Explore this thinking until you reach what feels like a fundamental, core belief about yourself or about life. If you're having trouble finding a core belief, here are some questions you can ask yourself when looking at a given thought, in order to go deeper: *Fears: "If that happened, what would that mean about me?" Beliefs: "What does this say about me?" Shoulds: "What makes me think that life (or I) should be this way?"*

Write down the core belief(s).

Take a minute to notice and be present with what you feel in your body when you tell yourself this core belief. Let awareness of the breath be your support as you ride the changing waves of emotion.

Allow memories/images to arise. Reflect: when else has this belief been present in my life?

Continue allowing memories and images to arise. What's the earliest moment you remember this belief operating or coming into your life?

Take a few minutes to write in your journal about that experience – what you remember happening, who was there, what you were feeling at the time. Be with whatever arises, letting go of any expectation that it should look or feel a certain way. Breathe. Feel and be with the changing waves of emotion. If the feelings ever feel too overwhelming, shift more of your awareness to the breath, or to the sensation of your body being supported by the earth.

Take a look at the Needs Wheel. What Needs were longing to be seen and understood in that moment in your life? Write those down.

Breathe and connect to those Needs now, taking a few minutes simply to embrace and empathize with yourself at that age, offering understanding and acceptance. If you like, offer this to yourself through touch and/or verbally. *For example, place your hand on your* *heart, or wrap your arms around your body, or say to yourself, "I see you just want to be loved, to be safe. I got you now."*

Close by releasing your memories and reconnecting to the presence of the earth and your breath, giving thanks for the life-serving Needs that your core beliefs were attempting to meet.

Later, during your day, if you notice a core belief arising, pause and take a minute to bring presence to the waves of sensation and the breath. Embrace yourself for that moment and offer appreciation for the Needs that are trying to be fulfilled. Breathe.

Tip – If this practice brings up new memories or history that feels emotionally overwhelming, it may be helpful to look at this through the lens of "emotional trauma" and get outside support. Consider speaking about it with someone you deeply trust or reaching out to a trauma-informed therapist. A good support person will help you unpack your experience openly and compassionately, without treating it or you as abnormal or unhealthy.

 Instant – Breathe. Take a moment to sense whether any pain from your past is being stimulated now or was stimulated earlier today. Do any of your reactions to situations seem familiar, like they are coming from you as a child or teen? Perhaps your tone of voice or the way you feel in your body seems younger. Look now at the Needs Wheel and consider which Need or Needs this "younger you" longs to have seen and understood. Breathe, and for this moment, simply embrace yourself at that age, offering understanding and acceptance.

 Deepening – Make it part of your daily practice to observe your reaction to situations when you feel triggered, even subtly. Notice especially when the feelings in your body and your habitual responses seem familiar, like they've been with you for much of your life. Take some time each week to unpack these moments, following the guidance of today's practice. As the beliefs, memories, and Needs behind these reactions become increasingly clear to you, let that awareness carry into the rest of your life. *For example, you might choose to breathe, embrace, and empathize with yourself the next time you start to notice that "younger you" start to arrive. Or you might share honestly with the person you're with that the way you're responding has less to do with them and more to do with experiences from your past.*

Unpacking Core Beliefs
Remembering

"Is it not perfectly ironic that it is the investigation of fear that makes us fearless? Just as it is the exploration of anger that teaches us to love, and the investigation of ignorance which brings wisdom. We learn to love by exploring what its absence feels like. We learn to be kind by examining how unkindness conditions the mind and body."
– Stephen and Ondrea Levine

Habit and Choice

"Between stimulus and response, there is a space. In that space is our power to choose our response. In our response lies our growth and our freedom."
— Viktor Frankl

Core beliefs are our habitual ways of thinking, and over time, the choices we made based on them became our unconscious, habitual ways of reacting to life. As we begin to recognize the pervasiveness of these habitual patterns of thinking and reacting in our life, we may think that we are powerless to change them. We may think that, because of our past or due to external circumstances, we have no choice but to think and act this way. One of the fundamental ways that we give up our power in life is by believing we have no choice but to act in habitual ways. Our practice today is to recognize that. When we understand and own how we contribute to our own suffering, we also rediscover our power to make new choices, choices that may better serve who we are today. Today, we invite you to reclaim your power.

Today...

Look in your journal at some of the thoughts and beliefs you have worked with so far in Ongo *(for example, in the Self-Empathy journal practice or in the Unpacking Core Beliefs practice from earlier this week)*. **Take a deep breath and exhale out any tension that occurs by re-reading them.**

Now, out of your own lists of thoughts, choose one that reflects a sense of choicelessness, inevitability, or lack of possibility for change.

For example, you might choose the thought "I don't have time to relax" or the thought "I'm too weak."

Read the thought you chose out loud. Breathe, then look at your Needs Wheel. Which Needs are being expressed by this particular thought? Write those Needs down next to the thought.

For example, next to "I don't have time to relax," you might write, "Rest" and "Ease."

Take a couple minutes to simply breathe and repeat those Needs out loud to yourself, slowly, one at a time, pausing in between words to experience how they feel in your body. Give spaciousness to just enjoy what this feels like. Breathe and release any anxiety around having to get on to the next step or get somewhere.

Look again at the thought you chose. Reflect on what actions you have been choosing that perpetuate that thought and what the Needs are behind those actions.

Now, in your journal, write "I choose to," then name the actions you have been choosing that perpetuate the thought.

Next, write "because it contributes to my Needs for," followed by the Needs behind those actions.

For example, after connecting to your Needs, you might rewrite "I don't have time to relax" as "I choose to spend most of my day responding to work-related tasks because it contributes to my Needs for order, security, meaning, and contribution."

Or you might rewrite "I'm too weak" as "I choose to shut down sometimes rather than try to 'be strong' because it contributes to my Needs for love and compassion" and "I choose to worry about 'being weak' because it contributes to my Needs for safety and acceptance."

Take another minute to read aloud your rewritten statement and notice how it feels. Again, allow spaciousness to enjoy what this feels like.

If you have time and interest, go back to the list and do this practice with another thought.

Tip – If you're having trouble identifying how you are choosing an action in your life and what Needs it's meeting, consider if that may be a choice to meet Needs of security, safety, or belonging. For example, you may be choosing to do certain things at work that you normally would not choose to do because you have a Need for the security that your job's paycheck provides. Or, you may choose to act in certain ways in public that you would not choose at home because you have Needs for the safety and belonging that conforming to societal expectations provides.

 Instant – In a moment when you notice yourself thinking or saying something that implies you don't have choice, pause and breathe. Reflect on what actions you have been choosing that perpetuate that sense of choicelessness. Look at the Needs Wheel. Consider why you keep choosing those actions. What Needs do they attempt to fulfill? Take a moment to acknowledge to yourself what you have been choosing and the Needs behind those choices.

 Deepening – As a daily mindfulness practice, anytime you notice yourself thinking or saying something that implies you don't have choice, let it be a signal to breathe and take conscious ownership of the choices you are making, as in the Instant practice above. Make it one of your commitments to, whenever possible, own the ways that you are presently contributing to what you experience, rather than seeing yourself as a victim of your thoughts or prisoner of your past.

Habit and Choice
Remembering

"We always have a choice. We don't do anything we didn't choose to do. We chose to behave that way to meet a need. A very important part of Nonviolent Communication is this recognition of choice at every moment, that moment we choose to do what we do, and we don't do anything that isn't coming out of choice. What's more, every choice we make is in the service of a need. That's how Nonviolent Communication works within us."
– Marshall B. Rosenberg, Ph.D.

Requests

"We need to free our minds if we are to find new paths through the dark forest of suffering. We need experimentation and playfulness in the face of difficulty, no matter how paradoxical that may seem."
– Mirabai Bush

The impulse to act in a habitual way can also be understood as a request to fulfill a Need. It is an invitation to ourselves – "Would you be willing to do this, because it would really contribute to these Needs?" To use one of the examples from the Habit and Choice practice this week, by asking oneself, "Would I be willing to spend most of today on work-related tasks, because it would really contribute to security?" we then have a choice of whether or not to say yes to the request. By taking conscious ownership of our actions, as the Habit and Choice practice supports us to do, we can recognize that our habits are, in fact, only requests and that we have the power to say yes or no to them. Knowing what Needs our habits are attempting to serve helps us to decide which habitual requests we want to continue saying yes to.

We also have the option to make new requests, inviting ourselves to take actions that may better serve the Needs we are aware of. For example, in the situation above, we might decide to request of ourselves an action that fulfills Needs for both security and rest, not just security at the expense of rest. So, we might ask ourselves, "Would I be willing to do work-related tasks until noon, then take a nap this afternoon, because it would contribute to both Needs of security and rest?"

Requests are where we take our practice "off the cushion." We have practiced listening to the Needs being expressed by our habits, beliefs, thoughts, and feelings. Today we will practice responding to those Needs by initiating action in our lives. This is what is called a "request" in Nonviolent Communication: an invitation, not a demand, to take a specific action in service of a Need.

Today...

Look at the Needs Wheel on page 271 and turn it slowly. Which Need or Needs are jumping off the page and feel enlivening to connect to in this moment?

Take a minute or two with each of those needs, feeling in your body how they touch you, what they mean to you. Breathe with those feelings and sensations.

What one simple action can you take to serve one of those Needs right now? Think small (*for example, choosing to drink your morning coffee outside in the sun today instead of in a bus on the way to work, in order to contribute to the Need for beauty*). Think of actions you can do right away so that you can give this gift immediately to yourself.

Take that action to nourish one of your Needs right now.

After, take a moment to acknowledge and thank yourself for giving to yourself.

Later today, do this practice again. Repeat as often as you like!

Deepening – As you grow in your practice of making requests of yourself, notice if there are certain requests that you regularly don't follow through on. For those requests, consider, are they:

- Doable? Sometimes we take on too much all at once. Try making a smaller request. *For example, if a request of yourself to "go to a yoga class after work" is something you are usually too tired to do, simplify the request to "do eight minutes of yoga right now," which might be something you are likely to follow through on.*

- Tangible and specific? Sometimes our requests are too vague. *For example, "Have more compassion for myself" isn't tangible or specific, but "Take five minutes after work to reflect on ways that I'm grateful for myself and acknowledge what I contribute to both my company and my family" is tangible and specific.* Naming a timeframe (i.e. "five minutes") can help.

- Dos rather than don'ts? *For example, "Don't judge myself" tells me what I don't want, but it doesn't offer any guidance for what to do instead. If I were to make that request into a "do" instead of a "don't," it might look like this: "Once today, if I notice that I'm judging myself, I'll take a minute to breathe and connect to the need that's there".*

Week 6

Finishing Business

Even after all this time
The sun never says to the earth
"You owe me"
Look what happens with a love like that
It lights the whole sky
— Hāfez,
translated by Daniel Ladinsky

Preparation – All Participants:

- Bring your copy of *The Ongo Book* and your journal.

Preparation – Group Guide:

- A day or two before the Group Gathering, remind everyone of the day, time, and place of the Gathering.

- Read "Leading Group Practice" (page 13) and do the points listed under "Responsibilities of the Guide."

- Bring a "talking stick" (a stick, stone, or object that can easily be held in one hand for Council) (as we did in Week 4's group).

- Lay one deck of Needs cards out in an attractive mandala or spiral in the center of the circle. Place the talking stick in the center.

Opening Meditation

Invite everyone to sit in the circle.

Ring a bell to signal the beginning of the sitting meditation.

After a moment of silence, read the guidance below to the group. Read in a way that supports the group to relax into the guidance, giving generous space and full breaths of silence between passages:

> Settle in where you are – on the floor, your chair, your cushion. Allow the body to feel the support of the earth beneath you.

Letting your eyes soften or close.

Take a deep breath in, fully filling the lungs. Breathing out, letting the belly soften.

Simply breathing and letting the belly soften a little more with each exhale.

Allow a couple minutes of silence, then read:

When we come to the middle of a practice period we awaken our internal sense to "Finishing Business." We acknowledge that we have opened our hearts to others and to ourselves. In that opening, we have also become aware that there is still more armor around our heart, protecting precious Needs. We are still creating separation from the life that we truly want to live. Finishing Business is our awareness of where we are and that the end is in sight. Finishing Business is saying what wants to be said, listening to those who long to have us hear them, and giving forth the forgiveness that transforms all that protection and armoring into acceptance, understanding, and belonging.

Sit in silence for three more minutes, then ring the bell three times to end the meditation.

Place your palms together and offer a bow of gratitude to the circle.

Council Round

With the talking stick that you brought in your hand, read this guidance to the group:

Mid-Ongo is a time when we may find ourselves needing to reconnect to the community and to ourselves. Enough weeks have passed that the excitement of starting Ongo may have faded, and enough weeks remain that the reality of Ongo ending has not yet set in. Like birth and death, beginnings and endings create a heightened sense of presence and give energy to practice. In between, we sometimes need support to remember why we're here, our Ongo intention.

Today, we will take some time to share with our circle in a Council Round how Ongo is unfolding for us. During the Council Round we will pass this talking stick around the circle to signal who has our attention.

Show the talking stick that you brought to the group, then continue reading:

The person speaking will have our full silent presence. While they are speaking, we will not comment on or respond to their words, nor will we be thinking about what we will say when it is our turn to speak. We will hold the space of empathy for each speaker. When it is our turn to speak, we will not refer to anyone else's sharing. Instead, we will speak from our own experiences and ideas.

> We will have one round of sharing. The topic is: "How is the Ongo journey going for you? How are you living your Ongo intention?" Feel free to share any celebrations, mournings, learnings, and challenges that are alive in your heart at this time around this topic. We will start with whoever first feels called to speak on the topic, then the talking stick will pass to the person on their left, and that person will share. We will continue that way around the circle until it comes back to the person who first spoke.
>
> Let us all be mindful about the length of our speaking so that there is time for everyone's voice to be heard and for another activity after this. At the same time, honor your own voice by giving it the space it needs to be expressed.

Check if anyone is unclear about the Council Round and needs to hear the instructions again. Once everyone is clear, invite everyone to take a breath together and to bring their presence to the circle. Read:

> How is the Ongo journey going for you? How are you living your Ongo intention? Who feels called to speak now on this topic?

Pass the talking stick to that person to begin the round of sharing.

Once the talking stick has made its way around the circle back to the person who first shared, take the talking stick and invite everyone to take a breath together.

Place the talking stick in the center of the circle.

Introduction to Finishing Business

Read to the group:

> Business, by most definitions, involves some kind of negotiation and exchange. We often engage our relationships in this way – a "this-for-that" approach. *If you listen to me, I'll listen to you. If I give to you, then I expect you'll give to me.* Love can become more like a commodity we are trading than a Need that is expressing life.
>
> We each will come to a certain point in our lives where we open to the reality that death is inevitable. Indeed, when we were born, we made a contract with death. Sometimes, it's not until we truly realize our life will end, or the life of someone we love will end, that we meet ourselves or the other person with consideration and love. We arrive to how we truly want to be in that relationship – loving, caring, understanding, and compassionate.
>
> When we say we are "Finishing Business," we are expressing a conscious awareness that this life has an end and that we would like to conduct our relationships with love and understanding. Finishing Business is the art of being present to all our relationships.

We are taking into deep consideration that any words we offer and any actions we take may be our last opportunity to connect with someone we hold dear. It is the practice of accepting that any moment could be our last breath. This acceptance holds within it a precious understanding that each interaction we have completes our destiny, our destination, which is life itself.

 Practicing Finishing Business

Invite everyone to form pairs and sit facing one another.

Read to the group:

> Imagine for a moment that this is your last day to be alive. Share for a moment with each other the feelings that instantaneously arise from imagining that.

Allow a minute or two for pairs to share, then read:

> Now bring to mind a person with whom you have "unfinished business," someone with whom you most would want to make sure you have finished business before you leave this life.

Allow a minute for everyone to reflect, then read:

> You and your partner will now take turns role-playing the people with which you each most want to finish business.
>
> Take a moment to decide who will go first.

Pause a moment for pairs to decide, then read:

> Person going first, tell your partner who the person is with whom you would like to finish business on your last day alive. Simply tell your partner this person's name and who they are to you. Your partner will role-play this person.

Allow a minute for pairs to share, then read:

> Now speak to your partner as if they were this person. Share with them what you long for them to hear. Finish business. Express what's in your heart – fear, joy, distrust, anger, expectation, relief, regret – whatever is there. Allow yourself a moment of freedom to complete with this person what you have been longing to complete.
>
> Partners in the role, simply receive it all with empathic listening and empathic reflection. Receive without judging or trying to "further the process." Simply respond with Needs words reflecting what you sense in their expression.

Let the dialogue flow until it settles to a close, then take a moment to breathe together and harvest what you learned.

Then, switch and begin again, so that the partner who was role-playing is now the person Finishing Business and the person who was Finishing Business is now helping by role-playing.

Check if anyone is unclear about the practice and needs to hear the instructions again. Once everyone is clear, invite everyone to take a breath together and to bring their presence to their partners for the practice.

Keep track of time. Allowing 10 minutes for a "Harvest" and "Closing," let everyone know when they are halfway through the available time for the practice. Remind them to switch if they haven't already so that both partners have a chance to finish business.

Ring a bell when it's time to shift to "Harvest." Invite everyone to thank their partners, then re-form the circle.

Harvest

Invite anyone who feels moved to share what touched them, what challenged them, what they learned, or what they discovered from today's practice with the group.

Close by offering gratitude to everyone for their sharing and practice.

Closing

Ask for a volunteer to guide the group next week. Give that person the deck(s) of Needs cards.

Remind that volunteer to read the pages on "Leading Group Practice" (page 13) and Week 7's Group Gathering before the next meeting. Everything they need to know will be in those pages.

Invite everyone to take a collective full breath together.

Invite everyone to each choose a Need card from the center that describes what they are taking with them from this sixth Ongo Group Gathering.

Starting with the person on your left, invite each person to share their Need with the group by holding their card face-out so everyone can see it. Go around the circle clockwise until everyone, including you, has shared.

Understanding, Acceptance, and Belonging

Out beyond ideas of wrongdoing and rightdoing,
there is a field. I'll meet you there.
When the soul lies down in that grass,
the world is too full to talk about.
Ideas, language, even the phrase 'each other'
doesn't make any sense.

– Jelaluddin Rumi,
translated by Coleman Barks

Opening Meditation

Greet your Buddy.

Decide who will read the remembering and who will time your silent sitting together.

The Buddy reading reads the following:

> Forgiveness is an invitation to know understanding, acceptance, and belonging. It allows us to join alliances, in our heart, with ourselves, others, and even the beliefs we think impossible to transform. It offers an opportunity to rewrite the stories of our past, present, and future and opens new pathways of reconciliation with people we thought we might not ever find peace with. Forgiveness is about giving forth energy to reconnect and restore our relationships, particularly with ourselves.
>
> Just hearing the word *forgiveness* can immediately bring up our defenses. The mind may say, "But what they did was unforgiveable" or "But I did nothing wrong, why do I need to forgive myself?" Forgiveness is not about wrongdoing or rightdoing. Forgiveness invites us into Rumi's field, out beyond those ideas, where we can lie down and feel the fullness of this world, this one beautiful life that will one day end.
>
> And when we come to that end, forgiveness asks us, Will our last breath let go into understanding, acceptance, and belonging? Or will it hold on, clinging, weighed down by unfinished business?

Sit together in meditation for 10 minutes.

Whoever is keeping time signals the other when 10 minutes have passed.

Close with a bow of appreciation to your Buddy for sitting with you.

Understanding, Acceptance, and Belonging

Decide who will be "A" and who will be "B."

Buddy A reads the following, slowly:

> Today, we will take turns asking each other a few open-ended questions about understanding, acceptance, and belonging. When it is our turn to respond, we are invited to share freely whatever response comes. Allow it to be a full exploration, taking time to explore what the word we're being asked about means to us. How does it live in our bodies? What physical sensations and feelings do we associate with it? What is our relationship to it when we're alone, with others, and in a group? How is it when it's fulfilled and not fulfilled? Or is there anything else that arises as a response to the question? If we notice that our attention is getting caught up in our own thoughts about what we're saying – for example, judgments about whether or not it's a "good" response, whether we're talking too much or too little, or even whether or not our response makes sense to our Buddy – simply notice, breathe, and return to presence with whatever wants to be spoken through us as a response to the question. We are allowing whatever arises from within simply to be given voice.
>
> When it is our turn to listen, we are asked to listen in silence, with our full presence. If we notice that our attention is getting caught up in our own thoughts about what's being said – for example, analysis, judgment, comparison, questions, or our own stories – simply notice, breathe, and return to presence with our Buddy. We will not offer any verbal response or confirmation of what we are hearing. We are allowing whatever rises as a response to our question to be given space simply to be heard.

Take a moment to check with each other if you both understood the guidance above for listening and responding. If needed, one of you can read the guidance out loud again.

Once both have understood, bring your presence to the practice:

1. A asks B, "What is *understanding*?"

2. B responds while A listens. When B is complete responding, B takes a breath and asks A, "What is *understanding*?"

3. A responds while B listens. When A is complete responding, A takes a breath and asks B, "What is *acceptance*?"

4. B responds while A listens. When B is complete responding, B takes a breath and asks A, "What is *acceptance*?"

5. A responds while B listens. When A is complete responding, A takes a breath and asks B, "What is *belonging*?"

6. B responds while A listens. When B is complete responding, B takes a breath and asks A, "What is *belonging*?"

7. A responds while B listens. When A is complete responding, A takes a breath and shares that they are complete.

8. Take three full breaths together.

Closing Harvest

Harvest by sharing any insights, learnings, or discoveries and any appreciations from your time together.

WEEK 6 SOLO PRACTICES

Seeing the Gift

"From the moment of birth, every human being wants happiness and does not want suffering. Neither social conditioning nor education nor ideology affect this. From the very core of our being, we simply desire contentment."
– Tenzin Gyatso, the 14th Dalai Lama

With our Core Belief and Self-Empathy practices, we can start to see that all our thoughts, feelings, and actions are expressing life-serving Needs, even those thoughts and actions that cause harm. Marshall Rosenberg, creator of Nonviolent Communication, called the latter "tragic, suicidal expressions of unmet [N]eeds," or more playfully, "gifts wrapped in shit." At the root of forgiveness is an understanding that recognizes this truth. We see the gift – the yearning to serve life – inside of every expression, even as we are also fully awake to the impact of those expressions on ourselves and others.

Today…

Carry with you a copy of the Needs Wheel (or your copy of *The Ongo Book* with the Needs Wheel in the Appendix bookmarked). Take it out two or three times today and look at the people around you. Silently guess what Needs are being expressed by each person you see. Don't think too hard about it – just see what Needs jump off the page. Even try guessing what Needs are being expressed by people who are silent – look at their body postures and movements.

Really take a moment to connect to the energy of those Needs, not just intellectually guessing them but feeling them in your body. *For example, if you're guessing someone is feeling pain around the Need acceptance, take a moment to connect to what the energy of acceptance feels like in your body.*

How does connecting to these people's Needs affect how you see them?

Try this with yourself also. Take out the Needs Wheel two or three times today and reflect on what Need(s) are most up for you in this moment? Again, really connect to the energy of those Needs in the body. Breathe with them. Close your eyes and feel what they mean to you.

How does doing this shift how you see your own thoughts, actions, or words?

Seeing the Gift
Remembering

"There is another peculiar satisfaction in really hearing someone: It is like listening to the music of the spheres, because beyond the immediate message of the person, no matter what that might be, there is the universal. Hidden in all of the personal communications which I really hear there seem to be orderly psychological laws, aspects of the same order we find in the universe as a whole. So there is both the satisfaction of hearing this person and also the satisfaction of feeling one's self in touch with what is universally true."
– Carl Rogers

Taking Inventory

"Sometimes the initial breakthrough doesn't result in peace or healing into anything. Indeed, sometimes people look and feel worse. But they are fuller. They have allowed suppressed and abandoned parts of themselves to surface and finally be served."
– Stephen Levine

By joining Ongo, and by walking this path of practice, all of us are expressing some form of a desire to open our hearts more to ourselves and to others. Through connecting to the body and the breath; through practicing seeing the Needs inside of actions, words, and thoughts, even the ones that trigger us; through acknowledging our limitations and opening to something greater than our minds can conceive, we are expanding our capacity to understand and be with ourselves and others.

Now, at mid-Ongo, is a good time to take inventory of what's left. What do we still want to open to? In Ongo, we sometimes use the word *forgiveness* to describe the act of opening our hearts to the thoughts, words, and actions that we have a tough time loving. For us, forgiveness does not imply blame, or that somebody did something "wrong," and it also does not mean a passive acceptance of harmful words or acts. Forgiveness, as we're using the word here, means being able to acknowledge, love, and empathize with the Needs behind a thought, word, or action, even if we don't necessarily agree with the thought, word, or action itself. Ultimately, it means deeply seeing the humanity in ourselves and others.

That's a lot to ask. So, today, we'll just name the work ahead.

Today...

Take several minutes to sit and be with the body and the breath, gently returning to presence with these whenever the mind gets lost in thought.

After, make two columns in your journal, one titled "Forgiving Self" and one titled "Forgiving Others." Take some time to reflect on your life at present and consider what beliefs/habits/behaviors/words/actions you would like to forgive yourself for. Write these down under the column of "Forgiving Self." Be sure to include even those things which you're not yet able to forgive yourself for. This is simply a list of what we hope and intend to one day be able to release.

For example, part of your list might look like this:

<u>Forgiving Self</u>

- forgetfulness, especially around things that are important to my loved ones

- the time I ignored a really supportive friend, because I was trying to gain acceptance from some of my other peers

- the moments with my dog when I speak or act from anger

- my belief that "I'm not enough"

- my frequent habit of working on the computer instead of physically exercising my body

Now, consider whom you would like to forgive in your life besides yourself, and write those names down under "Forgiving Others." Include which of their words or actions you would like to forgive each of these people for. Again, be sure to include even those people you are not yet able to forgive. We're setting an intention and naming a hope we have.

Take a few deep breaths. With each exhale, feel and send the energy of compassion, love, and acceptance into your being. If it's hard to connect to that energy, take another minute or two simply to say to yourself, "May I be free from suffering. May all those I interact with be free from suffering. May all beings be free from suffering. May all beings be free." If these phrases don't quite match what you are working with, then create your own loving-kindness intentional phrases and use them here.

Close by taking a moment to appreciate this desire to forgive in yourself. Celebrate your willingness to give energy and space to it today. Tenderly accept where there is still unwillingness and hurt.

Breathe and walk gently today.

Taking Inventory
Remembering

"[B]eing reconciled to our enemies or our loved ones [is] not about pretending that things are other than they are. True reconciliation exposes the awfulness, the abuse, the hurt, the truth. It could even sometimes make things worse. It is a risky undertaking, but in the end it is worthwhile, because in the end only an honest confrontation with reality can bring real healing. Superficial reconciliation can bring only superficial healing."
– Bishop Desmond Tutu

Forgiveness Meditation

"Forgiveness simply means that, as children of war, we wish to become people of peace. They say, if you don't forgive, you can become the oppressor. We must remember that we don't want to become the very thing that is hurting us."
– Lyla June Johnston

Forgiveness, like many other practices, develops its power in us through repetition. We may find ourselves practicing forgiveness many times with the same situation, each time unlocking a different dimension of understanding, acceptance, and belonging within our being.

Thich Nhat Hanh says, "If, in our heart, we still cling to anything – anger, anxiety, or possessions – we cannot be free." The understanding, acceptance, and belonging that comes with forgiveness is the true meaning of freedom. We become free to be fully present with ourselves and others, without holding on to the past. We become free to choose how we wish to live, without fear about the future.

Today...

Settle in.

Taking three full breaths, let the belly soften.

Invite into your mind the image of someone who stimulates a core belief you have about yourself. If this is your first time doing this meditation, we recommend choosing a light to medium weight – someone who does not greatly impact your life.

Notice what happens in the body.

Notice the "other" person in the situation who offered the stimulation for this core belief to arise. And notice how you have, just perhaps, put this person out of your heart.

Just feel their presence in your mind. Sense what you tell yourself about this person who helped to stimulate the core belief you have about yourself.

Now gently, as an experiment in truth, invite this person into your heart. Feel their approach to your heart. Notice whatever blocks their approach – fear, anger, shame, guilt, safety, trust. And notice the qualities that block the entrance to your heart to the person who offers stimulation to your core belief.

Then, just for this moment, let them through. Let them into your heart. Noticing in them, this "other," what may be alive. A desire to connect? To be understood? To belong? Whatever may be alive, just for this moment, let them in.

And say to them, in your heart, "I accept you as you are." "I accept you." "I forgive you for the action that stimulates my core belief."

It is so painful to put someone out of your heart. Just for this moment, let them back in. And whisper silently, in your heart, "I forgive you."

It can be so painful to hold on to protection, keeping them out of your heart. For now, simply give space in your heart for them to be – to be with all their humanness, which may have intentionally or unintentionally stumbled into your core beliefs about yourself.

Simply accept them. Love them.

And now, let them go. Sending them off, maybe with a blessing, in your own way.

Ahh, breath. Settle in more fully to where you sit.

Connect again to the core belief about yourself.

Say it to yourself in your mind.

Notice, where does it come alive in the body? Access that point. What arises? What images appear? Staying connected to this access point in the body, simply allow the images to pass through the mind. Bear witness softly to these images until you see yourself in your mind, possibly at an age when this core belief first arrived to you, or possibly at an age when this core belief took root in your believing.

See yourself at this age in your mind.

And now, gently, welcome you at this age into your heart.

Turn to yourself in your heart. Have mercy. You've been carrying this belief about yourself for so long – for protection, for safety. For so long carrying this belief – to find belonging, to find acceptance, to find love.

Turn to yourself in your heart and say to yourself, "I accept you as you are." "I forgive you for thinking this belief about yourself, for carrying this belief for so long."

It is so painful to keep you out of your own heart.

Whisper silently to yourself, "I forgive you." Have mercy. If the mind wants to try to block such forgiveness, touch it with understanding for such protection. Have mercy.

Calling yourself by your own first name, say "I forgive you" to you. "I accept you."

It can be so painful to hold on to protection, keeping you out of your own heart.

Simply give space now, for you to be, with all your humanness.

Simply accept. Simply love.

Let your mind – let your body, let your heart – be filled with loving-kindness for yourself. And for everyone, who also want only to be free of their own pain, to be at peace.

Let this love radiate, expanding outward to all those you love, that they too may forgive themselves in kindness, in love.

Let this loving-kindness include all beings, all hearts. All Needs of all sentient beings everywhere, touched by your loving kindness.

May all beings be free of suffering. May all beings be at peace.

May all beings live fully in their own authentic presence, in joy, in love.

May all beings be at peace.

May all beings be at peace.

Tip – Consciously choose the weights that you want to work with in this meditation. That said, sometimes, you may pick up what you think is a small weight and it can unexpectedly lead to a heavier weight in your meditation, a memory of a person or event that greatly impacted you. If this occurs, consider any or all of the following: do the meditation again with the new weight, call your Ongo Buddy for empathy and do the practice with their supportive presence, or contact a trauma-informed professional who can support you to work deeply with what has arisen.

Audio – There is a guided audio recording of this meditation available on The Ongo Companion Website at <u>ongo.global</u>. You can also make your own guided audio meditation by recording yourself reading the practice out loud. If you make your own, remember to speak slowly and allow lots of silence in between instructions so you can easily follow along when listening to it later.

Week 7

WEEK 7 GROUP

Forgiveness

"True forgiveness does not paper over what has actually happened in any superficial way. It is not a misguided effort to suppress or ignore our pain. And it cannot be hurried. It is a deep process, repeated over and over in our heart, that honors the grief and the betrayal, and in its own time ripens into the freedom to truly forgive."
– Jack Kornfield

 Preparation – Group Guide:

- A day or two before the Group Gathering, remind everyone of the day, time, and place of the Gathering.

- Read "Leading Group Practice" (page 13) and do the points listed under "Responsibilities of the Guide."

- Lay one deck of Needs cards out in an attractive mandala or spiral in the center of the circle.

Opening Meditation

Invite everyone into a standing position in the circle.

Ring a bell to signal the beginning of a standing meditation.

After a moment of silence, read the guidance below to the group. Read in a way that supports the group to relax into the guidance, giving generous space and full breaths of silence between passages:

> Today's meditation will be standing. If, at any point, it feels physically painful to stand, you are welcome to continue to follow the meditation from a seated position.
>
> Stand with your feet hip-width apart and rock slightly forward and back, finding the place where your weight rests evenly on your feet, rather than leaning on the heels or toes.
>
> Gently stretch the crown of your head toward the sky, and draw your chin in slightly toward your neck, feeling your spine relax as it comes into alignment.
>
> Breathe and roll your shoulders back, letting them relax, with your arms hanging freely by your sides.
>
> Let your forehead, eyes, and jaw be soft.

Take a few deep breaths. With each exhale, gently release any lingering tension in your body into the earth, starting from the top of your head, all the way down to the bottom of your feet.

Stand in silence for a minute, then read:

Bring your awareness to the sensations of the inhale and exhale, and the body, as it rests supported by the earth.

Stand in silence for a minute, then read:

Let your awareness expand to include your back body. Feel the space behind your head, neck, and spine. Feeling your connection to the past. Where your ancestors have given you both gifts and burdens to carry. Where you walk with both strengths and weights from your own lifetime. Breathe and simply feel it now.

Stand in silence for a minute, then read:

Gently exhale any tension there, down through your feet, into the earth. Letting the earth receive it and compost it.

Stand in silence for a few breaths, then read:

Let your awareness expand to include your front body. Feel the space in front of your head, chest, and belly. Feeling your connection to the future. Where your life impacts the generations to come. Where you have both gifts to offer and unresolved burdens that you will pass on. Breathe and feel it now.

Stand in silence for a minute, then read:

Gently exhale any tension there, down through your feet, into the earth. Letting the earth take it and compost it, to make new fertile soil.

Stand in silence for a few breaths, then read:

Let your awareness expand to include the space on both sides of you. Feel the space in your peripheral vision, out beyond your shoulders. Feeling your connection to all those who walk with you on this earth today. Your family and community. Those who are standing with you in this circle now. Those who support you with their presence, and those whom you support with yours. Breathe and feel it now.

Stand in silence for a minute, then read:

> This is the stance of a nonviolent warrior. Connected to the sky, the breath, and the earth.
>
> Standing with dignity, connected to all life – past, present, and future – without hiding, running away, or opposing it.
>
> Simply being awake to what is, and letting it be our home.

Stand in silence together for another minute, then ring the bell three times to end the meditation.

Place your palms together and offer a bow of gratitude to the circle.

Check-in

Read to the group:

> Today, we will continue our exploration of forgiveness. For many people, forgiveness can be a topic loaded with cultural and religious connotations. As a practice, it can also bring a lot to the surface, emotionally. Let's begin our continued exploration with a simple check-in to hear how it has been for us to explore forgiveness so far in Ongo. What has come up in your practices? How has it been to turn toward forgiveness, or not turn toward it? What new understandings or connections to forgiveness have emerged?

Invite anyone who feels moved to share their responses to these questions with the group.

Keep track of time. Allowing at least 45 minutes for the other activities, let the group know when there's just a few minutes left for sharing before the group will shift to the next activity.

Forgiveness

Read to the group (or invite others to take turns reading one or more of the paragraphs to the group):

> Forgiveness integrates our experience in a way that allows us to become free from suffering. It releases us of the burden of any resentment or hate we might be carrying. It's a recognition that our holding on is based on fear – fear that the past will repeat itself, fear that somehow harm will continue, fear that suffering will continue. Forgiveness is freedom from fear. As we touch this acceptance, this understanding, this belonging, on

any level, whether it's forgiving a person who was rude to us or forgiving the architects of war, we free ourselves from suffering.

Moving toward forgiveness also honors the heart's dignity, our own dignity. It returns us to the ground of love, reminds us of our compassion and unwillingness to harm ourselves or others. Though we may never be able to forgive the action, we can begin to see the Needs behind the action so we can return to seeing the human. Though the action itself may remain forever unforgivable, the human is always forgivable.

Forgiveness is not permission for the unforgivable action to continue, nor is it an excuse for the action having happened in the past. If, for example, this brings into question a current relationship where you are experiencing or expressing actions that are causing trauma, then before you dive further into this work, get you and your loved ones to safety. Your next step may be contacting a trusted person, therapist, or group that can help stop the action from continuing. Getting to safety is primary before diving deeply into this inner work.

When working with our past, we can acknowledge how different life would have been had the action causing the trauma never occurred. We can also acknowledge from a physically safe space that the action itself is no longer continuing and it is how we live with the residual trauma that matters most right now. When practicing forgiveness, we feel authentic regret for ours or others' actions. Forgiveness opens up the freedom within our own heart to find peace. Even when we experience great abuses, including physical and sexual violence, it is the holding on to anger, fear, and resentment that can destroy our lives, not the actions themselves. Choosing how we walk in our lives with what has happened is within our power. The biggest transformation we can make is to access understanding of Needs, separating out the actor from the action with acceptance, and touch forgiveness. In doing so, we have the ability to see the human inside ourselves as well as in others.

We develop these practices so we can cultivate and sustain the power that is always within us, the power to transform our own hatred and fear to live in peace, love, and forgiveness.

Ask if anyone would like to share anything that got stirred in them hearing these words about forgiveness. Invite anyone who feels moved to speak.

Forgiveness Meditation

Invite everyone to settle into a position where they can be comfortable for a longer guided meditation.

Once everyone is settled, read the guidance below to the group. Read in a way that supports everyone to be able to follow along at a meditative pace, with generous spaces of silence between instructions:

> Taking a few breaths, let the belly soften. Simply give this space to yourself right now.
>
> Invite in one of the core beliefs you have been working with in your practices. One of the things you often tell yourself –
>
> "I'm not enough." "I'm too sensitive."
>
> "There is never enough time." "It is always going to be a struggle."
>
> "I'm always wrong." "I'm always right."
>
> Whatever it is you've noticed through your practices in the last several weeks – the thoughts that always return. Maybe it phrases itself differently from time to time, but the essence is still the same. It still goes to this core belief. Bring that to mind now.
>
> And say it to yourself. Taking a few breaths as you settle in where you sit.
>
> Just say it to yourself in your mind.
>
> Then notice where energy comes alive in your body as you are saying this to yourself. Are there aches in your back? In your knees? Where is it? Where does it live in your body? Where does it move around?
>
> Access these points in the body, consciously breathing and connecting there.
>
> What images come to mind?
>
> Staying connected to these points in the body, allow all these images simply to pass through your mind like a slideshow.
>
> Bear witness softly to these images until you see yourself in your mind, possibly at an age when this core belief first arrived or possibly at an age when this core belief took root in you, when you began to believe it to be true.
>
> Just notice and begin to see yourself.
>
> See yourself at this age in your mind.
>
> Now gently welcome you at this age into your heart.

Hand in hand, bringing yourself into your own heart.

And turn to yourself in your heart. Have mercy. You have been carrying this belief about yourself for so long. For so long – for protection, for safety – for so long carrying this belief – to find belonging, to find acceptance, to find love.

Turn to yourself in your heart and say to yourself, "I accept you as you are."

Turn to yourself in your heart and say to yourself, "I accept you for thinking this belief about yourself."

Turn to yourself in your heart and say to yourself, "I forgive you for carrying this belief for so long."

It can be so painful to keep you out of your own heart.

Whisper silently and say, "I forgive you," to you.

And have mercy. If the mind wants to block such forgiveness, thank the mind for its protection and touch it with understanding. Have mercy.

Calling yourself by your own first name, say, "I forgive you."

Calling yourself by your own first name, say, "I accept you."

It can be so painful to hold on to protection, keeping you out of your own heart.

Simply give space now in your own heart for you to be with all your humanness that may have intentionally or unintentionally caused harm by believing any of these beliefs to be true. Simply give space.

Say, "I forgive you," to you.

Let your body, let your heart be filled with this loving-kindness for yourself.

Let this loving-kindness radiate outward to all those you love, that they too may forgive themselves in kindness and in love.

Let this loving-kindness radiate, expanding outward to all those you tell yourself are difficult to love, that they too may be free of their own pain and be at peace.

Let this loving-kindness include all beings, all hearts, all Needs of all sentient beings everywhere, touched in this moment by your loving-kindness.

May all beings be free of suffering.

May all beings be at peace.

May all beings live fully in their own authentic purpose in love.

Sit for another moment or two in silence, then ring the bell three times to signal the end of the guided meditation.

Harvest

Invite anyone who feels moved to share something that touched them or that they discovered from today's practice with the group.

Close by offering gratitude to everyone for their sharing and practice.

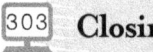

Closing

Ask for a volunteer to guide the group next week. Give that person the deck(s) of Needs cards.

Remind that volunteer to read the pages on "Leading Group Practice" (page 13) and Week 8's Group Gathering before the next meeting. Everything they need to know will be in those pages.

Invite everyone to take a collective full breath together.

Invite everyone to each choose a Need card from the center that describes what they are taking with them from this seventh Ongo Group Gathering.

Starting with the person on your left, invite each person to share their Need with the group by holding their card face-out so everyone can see it. Go around the circle clockwise until everyone, including you, has shared.

WEEK 7 BUDDY

Gratitude

"Gratitude unlocks the fullness of life. It turns what we have into enough, and more. It turns denial into acceptance, chaos to order, confusion to clarity. It can turn a meal into a feast, a house into a home, a stranger into a friend. Gratitude makes sense of our past, brings peace for today, and creates a vision for tomorrow."
– Melody Beattie

Giving Gratitude

Greet your Buddy.

Decide who will read the remembering (Buddy A) and who will read the first guided meditation (Buddy B).

Buddy A reads the following:

> If forgiveness is our practice of transforming resentment, hatred, and fear into living in love and peace, then gratitude is our practice to sustain that energy of love and peace in our life. When we touch with mindfulness what we give and receive in this life, we begin to notice that gratitude is a natural state of being that arises whether we are celebrating or mourning.
>
> Celebration goes beyond judging something or someone as "good," and gratitude goes beyond simply complimenting others. Our practices of mindfulness and empathy help us to go beyond these habits that separate us and touch into a deeper place of connection to life itself.

Pause for a moment simply to take a breath together.

Then, Buddy B reads the following meditation out loud, slowly, with pauses for both to follow the guidance:

> Take a breath to settle in just a little more, here and now.
>
> Take a few breaths to scan your body.
>
> Notice any tension or tightness and give a few more breaths to those areas. Simply letting in just a little more space.
>
> Now let yourself connect to celebration.

Celebration as a Need, an energy, an aliveness within your being. Notice how it moves within you. Notice its textures, sensations, movements, or stillness.

Now allow the image of a person to arise – a person who graced your life, for whom you are ever so grateful. Recall who they are to you. Recall their presence in your life.

Recall a specific moment of interaction you had with this person. What did they do? What did they say?

What are the feelings and sensations in your body as you remember this moment?

Take a breath. Place a hand on your belly. What Needs arise? What Needs are nourished by connecting to this memory? What Needs are nourished by having had this person in this particular moment of your life?

Now take a moment to write a gratitude. Make clear what the person did, what action on their part enriched your life. Make clear what feelings come alive as a result of what they've done. Make clear the Needs that are being nourished.

Once both of you have written a gratitude, take turns reading to each other what you wrote. Read just what you wrote: what they did, how you feel, and the Needs nourished. Breathe through any temptation to elaborate, complain, or compliment.

Receiving Gratitude

Buddy A now reads this meditation out loud, slowly, with pauses for both to follow the guidance:

Take a breath to settle in just a little more, here and now.

Letting yourself, again, connect to celebration.

Celebration.

Allow the image to arise of a person whom you have been waiting to appreciate you, a person for whom you would like to hear how grateful they are for your presence in their life.

Recall who they are to you. Recall their presence in your life.

Recall a specific moment of interaction you had with this person. What action did you take that you would like acknowledged? What did you say that you want to be heard?

What are the feelings and sensations you would guess were alive in them when they heard or saw what you offered?

Taking a breath, place a hand on your belly. What Needs arise? What Needs do you imagine were nourished for them in that interaction with you? What Needs do you imagine were nourished in this person by having your presence with them in that particular moment of their life?

Take a moment to write this gratitude, from them to you. Make clear what you did, what action on your part enriched their life. Make clear what feelings you guess came alive as a result of what you did. Make clear the Needs that are being nourished.

Hand what you wrote to your Buddy (or email it if you're meeting by phone).

Share just a bit of who this person is to you – again, breathing through the temptation to complain or compliment.

Taking turns, read out loud to your Buddy the gratitude that they want to hear.

As you hear the gratitude that you wanted to hear, take it in. Breathe and allow yourself to receive it.

Closing Harvest

Take a few moments to share what you learned from this practice. How was it to offer your gratitude out loud? How was it to receive gratitude?

Complete your time together with three minutes of silent sitting.

WEEK 7 SOLO PRACTICES

Gratitude List

"This could be our revolution:
To love what is plentiful
as much as
what is scarce."
– Alice Walker

Gratitude as a practice means giving our presence to all that enriches our life. Gratitude grows our sense of everyday joy, our knowledge of what feeds us, and our capacity to turn toward difficulty. At its deepest level, gratitude is a state of being that reflects our oneness with all that is.

Today…

Reflect on anything that is happening or has happened in your recent life that stimulates a sense of gratitude. What specifically happened that touched you? Was it something you said or did, or something someone else said or did? What Needs were touched?

Make a gratitude list with 10 happenings that you are grateful for, and name the Needs that are nourished by each happening.

For example:

> My body feeling comfortable, without pain - HEALTH, SUPPORT, STABILITY
>
> Enjoying hot tea with Catherine in the early morning sunshine on the porch - BEAUTY, SPIRITUAL EXPRESSION, AIR
>
> A friend calling us to share about their brother's passing - MOURNING, TRUST, EMPATHY
>
> Removing branches and leaves from our creek and seeing the current grow stronger - CONTRIBUTION, CONNECTION, RESPECT

If you're part of an Ongo group, share your list with them. This could take many different forms: an email sent out that everyone replies to, a messaging thread, a poster that everyone can write on, etc. Some Ongo groups have an ongoing gratitude list throughout Ongo that participants contribute to whenever they like.

Gratitude List
Remembering

"The great open secret of gratitude is that it is not dependent on external circumstance. It's like a setting or channel that we can switch to at any moment, no matter what's going on around us. It helps us connect to our basic right to be here, like the breath does."

– Joanna Macy

Sharing Gratitude

"Gratitude is so much more than a polite thank you. It is the thread that connects us in a deep relationship, simultaneously physical and spiritual, as our bodies are fed and spirits nourished by the sense of belonging, which is the most vital of foods. Gratitude creates a sense of abundance, the knowing that you have what you need. In that climate of sufficiency, our hunger for more abates and we take only what we need, in respect for the generosity of the giver."
– Robin Wall Kimmerer

When we extend our gratitude practice to others by letting them know specifically how they contributed to our life and what Needs of ours they touched, we invite a quality of connection that's richer and more meaningful than a passing "thank you." We're creating a world where connection can be based on joy, mutual giving, and appreciation.

Today's practice can also be a mindfulness practice: whenever you notice yourself about to praise or complimen>t someone, take a breath and do this practice instead.

Today...

Express a gratitude in-person to someone for how they contributed to your life.

Include in your gratitude:

- **Specifically what that person said or did that contributed to your life**
- **How you feel in relation to it**
- **What Needs their words or actions contributed to**

For example, "I want you to know how reassured I've been feeling having you walk us through this legal process by calling us each day, looking over our documents, and offering your advice. It contributes to my sense of TRUST, SECURITY, and PEACE OF MIND." Notice how this example names how one feels ("reassured"), what the other person specifically did ("calling us each day," "looking over documents," "offering advice"), and what Needs those actions contributed to (trust, security, peace of mind).

Sharing Gratitude
Remembering

"If we say thank you and really mean it, we have said yes to our belonging together. We have said yes to the fact that we are receiving something which under no circumstances can we give ourselves – a present. It's always another from whom I receive. When we cultivate that gratefulness to life, we not only cultivate trust in life and openness for surprise, we practice again and again saying yes to our limitless belonging to this great Earth household. That roots us and makes us at home; it gives us that great at-homeness."
– Brother David Steindl-Rast

Celebration and Mourning

*"If we learn to be aware of feelings without grasping or aversion,
then they can move through us like changing weather,
and we can be free to feel them and move on like the wind."*
– Jack Kornfield

The practices of mindfulness and Nonviolent Communication enable us to understand every thought and every feeling we have as a present-moment celebration or mourning. This understanding can free us from the tendency to judge our thoughts as being negative, something that "keeps us" from being present. Instead, we can see that thoughts are simply the mind's way to celebrate or mourn – they are like the mind's tears of gratitude and regret.

We can know, for example, that when we criticize ourselves for a choice we made, this criticism is simply an expression of mourning. We are mourning the Needs which weren't fulfilled in that moment of making the choice. We can hear the criticism as a kind of weeping rather than an assault. Similarly, when the mind is anxiously thinking about the future, trying to avoid repeating a past experience, we can recognize that these thoughts are a form of tears about what happened in the past. Or, if the mind is excitedly making future plans, trying to re-create a past experience, we can see that simply as a wave of fulfillment coming over us, celebrating the Needs that were touched by that past experience.

When we see this clearly, it becomes easier to live in the present moment and enjoy what we are experiencing. We can acknowledge the sentiment that's being expressed by our thoughts, feel that flavor of celebration or mourning in our bodies, and rest into the understanding of the Need that's being celebrated or mourned.

Today...

Sit for 15 to 20 minutes, being with the body and the breath.

During this time, whenever your attention gets caught up in thinking, notice whether the flavor is one of celebration or mourning.

> *For example, the thought "I'm so distracted – I should really calm down and focus on my breath" keeps coming up in my meditation. As I hear it in my mind, I notice it has a flavor of mourning.*

Breathe and feel whatever feelings and body sensations are present with that celebration or mourning.

> *For example, feelings of anxiety, restlessness, and tightness in my chest come with that mourning.*

Listen to the symphony of thoughts and feelings and sense what Need or Needs are being celebrated or mourned. Don't think about it too much – simply let the Need rise to the surface. Glance at your Needs Wheel if you want.

> *For example, as I continue to listen to those thoughts and feel those feelings, I sense that Needs of connection, spiritual expression, and peace of mind are being mourned.*

Breathe and rest into that understanding of what's precious to you. Let that natural settling lead you back to simply being with the body and the breath.

> *For example, breathing and understanding that those thoughts and feelings are really about how precious connection, spiritual expression, and peace of mind are to me, a sweet and tender feeling of appreciation rises in my being. As I rest into that feeling, I start to settle into a deep sense of stillness and presence. Now, being with the body and the breath feels effortless.*

Close the meditation by taking a moment to appreciate yourself and life for this time.

Once more during the course of the day, in a moment when you notice you are caught up in your thoughts, take a minute to simply breathe and hear the celebration and mourning that's being expressed inside. Feel whatever feelings are there, and sense the Needs that are being celebrated or mourned. Rest into that understanding.

Breathe.

 Audio – There is a guided audio recording of this meditation available on The Ongo Companion Website at <u>ongo.global</u>. You can also make your own guided audio meditation by recording yourself reading the practice out loud. If you make your own, remember to speak slowly and allow lots of silence in between instructions so you can easily follow along when listening to it later.

 Deepening – Practice seeing all expressions (thoughts, feelings, actions, words), in yourself and others, as present-moment celebrations and mournings. Breathe and rest into that understanding of what's precious to you and others as you go about your day. Let that inform how you relate to yourself and others.

Week 8

WEEK 8 GROUP

Celebration and Mourning

"If we can grieve with the griefs of others, so, by the same token, by the same openness, can we find strength in their strengths, bolstering our own individual supplies of courage, commitment, and endurance."

– Joanna Macy

 Preparation – Group Guide:

- A day or two before the Group Gathering, remind everyone of the day, time, and place of the Gathering.

- Read "Leading Group Practice" (page 13) and do the points listed under "Responsibilities of the Guide."

- Lay one deck of Needs cards out in an attractive mandala or spiral in the center of the circle. Place the Celebration and Mourning cards in the center.

 Opening Meditation

Invite everyone into a standing position in the circle.

Ring a bell to signal the beginning of meditation.

After a moment of silence, read the guidance below to the group. Read in a way that supports the group to relax into the guidance, allowing generous space and full breaths of silence between passages:

> In today's meditation, we'll explore walking with the same consciousness as in our sitting meditation. If it is physically painful for you to walk, you are welcome to meditate from a seated position. If seated, you can follow most of the guidance by resting your hands on your thighs and slightly lifting the left or right hand in place, according to the instructions, instead of your feet.
>
> Let's begin by feeling our feet on the floor and the support of the earth beneath.
>
> Breathe and bounce the knees slightly. Exhale and release any tension in the hips into the earth, letting the hips settle into alignment above the knees, and the knees above the ankles.

Slightly tuck your tailbone in and feel the length of your spine all the way up to the crown of your head.

On the inhale, draw the chin in slightly, bringing the head into alignment with the spine. Exhale and let any tension in the neck or shoulders release down into the earth.

Breathe and let the arms hang at your sides. Let the eyes rest and gaze soften to one point.

Feel how the body sways gently with the breath.

Feel the stability of the earth beneath the feet. Feel that support.

Stand in silence for a minute, then read, at the slow, steady rhythm of the breath, the following guidance:

Exhale and gently pour your weight onto your right foot and the earth beneath it. Coming to rest on that foot.

On the inhale, slowly turn to face the person on your left, letting the left foot turn with you. Exhale and gently pour your weight onto the left foot and the earth beneath it. Coming to rest on that foot.

On the inhale, slightly lift your right foot and take a baby step toward the person on your left. Exhale and pour your weight onto the right foot and the earth beneath it.

On the inhale, slightly lift your left foot and take another baby step toward the person on your left. Exhale and pour your weight onto the left foot and the earth beneath it.

Continue to walk around our circle this way, moving in baby steps, at the pace of the breath. Inhale and take a step. Exhale and shift your weight onto the forward foot. Throughout, let the body be relaxed, resting into the rhythm of the breath and the support of the earth beneath you.

Walk in silence for a few minutes, then read:

As we continue to walk, notice if there is anything there floating around in the mind or the heart. Listen to it, as you breathe and feel your feet touch the earth.

Does it feel like celebration, something you are appreciating or enjoying? Does it feel like mourning, something you seek or long for? Maybe a bit of both?

Allow yourself to feel whatever is there. However it feels in the body.

Walk in silence for another minute, then read:

> If something in the mind or heart keeps arising, hear what Need or Needs are being expressed. Not thinking about it too hard. Just let the Need rise to your consciousness and then pass, if it is there.

Walk in silence for a few more minutes, then read:

> This is an opportunity to witness ourselves through the stillness. Feeling the flavor of our moment-to-moment experience. Sometimes celebration, sometimes mourning. Sometimes both, sometimes neither.
>
> Sometimes there is a Need being spoken through the thoughts and feelings; sometimes it's unnameable. Just as quickly as we recognize and enjoy each of these aspects of our experience, we can release them all and return to the breath and the earth.
>
> Allow yourself this opportunity simply to be present to whatever is there, the symphony of your life.
>
> As Tenshin Reb Anderson once said, "Whatever arises is a gift, so we receive it completely and say, 'Thank you very much, I have no complaints whatsoever.'"

Walk in silence together for another few minutes, then ring the bell three times to end the meditation.

Invite everyone to turn and face the center of the circle again.

Place your palms together and offer a bow of gratitude to the circle.

Introduction to Celebration and Mourning

Read to the group:

> Meditation helps us notice how we live in a constant flux of celebrating what feels good in our lives and mourning what does not work. Celebration and mourning live hand in hand. When we touch one, the other is accessed. They ebb and flow. When we meditate, we notice how they wash through us like waves. In one moment, we celebrate the song of a bird, a memory of being loved, or the receiving of gratitude. In the next moment, we mourn the sound of a clock ticking, a memory of losing a loved one, or the pushing away of someone with our judgments. We begin to notice that this is just life expressing itself. We come to realize that this is what we are trying to do each time we speak – we are giving expression to the celebration and the mourning that flow through us in every moment.

Celebration and Mourning Circle

Pick up the Celebration and Mourning Needs cards from the center of the circle. Hold them in your hand and read the following guidance to the group:

> The practice of coming together in community to share mourning and celebration is one of our oldest human traditions. We come together to welcome, hear, and appreciate what each of us feels, with the understanding that this in itself has deep value. Grief and joy are not problems to be fixed or burdens to be carried – they are natural expressions of being alive and being human. Celebration and Mourning Circles are rememberings of who we are, affirmations of our humanity. They strengthen communities and the commitment to wisdom and compassion.
>
> Today's Celebration and Mourning Circle will be similar to our Council Circle practice. Our talking sticks will be "Celebration" and "Mourning."

Show the Celebration and Mourning Needs cards to the group, then read:

> We will begin with the Mourning card. Each of us is invited to speak to any mourning in our hearts. This could be something touched during the opening meditation, something present in your life right now. It could also be something touched freshly when the Mourning card comes to you, perhaps connected to humanity's mourning on the planet right now. When we hold the Mourning card, our role is not to judge what wants to be spoken through us, it is simply to give voice to it. Take your time and just let it speak, however it needs to, through words, tears, and breath. Let your presence to what is alive in your heart of mourning guide your expression, rather than just retelling familiar old stories or memories.
>
> As we listen to each other, consider that each person's expression is also our collective voice speaking. Engage your sense of curiosity and presence and breathe through any impulse to try to change someone's natural expression of mourning. This is an opportunity to place our trust in the empathic space that's been created and notice our own resistance or fears around expressions of grief and despair.
>
> When the person is finished sharing, like in the Empathy Circle, we will silently place Needs cards in front of them. Though we may want to offer many reflections, let's limit the number of cards we place to around eight so as not to overwhelm the person with our words.
>
> The person who shared will take three full breaths to read the cards, then place them back in the center, and we will go on to the next person.

Set the Celebration card to the side for this round and hold the Mourning card in your hand.

Check if anyone is unclear about the practice and needs to hear the instructions again. Once everyone is clear, invite everyone to take a breath together and to bring their presence to the circle.

Pass the Mourning card to whoever feels moved to start.

Once the Mourning card has made its way around the circle back to the person who first shared, take the Mourning card and invite everyone to take a breath together.

Place the Mourning card in the center of the circle and pick up the Celebration card. Read:

> Each of us is invited now to speak to any celebration in our hearts. Perhaps something touched today, or perhaps something else present in your life right now. Perhaps something that shows up freshly when the Celebration card comes to you. Again, there is no need to judge what shows up to be spoken; simply give voice to what's there. Simply be present to what is in your heart as you speak. In this round, we will not place Needs cards. When you are done sharing your celebration, simply pass the Celebration card to the next person.

Pass the Celebration card to whoever feels moved to start.

Once the Celebration card has made its way around the circle back to the person who first shared, take the Celebration card and invite everyone to take three breaths together.

Place the Celebration card back in the center of the circle.

Harvest

Invite anyone who feels moved to share something that touched them or that they discovered from today's practice with the group.

Close by offering gratitude to everyone for their sharing and practice.

Closing

Ask for a volunteer to guide the group next week. Give that person the deck(s) of Needs cards.

Remind that volunteer to read the pages on "Leading Group Practice" (page 13) and Week 9's Group Gathering before the next meeting. Everything they need to know will be in those pages.

Invite everyone to take a collective full breath together.

Invite everyone to offer a simple, nonverbal gratitude to each other with a bow, a hug, or whatever works best for each person.

Compassionate Boundaries

"We emphasize straightforwardness. You should be true to your feelings and to your mind, expressing yourself without any reservations. This helps the listener to understand more easily."
– Shunryu Suzuki

Opening Meditation

Greet your Buddy.

Decide who will keep time for the five-minute meditation.

Sit in silence together, being with the breath, the body, and the earth.

Whoever is keeping time signals the other when five minutes have passed.

Close with a bow of appreciation to your Buddy for sitting with you.

Introduction to Compassionate Boundaries

Taking turns, slowly read the following out loud to each other:

> Compassionate Boundaries is a practice of being true to our Needs. Through celebration and mourning, we can feel where our actions are aligned with our Needs and where they aren't. For example, sometimes we mourn that we said "yes" when we really wanted to say "no." Though we may have a habit of saying yes to contribute to harmony, sometimes setting a limit, saying no, or stopping an action may be the most compassionate and authentic choice.

> "No" is a complete sentence. When we are connected to Needs, we discover that saying "no" also is saying "yes" to other Needs that want our care and attention. "No" can be a protection of life itself. Though fear, guilt, shame, obligation, and duty all condition us to say yes when we actually mean no, saying no when we mean no can be one of the deepest practices of self-love we do. Rather than continuing to sacrificing our Needs for those of others, we free ourselves to trust that when we do say yes to another's request, we are doing so fully connected to our Needs.

> Saying no contributes to others as well. It gives them clarity and further information on how we would like to connect or interact differently. It also can be a preventive medicine, avoiding the creation of more unfinished business. Often our unfinished

business is connected to a boundary that we did not set or clearly offer on behalf of our Needs. Instead, we can mourn what has not worked and celebrate the honest relationships we are now building with ourselves and others.

Sit for a few minutes in silence, reflecting on a situation where you said yes to someone when what you wanted to say was no. Let your Buddy know when you have thought of a situation.

Once both of you have thought of a situation, go on to the practice below. Have your Needs Wheel accessible for this practice.

Compassionate Boundaries

Decide who will first be A and who will be B. Buddy A will follow the guidance below marked "A" and Buddy B will follow the guidance marked "B."

A: Share about a situation where you said yes to someone when what you wanted to say was no. Let go of any filters and fully express judgments, thoughts, blame, shame, etc., about the situation, yourself, or the other person/people involved.

B: Listen. Bring yourself into presence in whatever way works for you – i.e., breathing into soft belly. Allow your intention to be all about connection. Focus on the Needs – glance at your Needs Wheel. Simply notice when the mind wants to jump to advising, judging, fixing, consoling, sympathizing, commiserating, or even trying to anticipate the Needs. Simply breathe and listen.

B: When A finds a resting place in speaking, pause, then offer Needs guesses. Simply share the Needs words one at a time, taking a full breath between each one – anywhere from three to five needs. Don't try to figure out whether they are A's Needs or the other person in the situation's Needs. Simply offer any Needs words you are sensing.

A: Listen to the Needs being reflected. Sensing into these Needs, connect to yourself and the other person in your situation. Sense how these Needs can be held as equal. Sense, possibly, how some of these Needs may have been alive in the situation for you but that your Needs to contribute, to be of service, or to be safe overrode the voice of other Needs and said yes when you wanted to say no.

A: Share about the Needs that connected for you and any other Needs that have become clear through this process. Share what you are connecting to that may have been alive for you and for the other person.

B: Reflect back again just the Needs A has spoken to, one at a time, with a breath in between each one.

A: Touch your belly and be with these Needs that are being reflected back to you. Stay with them for just a moment longer. Maybe even touch any mourning of these Needs not having been able to express themselves clearly in the situation you were in.

A: Share how you imagine you could say no in the future when a similar situation arises or how you could have spoken directly to the "no" in the situation you were in. Use the vocabulary of Needs words in your expression.

Now switch roles.

Closing Harvest

Take a few moments to breathe in silence together. Notice any mourning about past choices and celebrations of future possibilities that may have arisen. Harvest by sharing what you notice, including any insights, learnings, or appreciations from your time together.

Also, take some time to share any appreciations that you have for your time together as **Ongo Buddies.** Next week, you will begin with new Buddies for your third month of Ongo Buddy Practice.

WEEK 8 SOLO PRACTICES

Mindfulness of Shenpa

"We could call shenpa 'that sticky feeling.' It's an everyday experience. At the subtlest level, we feel a tightening, a tensing, a sense of closing down. Then we feel a sense of withdrawing, not wanting to be where we are. That's the hooked quality. That tight feeling has the power to hook us into self-denigration, blame, anger, jealousy, and other emotions which lead to words and actions that end up poisoning us."
– Pema Chödrön

It is very difficult to respond to others compassionately and wisely if we are in a state of reactivity. In that state, we are more likely to battle whatever is happening, run away from it, or shut down to it – fight, flight, or freeze. In those moments, trying to "be compassionate" is a bit like trying to save others from drowning while we ourselves are in the water and barely staying afloat. So far in Ongo, we have emphasized working with this state of reactivity, or *shenpa* (Pema Chödrön's translation of the Tibetan Buddhist word for "attachment"), on our own, in the safety of our practice space.

However, it is also possible to practice with shenpa in the heat of live interactions. If we recognize the early signs of reactivity within us, as it arises, we can breathe, self-empathize, and choose how we want to respond, all while staying in the interaction. This is like climbing onto a raft from which we can more easily help others out of the water. Today's practice supports us to become more familiar with what our body's early warning signs of reactivity are and what it's trying to tell us in those moments.

Today…

Sit for 12 minutes or so, being with the breath, the body, and any celebrations and mournings that arise.

After, as you go out into your day, have your journal or a small notepad with you.

During the day, at least three times, whenever you feel a sense of being in a reactive state, even on the smallest level:

1. Breathe in … and out …

2. **Notice – what is your first response to this sense of being reactive?** For example, is it to brush it off? To ignore it? To blame the person that stimulated you? To blame

yourself for being stimulated? **Whatever your response is, take a moment to describe it in your journal.**

3. **Breathe in ... and out ... Feel the earth under your feet.**

4. **Notice – what thoughts, actions, or words stimulated you?** Try to trace the feeling back to the exact moment that it started. **Note it in your journal.**

5. **Breathe in ... and out ...**

6. **Bring awareness to what's happening in the body.** Where in your body do you notice the feeling of fight, flight, or freeze? Place your hand there. What does it feel like? What is its texture?

7. **Take a few breaths just to be with those sensations, not needing to change them or "get" anywhere – simply feeling them and resting in the flow of the breath.**

8. **Is there a Need or Needs calling for your attention?** Listen in to the body. **Write down whatever Needs are present.**

9. **Now, take two or three deep breaths and exhale any tension down through your body and into the earth.**

10. **Take another moment simply to smile and embrace with compassion the Needs that are present.** Let the earth support you in this. **Breathe.**

Instant – In a moment that you feel a sense of being reactive, take a deep breath. With the exhale, consciously relax your body. Notice what the signs of being reactive are in your body. Where do you feel it? What does it feel like there? Place your hand there and breathe. Notice whether your impulse is to fight, flee, or freeze (go numb). Breathe. If there is a Need that's screaming to be heard, acknowledge it and breathe.

Deepening – As you deepen in this practice, notice especially your "upgraded" versions of fight, flight, and freeze. For example, trying to "spiritually educate" yourself or someone else out of their present-moment experience (fight); focusing on positive affirmations rather than being present with something that is painful or stimulating (flight); practicing mindfulness entirely through the intellect while being numb to messy feelings (freeze).

Mindfulness of Shenpa
Remembering

Quiet friend who has come so far,
feel how your breathing makes more space around you.
Let this darkness be a bell tower
and you the bell. And as you ring,

What batters you becomes your strength.
Move back and forth into the change.
What is it like, this intensity of pain?
If the drink is bitter, turn yourself to wine.

In this uncontainable night,
be the mystery at the crossroads of your senses,
the meaning discovered there.

And if the world shall cease to hear you,
say to the silent earth: I flow.
And to the rushing water speak, I am.

– Rainer Maria Rilke,
translated by Joanna Macy

Turning Toward Shenpa

*"You have to choose. You can move through necessary pain and heal.
Or you can run from the pain and healing – and create much added
misery for everyone, including your descendants and yourself."*
– Resmaa Menakem

Today…

Continue to pay attention to moments when you feel a sense of being in a reactive state, even on the smallest level.

In one of these moments, make a conscious choice to wholeheartedly turn toward your present-moment experience rather than fight it, avoid it, or numb out to it. This turning-toward could take many different forms.

For example:

You notice you're trying to avoid thinking about a situation that's troubling you inside. Turning toward it, you choose to take a few minutes to self-empathize and really connect to the thoughts, feelings, and Needs that you're experiencing.

You notice that you keep wanting to fix or change someone because the way they're expressing is stimulating discomfort for you. You choose to let go of your impulse to offer them advice and instead turn toward them and empathize with their expression, taking a few minutes to connect to what they're feeling and what their Needs are.

You notice that you're trying to numb feelings of fear and anxiety. Taking a deep breath, you ask a friend to be with you and hold your hand as you allow yourself to breathe and feel fully the fear and anxiety.

You notice that you spent most of your walk to the store thinking about what tasks you need to get done later that day. You make a conscious choice to turn your attention to your breath, the sensation of your feet on the earth, and present-moment sounds, smells, and tastes. You spend the next few minutes walking with that intention and focus.

If you like, do this again later today. Choose to wholeheartedly turn toward your present-moment experience.

Turning Toward Shenpa
Remembering

"Feelings and emotions do seem very solid when we're caught up in them, and we are all habituated to express or repress them, escape from them, or want to do something about the mental and physical distress they cause. Can I be unconditionally with you in the presence of sorrow, fear, or whatever? Can I be fully understanding of the deep desire to get rid of it all, without knowing what to do about it, without depending on a technique, just letting it all happen? Everything is right here to be discovered, seen, felt, and listened to openly, gently, as the splattering rain, the passing clouds, and the songs of birds.

"The words that are spoken by one person may not be understood by the other this instant, but something much deeper than words is functioning when the mind is not caught up in fearing or wanting anything, or even the desire to help."

– Toni Packer

Asking for Help

"I'm not saying that we have to get totally liberated from all of our inner, violent learning before we look outside of our self to the world, or to see how we can contribute to social change at a broader level. I'm saying we need to do these simultaneously."
— Marshall B. Rosenberg, Ph.D.

The first two practices this week build our ability to recognize when we are being triggered in the heat of a live interaction. Often this awareness is enough to remind us of our practice, giving us the footing we need to turn toward the interaction and respond in a more enjoyable way. There are other times, however, where the awareness of being triggered by itself is not enough for us to find our footing while the interaction is happening and respond in a way we would like. These are the situations when people will often say that they "don't have time for self-empathy or mindfulness" – the conditions aren't there to support their practice.

Even in these moments, we can create the conditions we need, by requesting them. Taking action to find our footing – to make space for practice so that we can respond to others compassionately and wisely – is a gift to everyone. It is a gift because we are preventing immediate harm from taking place, either to ourselves or others. It is also a gift because when we then return to hearing others, it will be from an energy that is more likely to create the kind of connection that we all want.

Today…

Write down two requests that you could use in a live dialogue to ask for help:

- **A request for empathy.** *For example, "I want to be clear, and I feel like I'm not making a lot of sense. Would it be okay if I just vomited my thoughts out loud for a minute and you not take anything I say personally but instead try to help me find better words for what I'm trying to get across?"*

- **A request for space to self-empathize.** *For example, "I'm really not trusting that anything I say right now will actually contribute to the kind of connection I think we both want, so I'd like to go outside and clear my head. What you're saying is important to me – would you be willing to pick this up again in 10 minutes?"*

Write these requests on something that you can carry with you and pull out easily as a reminder anytime during your day (i.e., on a wallet card or in your smartphone).

Here are some useful tips for this kind of request:

- **Name what you're wanting to do.** In the examples above, the wants are for space to express ("vomit my thoughts out loud") and be heard empathically ("not take anything personally ... but instead try to help me find better words for what I'm trying to get across") and for space to self-empathize ("go outside and clear my head").

- **Name the need behind your action.** In the examples above, the Needs are for clarity ("I want to be clear") and connection ("the kind of connection we both want").

- **Consider the other person's Needs in your request.** In the examples above, the requests express consideration by suggesting that the other person not take the words personally and express consideration by proposing that they return to the conversation in 10 minutes.

If you get an opportunity, try out your request today.

Tip – Don't wait until you have no capacity left to respond compassionately to make one of these requests. At that point, your request will likely come off as a demand or threat, simply because you will have no room to hear anything other than a "yes." When possible, be preventative and make your request for empathy or space to self-empathize while you still have the ability to respond to the other person with some compassion or understanding.

 Instant – In a moment when you notice that you are triggered and unable to respond productively in an interaction, take a deep breath and consciously relax your body as you exhale. Then say, "Can we take a minute or two of silence? I notice I'm not with you anymore and I want to be. A short break will help me clear my head." Use that minute of silence to practice something that supports you to reconnect to yourself, to the other, and to life (i.e., mindfulness or self-empathy). After that minute of silence, thank the other person for honoring your request and resume the interaction.

 Deepening – Practice using the space created by your requests as time not only to find your footing but also to sense into what might be going on for the other person, and empathize with them. When you return to the conversation, let the first words you speak be informed by an understanding of all the Needs. For example, you may feel moved to express a regret about the impact of something you said earlier, or you may want to offer an empathic reflection for both of you (i.e., "I'm guessing we're both longing to be heard and understood right now.").

Week 9

Shenpa

"In Tibetan, there is a word that points to the root cause of aggression. The root cause of craving. It points to a familiar experience that is the root of all conflict, all cruelty, oppression and greed. And the word is 'Shenpa.'"
– Pema Chödrön

Preparation – All participants:

- Bring your copy of *The Ongo Book* and your journal to this Group Gathering

Preparation – Group Guide:

- A day or two before the Group Gathering, remind everyone of the day, time, and place of the Gathering.

- Read "Leading Group Practice" (page 13) and do the points listed under "Responsibilities of the Guide."

- Lay one deck of Needs cards out in an attractive mandala or spiral in the center of the circle. Place the Celebration and Mourning cards in the center.

Opening Meditation

Invite everyone to take their seats in the circle.

Ring a bell to signal the beginning of the sitting meditation.

After a moment of silence, read the guidance below to the group. Read in a way that supports the group to relax into the guidance, allowing space and silence between passages:

> Open up the lungs by taking a few deep, exaggerated breaths.
>
> Roll your shoulders back and exhale, releasing any tension there down into the earth.
>
> Roll your head, stretching the neck. Exhale and release any tension.
>
> Breathing, let the body gently settle into its seat. Settled, yet awake.
>
> Let the eyes soften, the eyelids partially or fully close.

> Being present.
>
> Breathing in, breathing out. No efforting.

Sit for a minute or two in silence, then read:

> Any time the mind begins to wander and run away from the stillness, return to the breath.

Sit for five minutes, then read:

> When the mind tries to pull on the stillness, return to the breath.
>
> No efforting. Just breathing in, breathing out.

Sit for five more minutes, then read:

> When the mind tries to attach to a particular thought or state of being, we lean into the breath.
>
> As we become more familiar with catching the attachment as it begins, our wisdom becomes stronger than shenpa.
>
> We can stop the chain of reaction. Stop being taken for a ride by our thinking.
>
> We can learn to relax into the place where that urge is strong, breathe, and get a bigger perspective on what is happening. The earth's perspective. The breath's perspective.
>
> When we pause, we find our connection. We become free to choose our response.
>
> Turning our presence to the stillness, a wide-open space emerges.
>
> No efforting. Just breathing in, breathing out, before we respond.

Sit in silence for five more minutes, then ring the bell three times to end the meditation.

Place your palms together and offer a bow of gratitude to the circle.

Introduction to Shenpa

Read to the group (or invite others to take turns reading one or more of the paragraphs to the group):

> Exploring shenpa leads us to looking at the ways we respond in the world. Shenpa directs us to our fight, flight, or freeze reactions. We can think of shenpa as something that happens in the body. Something happens or someone says something, and that stimulates a response in our body. How it feels for each of us may be different, but it's generally a kind of tightening or constricting, an impulse to fight, run away, or shut

down. Shenpa is that moment of all our attention going in one direction, toward one reaction.

So we take a breath to lengthen the pause between a stimulus and our response.

Then, we ask ourselves, "What is my intention here? Is my intention to get my way? Is my intention to make the other feel sorry? Is my intention to retaliate?"

If our intention is anything other than wanting to build connection, we're likely still standing in shenpa – for example, when we are attached to how we think things should go, or to how we think the other person should be, or to some other kind of outcome that we've righteously determined.

Even when we think we are practicing mindfulness or self-empathy, if we do it with an attachment to a particular outcome – like, to tune out our anger or to peacefully persuade the other person to agree with us – then what we are doing is practicing "shenpathy." We may think we are acting with wisdom and compassion, but it still smells like shenpa. You could say that most practice is simply about training our sense of smell. If we can smell it, we can avoid stepping in it.

Stepping In and Out of Shenpa

Invite everyone to take out their journal. Then read the following guidance:

> Take a minute to reflect on a situation where you did not respond in the way you would have liked, an interaction where you stepped right in to shenpa.

Pause a minute for everyone to reflect (including you) then read:

> Now, in your journal write down the words the other person said or the actions they did that were so stimulating or painful for you to experience. What did they say or do?

Pause for a minute for everyone to write, then pass out index cards or pieces of paper.

> Now, take the essence of what this person said or did and write it on a separate piece of paper that you can give to someone else to read.

After everyone has a chance to write down a stimulating message, ask everyone to hand their messages to the person on their left. Then read:

> When we step into shenpa, depending on the stimulation, we tend to take either a power-under position or a power-over position. We either blame ourselves or we blame others. Recognizing this is one way we can start to notice when we're standing in shenpa.

> Starting with me, we are now going to go around the circle and give voice to our power-under or power-over responses to what was said to us.
>
> The person on my left will read my stimulating message to me. I will respond from the place of shenpa, either blaming myself or blaming them. For example, if the message I wrote down was, "I am so tired of your excuses!," then the person on my left would say that to me, with energy. I would respond either with self-blame, like, "I know, I just fail you every time" or with blame toward them, like, "What excuses?! If you had been clear in the first place, this never would have happened!"
>
> We'll continue that way all the way around the circle, with each of us hearing our stimulating messages from the person on our left, and then each of us responding from either a power-under or power-over place, until we come back to me.

Check if anyone is unclear about the practice and needs to hear the instructions again. Once everyone is clear, invite everyone to take a breath together and to bring their presence to the circle.

Begin the practice by inviting the person on your left to read out your stimulating message to you.

After you have responded, invite them to turn to the person on their left, and continue the practice as described.

Once everyone has had a turn, invite everyone to return the papers to their original owner, the person on their right.

Once everyone has gotten back their own paper with their stimulating message on it, invite them to hand it next to the person on their right and then to open to the Needs Wheel on page 271 in the Appendix.

> We're going to go around the circle again, taking turns responding to these messages a second time. This time, we are going to engage the practices we have been cultivating in Ongo. The person on your right will read out your stimulating message to you. As you hear the words, simply take a breath and allow yourself to feel the shenpa in your body – that moment of tension or constriction.
>
> Once you feel it, take another breath and offer yourself empathy, connecting to the Needs that arise in you when you hear the message.
>
> Once you have connected to your Needs, take another breath and check that your intention is truly to connect.

Finally, offer a simple empathic guess of what you think might have been the feelings and Needs in the heart of the person who spoke those words to you. We will look at our Needs Wheel not as a way to over-think it but as a support to finding words in a challenging situation.

So, for example, the person on my right will say my message to me: "I am so tired of your excuses!" As I hear those words, I'll silently take a breath and feel my feelings of tightening inside. I'll then take another breath and self-empathize. Touching my hand to my heart, I'll notice I feel sad, and touching my hand to my belly, I'll notice the Need for understanding. Now I'll take a breath to check that I'm willing to connect with the other person. Finally, I'll make my empathic guess of what's going on for them: "When you say that, are you feeling frustrated and needing some mutuality and support?"

So, breathe with what we feel, breathe and self-empathize, breathe and check our intention, then empathize with the other person. These are all very important steps, because we don't want to respond out of fear or anger or shutdown. We breathe so we can come to the place of genuine willingness to connect and from there make our best guess about what's going on for the other person. We let go of any urgency to respond. We breathe as if we are not going to respond at all. Just breathe. Then, we let ourselves come around to the space where we can become curious about what's going on for the other person. Giving the gift for both people to step out of shenpa.

Check if anyone is unclear about the practice and needs to hear the instructions again. Once everyone is clear, invite everyone to take a breath together and to bring their presence to the circle.

Begin the practice by inviting the person on your right to read your message to you.

After you have responded, invite them to turn to the person on their right and continue the practice as described.

Once everyone has had a turn, invite the group to take a collective breath and sit together silently for three minutes. Then, ring the bell to signal the end of this practice.

Harvest

Invite anyone who feels moved to share something that touched them or that they learned or discovered from today's practice with the group.

Close by offering gratitude to everyone for their sharing and practice.

Setting up Ongo Buddy Practices

Invite everyone to sit next to their Ongo Buddies. Then, read to the group:

> Today, we will select new Ongo Buddies for the third month of Ongo. We suggest that any family members or life partners in the group be paired this month as a way to deepen those connections. If you do not have a family member or life partner in this circle that you will partner with, take a minute now in silence to breathe and feel into who you are called to continue your one-on-one practice with – someone whom you haven't already been Buddies with.

After a minute of silence, read:

> Now, turn toward that person. With this as our beginning, let's discuss who the pairings will be for this third month. We'll take five minutes for this discussion.

Keep track of time. Let the group know when there's just one minute left for the discussion.

After everyone has a Buddy, read:

> After this meeting, please take a moment to connect with your Buddy to schedule your first meeting together. Also, remember, if you or your Buddy aren't showing up consistently for your Buddy Practice together, please reach out to the group and ask if someone else might be willing to be your backup for the month.

 ### Closing

Ask for a volunteer to guide the group next week. Give that person the deck(s) of Needs cards.

Remind that volunteer to read the pages on "Leading Group Practice" (page 13) and Week 10's Group Gathering before the next meeting. Everything they need to know will be in those pages.

Invite everyone to take a collective full breath together. Invite everyone to offer a simple nonverbal gratitude to each other with a bow, a hug, or whatever works best for each person.

Empathy

*"For me, empathy is the thing which removes blocks to action,
not the thing which makes me feel better."*
– Dominic Barter

If you are paired with a family member, close friend, or partner, take a moment at the start of this practice to acknowledge each other's willingness and courage to be vulnerable allies on this path of learning. Remember that you are not here to teach each other or give any feedback other than the instructions in the practice. Instead, allow each of you to have your own pace with the learning. If something gets stimulated in a way that you can't be present to each other like you were for your previous buddies, then pause the practice. You can choose to return to the practice at another time or invite one of your previous buddies to join in the practices to offer support. Go gently.

Opening Meditation

Take a few minutes to meet your new Buddy, perhaps sharing something with them that they might not know about you yet.

After, decide who will time a five-minute silent sitting meditation.

Sit in silence together, being with the breath, the body, and the earth.

Whoever is keeping time signals the other when five minutes have passed.

Close with a bow of appreciation to your Buddy for sitting with you.

Sharing and Empathic Listening

Check if either of you would like a refresher on the Empathy Buddy Practice. If so, you can take turns reading out loud just the reading part under "Sharing and Empathic Listening" from the Week 2 Buddy Practice on page 46.

Then, decide who will share first and who will listen first. Have the "Needs Wheel" on page 271 in the Appendix accessible.

1. **Sharer shares about something happening in their life that's present on their heart and mind.** This could be something small or big, painful or joyful. The only request is that it be something that is alive and meaningful to the sharer.

2. **Listener listens with curiosity, mindful presence, intention to connect, and a focus on needs, all in silence.** If the mind jumps to advice, judgment, consoling, sympathy, or commiseration, breathe and return to curiosity, mindful presence, intention to connect, and a focus on needs.

3. **When the sharer comes to a breathing place, a pause, the listener looks at the Needs Wheel and offers confirmation with a simple, empathic guess about the feelings and needs that are being expressed.** *For example, "Are you feeling sad because you're needing acceptance?" or "Am I hearing a need for trust?" or "Are you needing to be seen?" or "I'm connecting to needs of respect and consideration; how are these landing for you?" or just Needs words, as in "Love?" or "Compassion?"* Offer just one line – one Need – at a time. Let it be received, then take a breath.

4. **Breathe together.**

5. **Sharer continues sharing whatever is still alive and present in their heart to say about the situation. When there is a pause, the listener offers confirmation with simple, empathic guesses about the feelings and needs that are being expressed.**

6. **Continue until sharer feels complete, often indicated by a relaxing of the energy.** It's important in this process that the listener follow the sharer's lead and does not try to be "right" about their guesses or analyze the sharer's story. Let the guesses simply be reflections of your presence with the sharer rather than an anxious exercise in trying to reflect every word you hear.

7. **Then switch roles.**

Closing Harvest

After both have had an opportunity to share and to listen, Harvest by sharing any learnings about yourselves and any appreciations from being listened to in this way.

Buddy Support

Discuss how you would like to support each other this month with doing the daily Solo Practices. This could look different for each Buddy, based on what each finds most supportive. *For example, one Buddy might want to send a daily text message or email to the other after they've done their Solo Practice. Another might want to have a short, weekly phone call to share their experiences of doing the Solo Practices that week.*

Also, discuss whether there is any mutual interest or openness to having empathy calls with each other outside of the regular Buddy practice. *For example, scheduling a second weekly call just for empathy, or agreeing to be available to each other for "on-call" empathy.*

WEEK 9 SOLO PRACTICES

Mindful Walking

"As you walk, you touch the ground mindfully, and every step can bring you solidity and joy and freedom. Freedom from your regret concerning the past, and freedom from your fear about the future."
– Thich Nhat Hanh

Mindfulness of the body and the breath is a practice that goes well beyond sitting. Ultimately, we want to extend mindfulness into all the activities of our life, whether we're moving, talking, typing, or washing the dishes. It can become one of the easiest and most reliable ways of connecting to many of the qualities we seek to embody in our life – qualities like ease, presence, space, stability, and connection.

Today…

Choose a place where you would feel comfortable taking a very slow, mindful walk. This could be anywhere, from your living room (it's okay to walk in circles or back and forth), to your porch or yard, to a local park or neighborhood.

Take 10 to 15 minutes to mindfully walk. You could do this any time: on your way to work, moving around the office or house, out shopping. As with sitting meditation, it can be helpful to set a gentle alarm or have someone let you know when the time has passed so you don't have to think about time during your walk.

The basic practice: bring awareness to the movement of the body, the lifting of the foot, and the foot's contact with the earth. Breathe with each step.

As feelings and thoughts arise, give space for them, and then gently bring your attention back to the body, the breath, and the contact between your foot and the earth. We do not need to avoid or block any thoughts or feelings to try and maintain some artificially calm "Zen" state – in fact, if we try to do so, we'll only make ourselves more agitated. Instead, give thoughts and feelings space. Then, with each exhale, gently bring your presence back to the breath and the earth.

Walking meditation is not a means to an end; its purpose is simply walking meditation. So, we don't need to hurry or become frustrated; we are simply appreciating what it is to be alive, which may include the busy thoughts passing through at times.

As you continue to walk, allow your awareness to expand to include the wonders of the world around you: the play of light and color, the symphony of sound, the dance of motion, and the feast of smells.

Breathe!

At the end, take a moment to give thanks to yourself for taking this time to slow down and enjoy life, and to Life itself for its treasures, so freely given.

If you like, take another mindful walk later today.

Audio – There is a guided audio recording of this meditation available on The Ongo Companion Website at <u>ongo.global</u>. You can also make your own guided audio meditation by recording yourself reading the practice out loud. If you make your own, remember to speak slowly and allow lots of silence in between instructions so you can easily follow along when listening to it later.

Instant – Right now, whatever you are doing, bring awareness to where the body is touching and being supported by the earth. For any movement you make, feel that movement through your skin and through your bones. Throughout, be aware of the breath. As you continue, allow your awareness to expand and include the rest of the world around you, being present to sound, light, touch, and smell.

Deepening – Inhabit your body whenever possible. Let runaway thinking and overwhelming feelings be a reminder to tune in to the felt sense of the body and its movements on the earth. Feel the breath and its relationship to movement. To take this practice even farther, practice yoga or Taiji (Tai-chi) and let those practices inform your awareness of the body and the breath when moving or still.

Mindful Walking
Remembering

"When my master and I were walking in the rain, he would say, 'Do not walk so fast, the rain is everywhere.'"
– Shunryu Suzuki

Practicing for All Beings

"I would say that the thrust of my life has been initially about getting free, and then realizing that my freedom is not independent of everybody else. Then I am arriving at that circle where one works on oneself as a gift to other people so that one doesn't create more suffering. I help people as I work on myself and I work on myself to help people."
– Ram Dass

One of the understandings that our practice brings us to is that we have more in common with the rest of the world than we think. Our struggles are not unique, though our core beliefs may tell us so. Our happiness is intertwined with that of others. If we lose sight of this and our practice becomes centered on personal growth and obsession over personal healing, we run the risk of reaffirming the very thing that we fundamentally wish to be free from – our sense of being separate from the wholeness of life. To realize the promise of practices like Zen, Loving-kindness, and Nonviolent Communication, our practice must ultimately be for the benefit of all beings, not just ourselves. Our Needs are not separate from the Needs of others. Marshall Rosenberg once stated to a group of students that his need for food has "never been fully met." When a confused student asked him why, he said, "Because, for my whole life, there have always been people who are starving."

Today…

Consider, whom do you want your heart to reach out to each day with your practice? Friends? Family members? Coworkers? Neighbors? Those whom you have a hard time opening your heart to? People in the news? Politicians? Individuals or groups in other countries? Victims of violence or disaster? Those who cause violence? Four-leggeds? Winged ones? Stones? Trees? Whose faces remind you that there are others who suffer in this world? Whose faces remind you of the importance of this practice that you are doing?

Gather images and/or create representations of these beings and place them in your practice space to remind you each day whom else you practice for.

Feel how their presence touches you – notice it in your body. Give room for those feelings to be expressed in you. Breathe with them.

Place an offering to these beings of something nourishing. *For example, place some flowers, a cup of water, or a small plate of their favorite foods in front of them.*

Close by offering a prayer or blessing or heart intention to these beings. Allow that felt sense of connection in the body to radiate out to their images – and beyond.

Practicing for All Beings
Remembering

Every second, what we feel
For our people & our planet
Almost brings us to our knees,
A compassion that nearly destroys
Us with its massiveness.
There is no love for or in this world
That doesn't feel both bright & unbearable,
Uncarriable.

– Amanda Gorman

Empathic Reflection

"[W]hen a person realizes he has been deeply heard, his eyes moisten. I think in some real sense he is weeping for joy. It is as though he were saying, "Thank God, somebody heard me. Someone knows what it's like to be me."
– Carl Rogers

Throughout Ongo, we have been steadily cultivating our ability to hear the life-serving Needs being expressed through others, no matter what their words or actions. Any Needs which we guess someone is expressing are only guesses, unless that person confirms our understanding. For that to happen, we must share our guesses with them.

Sharing our guesses is more than a way to confirm whether or not we are understanding someone. We are bringing a compassionate mirror to their experience. When we verbally reflect our guesses back to others, it offers an opportunity for them to recognize themselves in our words, to have a sense of being seen and known. It also offers an invitation for them to further clarify what they would most like to have heard and understood.

Empathic reflection is less about making the "right" guess and more about the willingness to be with another's truth – and expressing that willingness through our guesses, offering the trust that we are truly with them in the exploration of it, not just silently judging them or tuning them out. It requires us to be rigorously honest with ourselves about our motives for offering empathic reflection – we are not doing it to try to change the other person, get our way, or educate them about their Needs. We are joining them in the deep vulnerability of the heart, lending them the strength of our presence and our confidence in the basic okay-ness of their every expression.

Today...

Sit for a few minutes simply being with the body and the breath.

Then, bring your attention to any thoughts and feelings that are present. Look at the Needs Wheel and notice which Needs are being celebrated or mourned. Breathe and allow yourself to feel that celebration or mourning.

Later, during your day, continue to notice celebration and mourning in others' expressions.

In one or more of these moments of noticing, share your empathic guess with that person. Don't think about it too much – focus on the feelings and Needs and just let the words come out of whatever you notice, as if you're verbalizing what you're sensing on "the belly level" (as in our Self-Empathy practice, when we touch our belly).

An Ongo participant shared this example from their life:

> *"This morning, going out the door to work, my partner told me about how a couple of people had thanked him for something he wrote. Our dialogue:*
>
>> *Me: So their acknowledgment of you helps you to feel that you have contributed?*
>>
>> *Him: Yes! And that we are in this together!*
>>
>> *Me: Mutuality? Community?*
>>
>> *Him: Yes! Yes!*
>>
>> *Me: And you really love feeling a part of this effort, and that you are contributing?*
>>
>> *Him: Mutuality! I like that! Wow! Yes! Contribution! Yes!"*

If your guess connects, you'll likely see a visible softening in the person you're empathizing with – for example, a sigh, an exhale, a smile, a brightening of the eyes, a nod, or a release of the shoulders. Often they'll open up and share more about what's going on. If the guess doesn't connect, then the other person will say or do something that will offer more clues about what their feelings and Needs are.

Enjoy the connection, however it unfolds, and allow the conversation to flow naturally from there – perhaps making more empathic guesses, perhaps choosing other ways to connect. Remember, it's not about "getting the words right," nor is it about only listening or empathically reflecting without ever speaking your heart. We're simply making connection.

Anytime you notice yourself feeling nervous or tense, breathe, acknowledge the feelings and thoughts, and gently bring your attention back to the connection.

When it's time for one or both of you to move on, thank the other person for the connection in whatever way feels good to you.

Tip – In offering empathic guesses, focusing on Needs is more important than focusing on feelings. In fact, if your empathy guesses focus on feelings, it can often come off as "psychologizing" the other person. Also, remember that empathy is not agreement. You do not need to agree with the other person's perspective to be able to connect to its expression of humanity.

 Instant – If you're not in contact with anyone in person today, try empathizing with an expression in someone's email or social media post. *For example, Jesse once wrote this in response to someone's comment on Facebook: "I hear in your words a longing for deep consideration for those who are being left behind by the current political system. I hear it as compassion and mourning about what you are witnessing. Do these words speak to you?"*

 Deepening – Practice making empathic reflection your first response to others, particularly in moments when you sense a lot of charge in their expression. If someone expresses pain about something you said or did, whenever possible, choose to respond with empathy first rather than defending your actions or the intentions behind them.

Week 10

Speaking Truth

"[T]he most revolutionary act one can engage in is ... to tell the truth."
— Howard Zinn

Preparation – All participants:

- Bring your copy of *The Ongo Book* and your journal to this Group Gathering

Preparation – Group Guide:

- A day or two before the Group Gathering, remind everyone of the day, time, and place of the Gathering.

- Read "Leading Group Practice" (page 13) and do the points listed under "Responsibilities of the Guide."

- Lay one deck of Needs cards out in an attractive mandala or spiral in the center of the circle.

Opening Meditation

Invite everyone to take their seats in the circle.

Ring a bell to signal the beginning of the sitting meditation.

After a moment of silence, read the guidance below to the group. Read in a way that supports the group to relax into the guidance, allowing space and silence between passages:

> Settle in. Take a few deep breaths. Deeply drawing in the in-breath. Deeply relaxing the out-breath.

> Letting go and letting the belly soften a little more with each breath.

> Letting the shoulders drop just a little more. Letting the crown of the head and the spine extend upward just a little more.

> Letting your body sit. Letting your being arrive.

> Resting into the gentle flow of the breath. Resting into the support of the earth.

Sit for five minutes, then read:

> Give whatever is there space to be, not trying to change it or get away from it. Even if it's uncomfortable at first. Give it space to be and express itself in your body.
>
> Let the breath be your companion. Let the earth hold you. Be awake to it all.

Sit for five minutes, then read:

> Sitting this way is a ceremony. A ceremony of honoring our enough-ness.
>
> We are not sitting here to get somewhere else. This sitting is not a means to an end. We are here to honor our wholeness, our completeness.
>
> Sitting is a radical act. By taking our seat, resting our hearts and minds and souls into the breath, into this connection with the earth and with all life, we are honoring that all of this life is enough.
>
> Even our thoughts of not being enough, or wanting more, or seeking a different kind of experience. We don't try to get away from those things. We honor them. We include them when we sit.
>
> This is enough. Just this.

Sit in silence for five minutes, then ring the bell three times to end the meditation.

Place your palms together and offer a bow of gratitude to the circle.

Introduction to Speaking Truth

Read to the group (or invite others to take turns reading one or more of the paragraphs to the group):

> Speaking truth is the continuation, an integration, of everything we have been practicing. When we speak our truth, we embrace all of who we are. Living this practice in our lives, bringing this wisdom and compassion out in the company of others, asks us to be completely ourselves, to bring forward our truth in words and actions.
>
> Zen Master Suzuki Roshi described practice as burning the candle at both ends. In the context of speaking truth, that means we practice with both edges of our comfort zone as speakers. If our tendency is to withhold our voice, then we practice speaking more often. We start to do it in the places that feel a little bit safe, where we feel a little bit of trust, rather than places that feel completely unsafe to us, where we have no trust. If we tend to speak up a lot and in all kinds of circumstances, then we practice coming back to our breath more often, bringing more silent empathy and

listening to situations rather than our voice. So we work the practice on both ends of the spectrum. There isn't a right or wrong with any of this. It is an invitation to explore what's there for you at the edge of your practice – and where there are places in your life that you can start to melt away that edge.

Sometimes what we are most afraid of when we speak our truth is not so much the words themselves, but of what will happen once we do speak. This is where all the practices we have been working on come in: our practices of empathy for self and others, our meditation and mindfulness practices. We see that we have the tools we need to be able to bring compassion into the moments when the painful things come to light, whether they are within ourselves or with someone else. Speaking our truth may open up things that may be a little "ouch-y," but when they appear we can bring our empathy, we can bring our presence. In that way, something starts to shift, something starts to transform.

Speaking truth is not the same as speaking what we think *about* somebody else or what we think *of* something. It is not about vomiting our thoughts out into the world. It requires as much deep listening to ourselves as it does willingness to open our voice and share with others. We are listening to the life energy, to the divine energy, to the grace that wants to move through our voices into the world.

This practice is not an all or nothing. In other words, it is all practice. We get to choose what edges we want to work with.

Practicing Speaking Truth

Invite everyone to take out their journal and have the "Needs Wheel" (page 271) and "Feelings" (page 272) pages in the Appendix accessible. Then read the following:

> Take a moment to think of a relationship you have with another person – this could be a co-worker, a friend, or a family member. Think of a relationship in which there's something you feel hesitant to say, where you feel scared to open your voice, and yet there is something within you that still wants to be spoken.
>
> Maybe, up until now, you haven't been willing to speak it because it feels too vulnerable, or you're not sure you could say it and be understood or heard in the way you would like.
>
> Think of such a situation in your life and write down what wants to be spoken. We will take four minutes right now to reflect and write down our expression.

Gently ring a bell after four minutes, then read:

> Next look at the Needs Wheel. Which Need or Needs are being expressed inside of what you are wanting to say to this other person? What are the Needs you are trying to communicate through your words? Don't think about it too hard, just look at the Needs Wheel and see which words jump up, then write those words next to your statement.

Gently ring a bell after two minutes, then read:

> Now see if there is a way you would like to rewrite your original statement, what you'd like to say to this person, that perhaps more clearly communicates the Needs that are there. You don't necessarily have to, but take a look at what you first came up with and take a look at the Needs you are trying to communicate. See if there is a way you can distill what you have written into a concise one- or two-sentence statement that better expresses your truth, including the Needs you are trying to communicate. Next, take a moment and rewrite this statement. See if you can get it down to just one sentence you'd like to say.

Gently ring a bell after two minutes, then read:

> Now, as you look at this new statement that you'd like to share, imagine your worst fear of what the other person might say back to you. What is the nightmare response you think you would hear back, even if you know they wouldn't actually say it? What is it that you might hear from this other person that stimulates your fear about even speaking up? Write that down. Write down whatever it is you are afraid they might say as a response or reaction to your words.

Gently ring a bell after two minutes, then read:

> The last step before we open up to the full practice is to write down your empathic guess for this person. Look at what you wrote for their nightmare response, and take a look at the Needs Wheel. What Need or Needs might the other person be speaking to?
>
> Once you connect to the Need or Needs they might be speaking to, write a simple, empathic guess. For example: "Are you needing understanding?"
>
> If you want, you could put in a feeling too. For example: "Are you feeling angry because you are wanting connection?"

Don't make it complicated. Just make a very simple guess around the Needs and, if you'd like, the feelings that might be going on for that person. Use Needs from the Needs Wheel and feelings from the feelings list.

Hand out index cards or pieces of paper.

On this paper, write down the nightmare response you're afraid of. Write it clearly, so that it's readable by others.

After everyone has written down their nightmare responses, read the following:

We will go around the circle taking turns. As if we are beginning a dialogue or conversation with this other person, we will engage in a short role play. When it's your turn, give the person on your right the nightmare response that you wrote down. You will start the dialogue by saying the statement you've been nervous about saying to this other person. Simply express your truth. The person on your right is going to answer by reading back to you the nightmare response on the card you just gave them.

When you hear the nightmare response, breathe and offer them your empathy guess. That's as far as we'll go with the dialogue for this practice.

Here's an example of how this will work. I'll use a real example from another Ongo, where the person was practicing speaking to their elder parent. I'll call them "Person A." In the first part of this practice, Person A rewrote what they wanted to say to highlight the Needs of safety, security, and well-being. So, Person A begins the dialogue by saying this rewritten statement to Person B, who sits on their right: "When I hear that you are not remembering where the money you are taking out of your account is going, I feel concern about your safety, security, and well-being." Person B then says to Person A the nightmare response on Person A's card, "I am completely capable of taking care of myself. You don't need to worry." Person A then responds with the empathic guess, "Are you feeling cautious and needing connection, understanding, and choice?"

Then we would continue around the circle, with Person B practicing their dialogue with the person on their right.

So, we're just going to do those three steps. You'll say your statement to the person on your right, they will respond with your nightmare response, and then you'll offer your empathic guess of what might be going on for them.

Check if anyone is unclear about the practice and needs to hear the instructions again. Once everyone is clear, invite everyone to take a breath together and to bring their presence to the circle.

Begin the practice by giving your nightmare response to the person on your right. Go around the circle until everyone has had a turn.

Invite the group to take a collective breath together, followed by sitting together in three minutes of silence.

Close the practice by ringing the bell.

Harvest

Read:

> There's a lot that comes up for each of us when we connect to these messages and what they represent – all the fears and the vulnerability. Let's take a moment to celebrate each one of us, all of us in this circle, and our willingness to practice with these relationships.
>
> Let's Harvest this practice. What did you learn? What are you appreciating about yourself or this practice? What are you mourning?

Invite anyone who feels moved to share with the group.

Closing

Ask for a volunteer to guide the group next week. Give that person the deck(s) of Needs cards.

Remind that volunteer to read the pages on "Leading Group Practice" (page 13) and Week 11's Group Gathering before the next meeting. Everything they need to know will be in those pages.

Invite everyone to take a collective full breath together. Invite everyone to offer a simple nonverbal gratitude to each other with a bow, a hug, or whatever works best for each person.

Speaking from the Heart

"[T]rue communication comes out of a powerful willingness not to protect oneself or even to be right. It comes from a longing for the truth, as painful as that may be at times. It comes out of direct perception ... To the little mind, communication gets you what you want. To the great heart, communication is the ability to commune in beingness itself."
– Stephen and Ondrea Levine

Opening Meditation

Greet your Buddy.

Decide who will time a five-minute meditation and who will read the reading following the meditation.

Sit in silence together, resting attention on the breath, allowing the body and mind to settle.

The Buddy keeping time signals the other when five minutes have passed.

Close with a bow of appreciation to your Buddy for sitting with you.

Introduction to Speaking from the Heart

The Buddy reading reads the following out loud:

> Just as the breath or our body sensations can help draw our attention to the present moment, so too can our speech. When we speak our present-moment experience, our words themselves become an instrument of mindfulness, bringing conscious awareness to what's here. Rather than reliving resentments from the past or fantasizing about the future, mindful speech invites us to wake up to the now. Though it can take many different forms, it always begins and ends with listening – to ourselves and others. Because everyone's Needs are interdependent, and all express some aspect of truth, we listen to it all and speak when it is our turn to speak.
>
> This is different from our habitual speech, where we tend to prejudge what we should or shouldn't say based on our core beliefs about ourselves and others. With mindful speech, we speak what wants to be spoken through us in the moment. We hear what's alive in our heart and the hearts of others. We connect to the breath, feelings in the body, Needs that are present, and any requests that arise. Out of that, we speak what

we, as an integral part of the whole of life, sense is our responsibility to say. Even after we begin speaking, this listening continues until we sense that there is nothing more that wants to be said. Then the practice begins again.

This is the secret recipe for speaking from the "HEART": four parts H-E-A-R-ing, only one part T-alking.

Speaking from the Heart

Taking turns, slowly read the following guidance out loud to each other:

Today we'll have a conversation based on speaking from the heart. We will take turns sharing and leading the conversation while the other listens and responds, building the empathic connection.

One of us will begin by sharing something that is alive and present on our heart and mind. It could be something that occurred recently, a situation we want to review. It could be something in the future that our mind is anticipating. Essentially, this is like when we call a friend to connect and share stories from our life. We will share naturally and pause whenever we want.

The other person will begin by listening and connecting to the Needs that they sense in the first person's sharing. At the same time, they will also be connecting to the Needs inside that may be stimulated by what they're hearing. When we're the one listening, we are simply allowing our presence to include both the person sharing and ourselves. Perhaps a similar story is rising up in us, or a connection to something else.

When the person sharing pauses for reflection, the listener can choose how they want to respond – either with an empathic guess of what they're hearing in the first person's sharing or by sharing what comes alive in their own heart as a result of listening. When listening, if we sense that it might contribute to connection, we offer empathic reflection of what we're hearing. If we choose to share what comes alive in our own heart, we are choosing from a place of connection to Needs rather than habit. In other words, we're not sharing as an attempt to analyze, fix, or otherwise change what we just heard. We are sensing what is happening in our body and connecting to any Needs that want to be expressed. We may notice if there's any request that wants to be made.

Throughout, we won't worry if this is the "right" moment for listening or sharing. We won't worry if we will say the "right" thing. Our practice is to breathe and be present with what arises.

When the listener chooses to share, then the roles reverse, and the person who shared now listens. We will continue in this dance of back and forth, letting the empathic conversation unfold for at least 15 minutes. We will share what we want to have heard and listen to what is spoken, in some moments offering empathic reflection and in some moments expressing our own truth. This is about having a natural conversation, but with the conscious intention to connect.

Take a moment to check with each other if you both understood the guidance above for listening and responding. If needed, one of you can read the guidance out loud again.

Once both have understood, decide who wants to start sharing and continue from there as described in the guidance.

Closing Harvest

Harvest by sharing any insights, learnings, or discoveries and any appreciations from your time together.

Take a moment to share a gratitude with each other for the conversation and for each other's contributions to the conversation.

Take a few minutes to close together with a silent sitting meditation offering a silent gratitude to yourself for anything that you appreciate about your contributions to the conversation and for speaking from the heart.

WEEK 10 SOLO PRACTICES

The Courage to Speak

"I often talk to people who say, 'No, we have to be hopeful and to inspire each other, and we can't tell [people] too many negative things' ... But, no – we have to tell it like it is. Because if there are no positive things to tell, then what should we do, should we spread false hope? We can't do that, we have to tell the truth."
– Greta Thunberg

Your voice matters. From the moment you were born, your unique song, first in sound, then later in words, communicated truths about the world. These were important truths, about Needs dear to you and those around you, Needs like love, safety, and belonging.

Sometimes our voices, and the Needs they express, are marginalized by our families, organizations, or societies because the truths we speak can be uncomfortable for others to hear. Our truths can surface long-buried pain or grief that people are afraid to look at or feel. They may believe it will destroy their lives. We may ourselves become afraid to speak up, for fear that our lives will be destroyed by the consequences.

In nonviolence, we find the courage to speak by joining alliances. When we speak, we speak not only to benefit ourselves, but also to contribute to others. We speak not only to our own Needs, but also to a shared higher purpose that unifies, rather than divides. Rather than shrink to avoid individual destruction, we grow to inspire collective creation. Today's practice offers a template for finding the courage to speak, by remembering who you stand with, what you stand for, and how you'll get there ... together.

(An example of today's practice can be found on the page following the practice.)

Today...

Use the template on page 219, or draw your own in your journal, for the practice below.

Take a deep breath. Settle into presence with the body, the breath, and the earth.

Reflect, what is a current situation in your life where you wish you or someone else would speak up? Write this down on the template, in the rectangle on the lower left,

noting in particular *what happened* that you want addressed. This could be from any context: home, work, school, wider community, etc.

Now, take a moment simply to breathe and consider, who might it contribute to if you spoke up? *For example, would it teach your children the importance of speaking up for one's own Needs? Would it support someone with less social standing than yourself? Would it give voice to the voiceless (i.e., trees, animals, people who aren't in the room where the conversations are happening, future generations)? Would it benefit your organization or community?*

Bring that person or group to your mind. Breathe and feel your connection to them. Feel what they mean to you. Then, on the template, draw an image of that person/group or write their name(s) down in the heart.

Now, look at the Needs Wheel. In this situation, what Needs are *you* wanting to have met? Write these down on the template, in the left side of the left circle (leaving blank the space where the two circles intersect). In other words, what important values do you want voiced in this situation?

Bring to mind the person or group that you want to hear these Needs. Look at the Needs Wheel and consider, what Needs might *they* be trying to meet? Write these down in the right side of the right circle (leaving blank the space where the two circles intersect). In other words, what is important to them? What are their words and actions attempting to express (even if you don't enjoy *how* they're being expressed)?

Take a deep breath. Looking at all the Needs you wrote down, what do you sense is the higher purpose that unites you? Write this down in the space where the two circles intersect. This could be a Need that you've already written down which is important to both you and the other(s). Or, this could be a Need that has not yet been named. This could also be something more elaborate than a one-word Need – it could be a shared desire for a particular outcome.

Take a moment now to reflect on the situation (in the rectangle) in light of this higher purpose. Breathe and feel where your body contacts, and is supported by, the earth.

What doable request can you make that you imagine would move everyone toward that higher purpose? Write this down in the arrow.

Breathe and look at your completed template – who you stand with, what you stand for, and how you propose getting there, together. Feel whatever is present in your body as you take it in.

Later, if you choose to speak up and share this truth in a live situation, here's one way you can use this template to guide you:

1. Breathe and see the situation in front of you. (Rectangle)

2. Breathe and connect in your heart with those you want to contribute to. (Heart)

3. Name out loud how you see the current situation (Rectangle) doesn't serve the higher purpose that unites everyone present. (Intersection of Circles)

4. Make the request that you sense will move everyone toward the shared higher purpose. (Arrow)

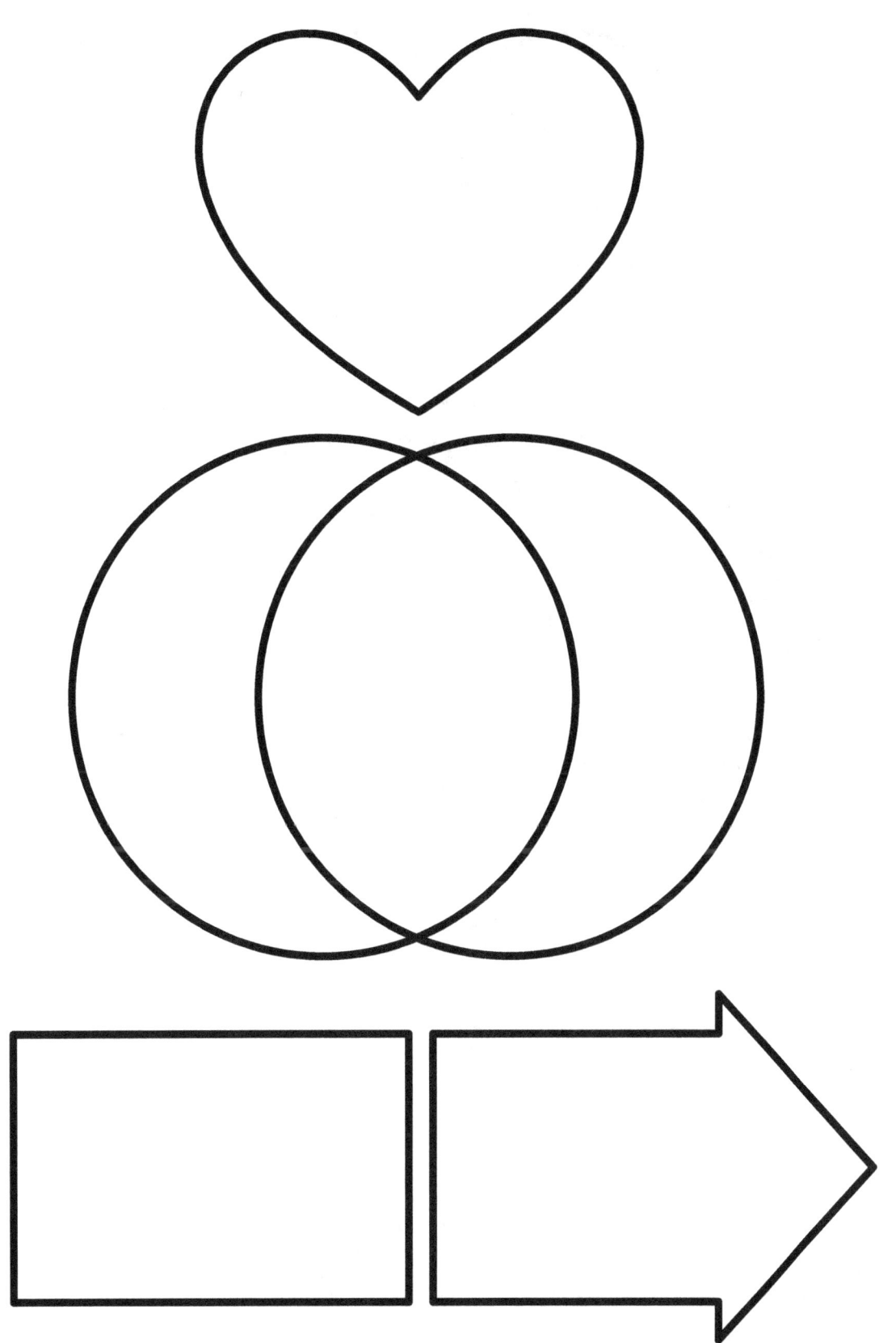

Who I contribute to by speaking up: Everyone who has worked so hard to ensure the success of this project, and all those who will be affected if it falls apart.

My Needs: Consideration, Space, Meaning, Mutuality, Trust, Connection

Higher Purpose everyone shares: We all want this project to succeed, and we all are needing Trust

CEO's Needs: Contribution, To Be Seen, Belonging, To Matter, Safety, Trust

Situation: In meetings, one CEO speaks so much and so often that we don't get to some urgent agenda items, nor is there time for others with time-sensitive concerns to be able to speak.

Request: For everyone, including the CEO, to only speak if they have a question or comment that requires everyone's immediate attention. Also, request that smaller meetings be held for all other comments, involving only those people who need to be part of those discussions.

The Courage to Speak
Remembering

*"The nonviolent approach does not immediately change the heart of the oppressor.
It first does something to the hearts and souls of those committed to it.
It gives them new self-respect; it calls up resources of strength and
courage they did not know they had."*
– Dr. Martin Luther King Jr.

Connecting Requests

"Truth arises when my truth is offered but not placed above the truth of others."
– Tenshin Reb Anderson

Few of us have been educated in how to share our truth or to listen deeply to others. We may have been taught that it isn't safe or socially acceptable to speak our truth and that it's prying to be curious about others'. Nonviolent Communication offers a different perspective: that the truth, whether expressed through ourselves or others, is a gift to all because it allows us to recognize our common humanity. It inspires us to give to one another, not out of fear of punishment or hope for reward, but out of joy and compassion.

Connecting requests are requests that invite others to share their truth and deeply listen to ours. They can help build connection in dialogues where our own sharing and empathic listening aren't enough to establish a sense of mutual understanding. In those moments, we can request:

- Reflection, when we want to have the confidence that we're being understood. *For example, "Would you be willing to tell me what you're hearing me say? I would love to know if my words are making sense."*

- Response, when we want to connect with the other person's truth. *For example, "Would you be willing to tell me how you feel, hearing what I said, because your truth is important to me?"*

As with any request, it helps to name the Needs that the request serves so the listener can connect to the intention behind it *(i.e., in the examples above, "I would love to know if my words are making sense" and "because your truth is important to me").*

Today…

Write down two connecting requests that you could feel comfortable making in a live dialogue, one for reflection and one for response. Write them on something that you can carry with you and pull out easily as a reminder anytime during your day (e.g., on a wallet card or in your smartphone). Remember to include the Needs behind the request in your expression. See the bulleted text above for examples.

Later today, if you're in an interaction where you want to trust that you're being understood and you sense it might benefit the connection, share your request for reflection.

If you're in an interaction where you would like to connect to the other person's truth, share your request for response.

Remember:

- A request is an invitation, not a demand – making a request means that you are willing to hear "No."
- Continue to be present to the Needs that you sense in yourself and others, and offer empathic reflection when you sense it may be beneficial.
- Breathe!

Connecting Requests
Remembering

*"My daily experience, as of those who are working with me,
is that every problem lends itself to solution if we are determined
to make the law of truth and nonviolence the law of life.
For truth and nonviolence are, to me, faces of the same coin."*
– Mohandas Gandhi

Right Speech

*"I raise up my voice – not so I can shout
but so that those without a voice can be heard."*
– Malala Yousafzai

In Buddhism, Right Speech is defined as having five characteristics: it is timely, true, spoken in a way that creates connection, beneficial, and spoken out of compassion. Right Speech grows out of our spiritual understanding and practice and supports its further development. For example, our practice of empathic reflection, which grew out of and supports our Ongo learning, can also be a practice of Right Speech.

Right Speech is more than what we say in any given moment. It involves all of our Ongo practices, from Week 1 until now. Today's practice illustrates this, by offering a way to practice Right Speech that utilizes everything you've practiced so far.

Today...

Set an intention to speak whenever it's of service. In your own way, ask for life's support in this. This is like our practice of Life's Inbox. We are taking the decision to speak out of the realm of our judging mind and putting it into the hands of Life.

> *For example, set the intention, "Life, please help me to get out of my own way today and be of service to you. May any words I speak and any actions I take be of benefit to all. I humbly ask for your guidance in this."*

Throughout the day, be present to the Needs that you sense, whether they arise in you or in the expression of others. This is like our Seeing the Gift practice from Week 6. Breathe and feel whatever feelings arise in the body from connecting to these Needs.

If you sense that it would be beneficial to voice one of these Needs to others, take a moment to consider what request you would like to make of those you're speaking to that would serve this Need.

> *For example, standing on a train, noticing a Need of well-being arise as you witness an elderly woman struggling to stand beside you, the request might be for one of the younger people who are sitting in the seats to offer their seat to the elderly woman.*

Check if your request is:

- **Tangible and specific.** *For example, "Would you be willing to be nice to this woman?" isn't tangible or specific, but "Would you be willing to offer your seat to this woman?" is.*

- **A "do" rather than a "don't."** If your request is to not do something, then it actually isn't something that someone can act on. *For example, "Would you be willing to not take all the seats?" doesn't actually give clarity as to what the others can do, but "Would you be willing to offer your seat to this woman?" does.*

- **An invitation, not a demand.** Do you have the willingness within yourself to be curious and open to other possibilities if the reply to your request is no?

Once you know what request you would like to make, consider if it would be beneficial to make it at this time. If so, make your request and share the Need behind it.

For example, you might say to the younger person, "Would you be willing to offer your seat to this lady? I would love to contribute to her well-being."

Continue to be present to the Needs you sense, even if others are unwilling to meet your requests. Let yourself be curious about the Needs of those who are saying no, and offer empathic reflection if you sense it might be beneficial.

For example, hearing "No" to your request of the younger person, and noticing their withdrawn posture, you sense Needs of love, empathy, mattering, and respect. You share your guess with them, "Sounds like you're having a rough day. I'm guessing you'd like some love and respect, too?"

Remember that none of this is about "getting it right" or "getting your way." We speak in service of the Needs we're connected to because we want to contribute to all of life. We make requests because it gives opportunities for others to also contribute. We offer empathic reflection because we want to make connection. If our specific words or actions don't seem to be contributing or creating connection, then we can turn our curiosity to what will, by being present, listening, and offering silent loving-kindness. If we're too triggered to do that, then we can practice self-empathy and mindfulness of shenpa.

Week 11

WEEK 11 GROUP

Dialogues of the Heart

*"Dominator culture has tried to keep us all afraid,
to make us choose safety instead of risk, sameness instead of diversity.
Moving through that fear, finding out what connects us,
reveling in our differences; this is the process that brings us closer,
that gives us a world of shared values, of meaningful community."*
– bell hooks

Preparation – All participants:

- Bring your copy of *The Ongo Book* and your journal to this Group Gathering.

Preparation – Group Guide:

- A day or two before the Group Gathering, remind everyone of the day, time, and place of the Gathering.

- Read "Leading Group Practice" (page 13) and do the points listed under "Responsibilities of the Guide."

- Lay one deck of Needs cards out in an attractive mandala or spiral in the center of the circle.

Opening Meditation

Invite everyone to take their seats in the circle.

Ring a bell to signal the beginning of the sitting meditation.

After a moment of silence, read the guidance below to the group. Read in a way that supports the group to relax into the guidance, allowing space and silence between passages:

Take a breath to settle into where you sit and connect to your body.

Rock your body slightly right and left, forward and back a little bit, and allow yourself to find center.

Find the place where your spine is naturally stacked and supporting itself without having to strain or feel like you're holding yourself up or falling over.

In this moment, notice if any muscles are working that don't need to be.

Notice that the ground is supporting you.

Take a deep breath. On the exhale, allow your mind and your body to settle into this place, in this moment, right here, right now.

Feel the presence of the others in this circle who are sitting with you in this moment.

Allow your mind to settle into the possibility, the possibility that this moment is enough.

Let your breath and the earth teach you what that feels like.

Allow five full minutes of silence then read:

Allow yourself to bring to mind interactions – interactions with others from your day or from your week. If it helps, you can start at the beginning of your day and review what you did and whom you interacted with.

As you review, don't get too hung up on the details. It is more about reviewing your day from a heart place and the space of mindfulness.

As you review, allow yourself to notice what moments you are celebrating.

Allow yourself to notice moments you are mourning, any moments that feel stuck or unresolved. This isn't the time to fix or resolve those moments but rather to open your heart to them.

Feel how they touch you. If you get distracted or caught up in your stories about the events, allow yourself to come back to your body and your breath.

Settle in.

Allow 10 full minutes of silence then read:

We are not going to ring a bell to close the meditation in today's gathering. We are going to bring this meditation into every dialogue and interaction we have in our circle today, bringing our practice into our words.

Introduction to Dialogues of the Heart

Read to the group (or invite other participants to take turns reading paragraphs to the group):

As you listen to these words, even if you are the one reading them, continue to feel the presence of the body and the breath in each moment. From this place of connection, consider the interactions that arose during the meditation, during the review of your week. Consider whether there is any interaction you would like to practice with, perhaps trying out some different choices than the ones you made in the original conversation. Perhaps working with some difficult dynamics or responses, things that were painful for you to hear and challenging for you to respond to in the way you would have liked. Or maybe there is an interaction you're anticipating having that you'd enjoy preparing for. Is there an interaction you haven't had yet but are thinking about? Or scared of even considering? Here, in this safe container, you can play with that interaction.

We don't walk into these conversations expecting an outcome or wanting to change the other person. We begin with our intention to connect. Humans of any age, when they sense that the person who is speaking with them is coming from an intention to connect, naturally relax. And the intention to connect can come quite naturally to us when we're in a lighthearted conversation with few consequences.

Then there are the situations where the mind says, "But I know what is right! I have the answer. They have to listen to me." When it comes to challenging dialogues, especially when we feel something is at stake like somebody's health or well-being, we can easily forget about connection in our desire to protect or contribute. In those moments, we have the opportunity to practice returning to that intention to connect.

For example, Catherine recalls a situation with a 15-year-old girl from one of her "Play in the Wild!" quests. During a group dialogue at the beginning of the quest, the girl requested to bring her cigarettes on the trek. She agreed with the community of students and leaders to limit herself to no more than three cigarettes a day, to be at least 300 feet away from everyone while she smoked, and to make sure that none of her butts were left behind in the outdoors.

When it came time for an eight-hour vision quest in which the students would sit by themselves in the forest, Catherine expressed to this girl, "I can't imagine having you sit for eight hours on a vision quest, spending the day smoking. I'm wondering if you'd be willing to try these eight hours without your cigarettes." The girl said, "Yeah," and handed over her cigarettes to Catherine.

As soon as the vision quest was over, she came running back to Catherine and said, "Hey, can I get my smokes back?" In that instant, Catherine noticed a moment of internal choice. As she handed the cigarettes back to the girl, she said, "I'm noticing that I'm hesitant to give these back to you. I can't make or change anything about you or your choices. But when you take a cigarette and the smoke into your lungs, I'd love to hear back from you what Needs are met for you."

The girl took the cigarettes and walked off. Almost immediately, she came running back and said, "You know, I really connected to the Need of belonging, so that makes me think I'd much rather hang out with people than smoke my cigarettes."

That was her last cigarette. Her choice.

This is an example of returning to the intention to connect, even when it's challenging to do so, as part of our practice of wisdom and compassion. If Catherine had just told the girl not to smoke and all the reasons it was bad, it wouldn't have allowed the girl her dignity or the space to find out what was true for her. If we bring connection as our simple intention, as opposed to wanting to get our way and change the other person, something melts away and wisdom and compassion take over.

Practicing Dialogues of the Heart

Invite everyone to look at the "Communication Flow Chart" on page 275 in the Appendix and to take out their journal. Then read the following:

> The Communication Flow Chart is a simple map of our choices when we're in a dialogue or conversation. It brings together a lot of the skills we've been practicing so far in Ongo. When we're in an interaction, we always have self-empathy as our first option. This is where we take a moment to breathe and notice what we're feeling, what our Needs are, and consider what we might want to request.
>
> From that place of self-connection, we then get to breathe and move down the chart to check our intention. Are we in this conversation because we're curious and want to connect with this other person? Or are we still, in some form, wanting to get our way, constricted and tight? If that is where we find ourselves, we go back up to self-empathy.
>
> If we find when we breathe and check our intention that we are ready to connect with this other person and are genuinely curious about their experience, we have a choice. We can choose to empathize with what's present for them, or we can choose to express – our practice of speaking truth. We also sometimes call speaking truth "empathic expression" because it's an honest expression that's helping to build empathic connection.
>
> Today, in our practice of wise and compassionate dialogues, we will use the Communication Flow Chart as a map of our choices while we are in dialogue. We will take turns bringing forward interactions with which we would like to try out some of these choices.

When you have a situation you would like to play with, you will ask another group member to play the role of the person in your situation. You will tell that person a little bit about the situation – just the basics without a lot of story. You will begin to express what it is you want to say, bringing your practice to your words, engaging the pause or the breath when you notice that you're getting caught in a reaction. They will respond authentically to you, without trying to overthink how the person they're playing would "actually" respond. The point is to create an opportunity for you to practice the skills of mindfulness and Nonviolent Communication, not to attempt a perfect simulation of the other person.

Your body and breath will be your ground for the entire interaction. Let it be a place you can go to to resource and respond from. Anytime you get lost or confused, take a moment to look at the Communication Flow Chart and consider which choice you want to make. In general, if you're feeling lost, it's probably best to go to self-empathy first.

For the purpose of this practice, we will name out loud when we are choosing self-empathy. Allow yourself to pause the conversation and take the time to acknowledge out loud what you're thinking, feeling, needing, and wanting to request before choosing how you want to respond next. Remember that this isn't just about the words – take the time to actually feel and be with what you're naming. Breathe with it, then go down to check your intention on the flow chart.

This is the beginning of shifting to connection rather than just trying to get our own way. Trying to get our way is a strategy of protection – to protect something important to us. When we recognize that the protection is there and what the protection is about, then often we can start to make the shift that we need to be able to connect.

Because this practice is about connection rather than trying to get our way, we won't role-play our dialogues all the way until an agreement or solution is reached. Simply practice with your interaction until you feel a sense of relaxed empathic connection that isn't dependent on the other person changing how they're responding to you. This will be an intuitive sense in the body. It is from this quality of empathic connection that we trust resolution or new strategies will emerge. Therefore, we practice to arrive to the empathic connection.

Check if anyone is unclear about the practice and needs to hear any instructions again. Once everyone is clear, read:

> Let's take a couple of breaths together now as we step into this vulnerability and trust moving deeper into our practice.

Gently ring a bell and invite whoever would like to go first with practicing a dialogue.

After each dialogue practice, take a collective breath together followed by a minute of silence for integration of the experience. Complete the silence by gently ringing a bell and asking for the next person who would like to practice.

Harvest

Read:

> This practice reminds us of our collective humanity. If we are reactive, lost, or stimulated, then there's a really good chance that something inside the other person is reacting to the interaction as well. So we let go of our agenda and dance in the empathic connection. We can begin to see just what's right in front of us. We pause, breathe, and peel back the layers of confusion and disconnection so that we can return to the connection that is trying to happen, just in that moment in front of us.

Let's Harvest this practice. What did you learn? What are you appreciating about yourself or this practice? What are you mourning? What are you celebrating?

Invite anyone who feels moved to share with the group.

Closing

Ask for a volunteer to guide the group next week. Give that person the deck(s) of Needs cards.

Remind that volunteer to read the pages on "Leading Group Practice" (page 13) and Week 12's Group Gathering before the next meeting. Everything they need to know will be in those pages.

Invite everyone to take a collective full breath together. Invite everyone to offer a simple nonverbal gratitude to each other with a bow, a hug, or whatever works best for each person.

The Hook

"In spite of everything, I still believe that people are really good at heart. I simply can't build up my hopes on a foundation consisting of confusion, misery, and death. I see the world gradually being turned into a wilderness, I hear the ever-approaching thunder, which will destroy us too, I can feel the sufferings of millions and yet, if I look up into the heavens, I think that it will all come right, that this cruelty too will end, and that peace and tranquility will return again."
– Anne Frank

Opening Meditation

Greet your Buddy.

Decide who will read the remembering (Buddy A) and who will time a five-minute meditation (Buddy B).

Buddy A reads the following out loud:

> "[There is] a cartoon of three fish swimming around a hook. One fish is saying to the others, 'The secret is nonattachment.' That's a shenpa joke; the secret is, don't bite that hook. If we can learn to relax into the place where the urge is strong, we will get a bigger perspective on what's happening." – Pema Chödrön

Sit in silence together for five minutes.

Buddy B signals Buddy A when five minutes have passed.

Close with a bow of appreciation to your Buddy for sitting with you.

Introduction to Not Biting the Hook

Buddy B reads the following out loud:

> This week's Buddy Practice engages everything we have been practicing so far in Ongo: mindfulness of body and breath, a consciousness of Needs, empathy and self-empathy, turning toward a power greater than ourselves, awareness of core beliefs, finishing business, forgiveness, celebration and mourning, mindfulness of shenpa, and speaking truth.

Difficult dialogues request us to step out to the edges of our practice. We get to notice the moment of "getting hooked" when words stimulate our old, habitual responses. We notice, we breathe, we return to self-empathy. By returning to the energy of the Needs, we are practicing in dialogue what we practice in our meditation. We are increasing the space between stimulus and response. One of the steepest learning curves in Nonviolent Communication is becoming aware of how we hear things and noticing how that stimulates our reactions more than what others actually say or do. If we take a breath to "not bite the hook," to not let the stimulus steer us away from connection, then we have a chance to stay connected to Needs and retain our ability to listen with empathy to ourselves and the other person.

For this practice we will refer to the "Communication Flow Chart" and "Needs Wheel" in the Appendix.

Not Biting the Hook

Sit in silence together for a few minutes, reflecting on any dialogues from your life that you would like to bring to this practice. It can be a dialogue you are planning to have with someone or one that you have already had and did not enjoy how it went.

Decide who will be A and who will be B first. Buddy A will follow the guidance below marked "A" and Buddy B will follow the guidance marked "B."

A: Tell B the name of the person they will "role-play" and who that person is to you. Avoid sharing other details and background about this person – it's not necessary for this practice and may become a distraction.

A: Tell B what you are most afraid of hearing from this person as their first response to you – your "nightmare" response. This is what B will say to you, as their first response in the dialogue you are about to have.

A: Look at the Communication Flow Chart. Use this as your guide for the dialogue.

A: Begin at the top of the Communication Flow Chart by practicing Self-Empathy out loud until you feel a sense of clarity about your Needs and what you would like to request.

B: While A is practicing Self-Empathy, simply offer silent empathic listening.

A: Look at "Check Intention" on the Communication Flow Chart.

- **If you sense you want connection, then proceed to "Speaking Truth."**

- **If you sense you still want to convince the other person you are "right" in some way, get them to do what you want, or try to tell your Buddy more about the story, then return to "Self-Empathy,"** until you are clear about your Needs and wanting to make connection.

A: Say out loud to B what you would like to express to this other person. Feel free to use your own words, but use the principles that you've learned: be connected to your Needs, name your Needs and your request, and be present to your body and breath. Remember to use a connecting request if you think it would support mutual understanding in the connection.

B: Respond to A with the "nightmare" response that they gave you above.

A: Notice if you are "getting hooked." What emotions are stimulated? What thoughts? Simply notice, breathe, then choose where to move on the Communication Flow Chart:

- **If you are "hooked," name your "hooks" out loud. Go to "Self-Empathy" and self-empathize out loud.** When you get the sense that you have returned to an intention to connect, choose where you would like to move next on the Communication Flow Chart.

- **If you can hear the Needs behind the nightmare response, go to "Empathic Listening" and make an empathic guess.**

- **If you would like to continue to express what is alive in you, go to "Speaking Truth."**

B: Continue the dialogue in your role by simply responding to A in whatever way feels authentic to you. Don't over-think it or try to imagine what the person you're playing would say. Simply respond in whatever way is authentic to you.

A: Continue to use your Flow Chart to track where you are in the conversation, staying with your practice of self-empathy then choosing expressing, listening, or offering an out-loud empathic guess.

Arrive to a stopping point after 15 minutes, then take a moment to breathe together. Harvest whatever you learned.

Now switch roles, with the person who was role-playing bringing forward the situation they would like to work with, and the person who just practiced offering support through role-playing.

Closing

Take a few minutes to sit in silence together for completion.

WEEK 11 SOLO PRACTICES

Harvesting

"You don't have to be brilliant. It's enough to become progressively less stupid."
– Marshall B. Rosenberg, Ph.D.

Harvesting is a practice of consciously reflecting on learning experiences through the lens of celebration and mourning. We celebrate any life that was enriched and mourn any life that wasn't. Harvesting creates meaning of the past, enjoyment in the present, and direction for the future. As we are about to enter our last week of Ongo, it's a good time to Harvest our Ongo journey.

Today…

Sit in your practice space and take some time to reflect on your experience of Ongo.

Consider the Ongo Intention that you started with. Revisit the last three months in your mind and heart, perhaps looking back over any journal entries and practices you did.

Take time to breathe, feel, and be with anything that touches you – celebrations and mournings. Take time to acknowledge and appreciate any growth and change that has occurred.

In your journal, write:

- **One or more celebrations of anything you did or said this Ongo.** Write down what you specifically did or said and what Needs it touched. With each celebration, take time to breathe and savor!

- **One or more mournings of anything you did or said this Ongo.** Write down what you specifically did or said and what Needs are being mourned with that. With each mourning, take time to breathe and be with the mourning in the body.

- **Any insights that come as you're being with these celebrations and mournings.**

- **Any questions that are still alive for you in relation to practice** (any aspect – mindfulness, empathy, speaking truth, etc.).

- **Any actions/requests for yourself or others that come out of these celebrations, mournings, insights, and questions.**

If you are part of an Ongo group:

- **Reflect on the members of your Ongo circle, considering in turn your connection to each person.**
- **Create an offering to express whatever you would like about your Ongo journey to the community at the closing gathering.** It might be a poem, a song, ... or use your imagination!
- **Bring your offering to the final Group Gathering.**

Take a deep breath and acknowledge yourself for all your efforts this Ongo to become "progressively less stupid"!

 Deepening – Harvesting can be quite powerful as a daily reflection, especially when we are also present to the impermanence of our lives. Each evening, take some time to Harvest the day in your journal, with the understanding that this could be the last day, week, or month of your life. This practice can also be done in your mind, without a journal, as a nightly reflection before you fall asleep.

Harvesting
Remembering

"To be truly happy in this world is a revolutionary act. ... It is a radical change of view that liberates us so that we know who we are most deeply and can acknowledge our enormous ability to love."
– Sharon Salzberg

Post-Ongo Support

"Guidance wasn't whispered in my ear by angels. It came through trial and error, as it does for most of us non-saints."
— Mirabai Bush

As this Ongo draws to a close, we may wonder what our practice after Ongo will look like. It can be valuable, while we're still in Ongo, to take some time to connect to what Ongo has meant to us and to consider what actions we want to take to give us support after Ongo.

Today…

Take 10 minutes to sit with the breath and the earth.

After those 10 minutes, ask this question into the stillness: "Do I have any requests for myself or others that could contribute to my need for support after Ongo ends?"

Write down anything that comes.

Take a minute to check, Are the request(s) you wrote down:

- Specific (you know exactly what action to take)?
- Doable (small enough that you can easily follow through on them)?
- Dos and not don'ts?
- Invitations and not demands (they feel enjoyable and not burdensome)?
- Supportive of your vision of life after Ongo?

If not, rewrite your request(s) so that they are.

Place these requests in a place where you will see them and be reminded to act on them.

Post-Ongo Support
Remembering

"Religion is everywhere. We have to understand our teaching in this way. We should forget all about some particular teaching; we should not ask which is good or bad. There should not be any particular teaching. Teaching is in each moment, in every existence. That is the true teaching."
– Shunryu Suzuki

You Are Here

"It's like you never can do it and still you try. And, interestingly enough, that adds up to something, it adds up to appreciation for yourself and for others. It adds up to there being more warmth in the world."
– Pema Chödrön

We will close our Ongo practice this week with a two-part practice that begins in the morning and ends in the evening. We will return to the place where we began this whole journey – right here. In fact, we are inseparable from "here." Here is wherever we are. Our place of practice is wherever we go.

Today, in the morning…

Choose a place where you can sit for twenty minutes in the midst of your everyday life. *For example, at the kitchen table where you drink your morning coffee, at your desk at work, in the driver's seat of your (parked) car, or in the seat on the bus you ride regularly.*

Set a timer for 20 minutes, then sit down in this ordinary, everyday seat.

For the first few minutes, sit with the eyes closed, present with the body, the breath, and the support of the physical seat that is holding your body in this moment. Rest into the texture of the breath, as it flows in … and out.

Then, with your eyes still closed, gently expand your attention to include the smells and sounds of this familiar place. Sit for a few more minutes with this awareness that includes the space around you.

If the mind wanders to thoughts, return to the simple intention of being here, with breath, smells, and sounds, in this familiar space. There's nothing wrong with wandering – just keep returning here.

If certain thoughts or feelings in the body persist, be open and curious about what Need they're expressing in the present moment. Remember, every thought, every feeling, every sensation is a *present-moment* expression of a Need. They're revealing some aspect of who you are in *this* moment.

Wiggle your toes. With your eyes still closed, sense where your feet are right now. Notice *you* are a part of this familiar space. Right here. Right now. Breathe and rest into that precious understanding.

After a few minutes, slowly open your eyes and breathe. Look around, taking in what is around you and includes you, while staying present in the body.

Now, look at your hands. Notice how they are part of the body of this being, sitting in this place, right now. Take a breath with these hands that hold history as well as future possibility.

Notice your unique place in this familiar space, at this moment.

Notice belonging in this space. In this world.

Notice your own mattering. How it matters what you choose to do with these hands, that are part of this body, of this being, sitting in this place, right now.

As thoughts arise, return to the breath. Allow yourself to let go of trying to conceptually understand your belonging and mattering and feel the earth beneath your seat. Remember that something greater than you is holding all of it, including you. Release into that. Simply rest into the body, the breath, and the earth.

At the end of the 20 minutes, take a deep breath and bring your hands into prayer position. Bow outwardly to the world around you with a simultaneous inward bow acknowledging your place in this world. May all beings know they belong. May all beings know they matter.

In the evening...

Return to the practice space you created for Ongo.

In your journal or on a piece of paper, trace your hands.

Inside the hands, color, write, or draw any insights or Needs that have arisen or stayed with you from the morning's practice. What did you learn about being part of the whole design of Life? What Needs guide your actions in the world?

Afterwards, remove or put away any Ongo-specific items or decorations.

Clean, re-set, and refresh your practice space. Place the drawing of your hands there.

Take a moment to acknowledge and give thanks to some of the causes and conditions that have supported you in your Ongo journey. This might include teachers, family, friends, community, helpful teachings, and nurturing environments and places.

Then, take another moment to dedicate any and all merit gained from these three months of Ongo practice to the benefit of all beings, that all may be happy and free from suffering, including any specific people or groups that you'd like to send blessings to.

Take a deep breath.

Is there anything more that needs to be done for closure? If there is, do it.

Next week will begin a new chapter in your practice.

Audio – There is a guided audio recording of this meditation available on The Ongo Companion Website at ongo.global. You can also make your own guided audio meditation by recording yourself reading the practice out loud. If you make your own, remember to speak slowly and allow lots of silence in between instructions so you can easily follow along when listening to it later.

Instant – Right now, close your eyes and take a deep breath. Notice the smells and sounds around you. Wiggle your toes and feel yourself in this space, in this moment. Then, take a deep breath and open your eyes. Look around at your surroundings. Finally, take one more deep breath and look at your hands. Feel how they are a part of this body, which is a part of everything. Feel how what you choose to do with them matters. Now, act.

Deepening – Let the morning meditation become a practice that you do in different contexts in your life: at work, at home, out in the community. Sometimes, it may be a shorter; sometimes, longer. For example, sometimes, you may find that simply breathing and looking at your hands is the return to presence needed in the moment.

Week 12

Ongo Harvest

"If the world is to be healed through human efforts, I am convinced it will be by ordinary people, people whose love for this life is even greater than their fear."
– Joanna Macy

Preparation – All participants:

- Bring your offering to the group from your Day 1 Solo Practice last week.

Preparation – Group Guide:

- A day or two before the Group Gathering, remind everyone of the day, time, and place of the gathering, and to bring their offering (see above).

- Read "Leading Group Practice" (page 13) and do the points listed under "Responsibilities of the Guide."

- Lay one deck of Needs cards out in an attractive mandala or spiral in the center of the circle.

Opening Meditation

Invite everyone to take their seats in the circle.

Ring a bell to signal the beginning of the sitting meditation.

After a moment of silence, read the guidance below to the group. Read in a way that supports the group to relax into the guidance:

> Let us sit together in silence for these next 20 minutes, being present to ourselves, our Ongo circle, and this one precious life we share. There's nothing special we have to do. Let's just be here together for this one last time.

Sit in silence together for 20 minutes, then ring the bell three times to end the meditation.

Place your palms together and offer a bow of gratitude to the circle.

310 Closing Harvest

Read to the group:

> For three months, we have taken this journey of wisdom and compassion together, building a community of support for our practice. As this Ongo comes to a close, we can feel the preciousness of each moment and each connection we have experienced in our time together.
>
> Let us give space now for this preciousness to be expressed by bringing our presence to each member of our circle for a closing Harvest. We are each invited to share any celebrations in our hearts of our time in Ongo, any mournings that are present, and any learnings that want to be shared out loud. This is also an opportunity to share any offerings that we have prepared for our community.
>
> As with our Empathy Circles, when someone is sharing, the rest of us will bring our silent listening presence. When each person is finished sharing, those of us listening will, in silence, place Needs cards in front of them, offering a sense of confirmation that we have heard their sharing.
>
> We can start with whoever first feels moved to share, then go around the circle clockwise from there.

Invite anyone who feels moved to begin the Harvest.

Continue around the circle clockwise until everyone, including you, has shared and received Needs cards.

After, invite the group to take a collective breath together followed by a minute or two of silent meditation. Ring the bell once to end the Harvest.

311 Honoring Ceremony

Invite everyone to stand in a circle.

Read:

> Let us complete this journey together by honoring ourselves as individuals and as community.
>
> As a community, we will collectively say to each member of the circle, "It is an honor to know you," followed by their first name.

When a person is named, that person will respond by saying, "Thank you for walking with me."

Then we will all bow to each other, as we do after meditation, with our palms together in front of our hearts.

We will then go on to the next person in the circle and start again: "It is an honor to know you …," and the person responding, "Thank you for walking with me." Then we all bow to honor that connection and continue around the circle.

Let's begin with the person on my left, and continue around the circle clockwise from there.

Check if anyone is unclear about the ceremony and needs to hear the instructions again. Once everyone is clear, invite everyone to take a breath together and to bring their presence to the ceremony.

Begin the ceremony by turning toward the person on your left, then continue as described in the guidance.

After the last person (you) has been honored, ring the bell three times to signal the end of Ongo.

Pure Meeting

"This is a story of pure meeting. There's no instruction, no test, no program, no content. There are no words, nothing you could put a finger on other than a smile shared between two people who are appreciating together the profound beauty of the flower that is our life."
– Norman Fischer

The final Ongo Buddy Practice is an open space for you and your Buddy to use in whatever way you both need to further your integration and completion of the Ongo journey. This can be an opportunity to review a Buddy Practice that you would both enjoy exploring more deeply. It is also an opportunity to discuss what would support your post-Ongo transitions, as you complete the cycle of four Buddy meetings together.

Thank you for walking with each other.

Thank you for your journey in Ongo.

WEEK 12 SOLO PRACTICES

Five Days to Live

Walk around feeling like a leaf.
Know you could tumble any second.
Then decide what to do with your time.
– Naomi Shihab Nye

This week's Solo Practices offer a way to create a daily practice that can continue well beyond Ongo. Knowing our own impermanence – and the impermanence of everything and everybody around us – can help to clarify our priorities. What would you want to practice in your life if you only had one week left to live?

Today…

Take some time to sit, being with body and breath.

While sitting, invite in the question, "If this were the last week of my life, what's one Need, one quality of life, that I would like to be or express more fully?" See what arises and write that word or phrase down. *For example, "play" or "respect for all life."*

Then, invite in a second question, "If this were the last week of my life, what's one quality of life that I would like to contribute more of to one of my relationships?" This could be a relationship with a loved one, close friend, family member, or someone you connect with on a regular basis. **Write down what comes.** *For example, "empathy in my relationship with my partner."*

Finally, invite in a third question, "If this were the last week of my life, what's one quality of life that I would like to contribute more of to my community?" Community could be your circle of friends, neighborhood, town, workplace, tribe, or some wider grouping of people that you're in touch with on a regular basis. **Write this down.** *For example, "I'd like to contribute gratitude to and among my neighbors."*

Allow these to be open questions throughout your day. Carry your journal or a small notebook with you and note any other responses that come to you.

Four Days to Live

"There is a vitality, a life force, an energy, a quickening that is translated through you into action, and because there is only one of you in all of time, this expression is unique. And if you block it, it will never exist through any other medium and it will be lost. The world will not have it. It is not your business to determine how good it is nor how valuable nor how it compares with other expressions. It is your business to keep it yours clearly and directly, to keep the channel open. You do not even have to believe in yourself or your work. You have to keep yourself open and aware to the urges that motivate you. Keep the channel open ... No artist is pleased. [There is] no satisfaction whatever at any time. There is only a queer divine dissatisfaction, a blessed unrest that keeps us marching and makes us more alive than the others."
– Martha Graham

Today...

Consider the Need that you would like to express more fully in your life (your response to the first question from Day 1's practice).

Sit for a few minutes and feel the energy of that Need in your body. If it helps, follow the Being Needs guidance from Week 2, Day 5, of the Solo Practices.

Take one action today that expresses that energy. *For example, if "play" was the Need, you might choose to dance to a favorite song or invite someone to play a game with you.*

If this action doesn't feel easy or joyful to do, check:

- **Is this request you're making of yourself truly an invitation and not a demand?** If not, change the request so it feels like less of a "have-to" and more of a "love-to."

- **Is it specific and doable, rather than vague and wishful?** If not, change the request so it's smaller and more tangible.

- **Is it a do, rather than a don't?** If not, change the request so it's clear what you want to do instead of focusing on what you don't want to do.

After doing the action, take a minute to visualize any happiness and fulfillment you experience extending out to all beings who long for this Need to have greater expression in their lives.

Three Days to Live

*"Since the world is round
There is no way to walk away
From each other, for even then
We are coming back together."*
– Amanda Gorman

Today…

Take a few minutes to acknowledge and give thanks for some of the ways others have contributed to your life recently. You might choose to visualize some of those moments, write them down in a gratitude list, or simply say them out loud.

Then, consider the quality of life that you would like to contribute more of to one of your relationships (your response to the second question from Day 1's practice).

Sit for a few minutes and feel the energy of that Need in your body, what it feels like as you connect to the vision that you hold for this relationship.

Take one action today to bring that quality alive in this relationship. *For example, if "empathy" was the quality you wanted to bring more alive, you might choose to invite your loved one to share what's on their mind and heart while you listen with presence and empathic reflection, without interjecting your own opinions or advice.*

Allow yourself to be brave in your action, as if this truly was your last week to live. Often we forget that when we act in true service of Needs, it is a gift for everyone, not a burden or imposition. Who wouldn't want to be invited into a deeper, fuller, more intimate experience of life?

After doing the action, take a minute to visualize any happiness and fulfillment you experience extending out to all relationships everywhere who long for this quality of life to be expressed more fully.

Two Days to Live

"True compassion is more than flinging a coin to a beggar; it comes to see that an edifice which produces beggars needs restructuring."
– Dr. Martin Luther King Jr.

Today…

Take a few minutes to bring to mind those in your community whose suffering you long to relieve and whom you would want to benefit from your practice.

Feel how their presence touches you – notice it in your body. Give room for those feelings to be expressed in you, including any pain or mourning. Breathe with it all.

Then, consider the quality of life that you would like to contribute more of to your community (your response to the third question from Day 1's practice).

Sit for a few minutes and feel the energy of that Need in your body, what it feels like as you connect to the vision that you hold for this community.

Take one action today in your community to contribute more of that quality. *For example, if "gratitude" was a quality that you named, then you might choose to do the Sharing Gratitude practice from Week 7, Day 3, with the people in your local town.*

Allow yourself to be brave in your action, as if this truly was your last week to live. No one after you may ever even think to do this action in your community. Social change begins with us. What kind of world do we want to live in? What kind of community would we like for the generations to come?

After doing the action, take a minute to visualize any happiness and fulfillment you experience extending out to all communities everywhere who long for this quality of life to be expressed more fully.

One Day to Live

"Friends, we have arrived."
– Shantum Seth

Today...

Sit for 20 minutes. Sit as if these are your last minutes on earth and all your other affairs are complete.

Breathe.

Invite awareness and presence into each moment: shape, color, sound, breath, heartbeat, sensation, thought, emotion, "you," and all the Life around "you."

For just this one time, sit as if you no longer had to worry about becoming a better person. Just be with the preciousness of what is here – because you may never experience it again in this form.

Afterword: Continuing Ongo with Integrity

"Ongo is a tool that is needed for people like me. People who are passionate about life on earth and keeping it livable. I learned to accept this moment and then connect with others as we move toward action to make the world better ASAP."
– participant in Citizens' Climate Lobby's Peer Support - Ongo Program

The Ongo Book was written with a specific progression of practices that we have found to be deeply liberating in both our own lives and the lives of others. However, because nonviolence itself is broader than any one form or teaching, we do not consider our progression, or the forms of practice we offer, to be the only path that Ongo can take.

Some Ongo Book groups, buddies, or individuals may find, after journeying several times through the twelve-week progression of this book, that they would like to retain the structure of Ongo but are ready to expand the breadth or depth of their learning beyond the offered practices. We encourage them to play with changing the forms of Ongo practice, while still keeping the purpose and structure of Ongo intact. This chapter contains guidance for how to do that. In it, we offer several essential principles to always keep in mind, suggested guidelines for introducing new forms to an Ongo group, and a general template for creating your own Ongo Group Practices.

Essential Principles of Ongo

These essential principles define what stays constant about Ongo, even when the forms of practice change. They are what distinguishes Ongo Book groups from other kinds of groups (i.e., meditation groups or Nonviolent Communication practice groups). When diverging from the forms in *The Ongo Book*, remember the following:

1. **Our shared purpose is to *be* nonviolence in the context of our daily lives, and we gather to practice, offer mutual support, and learn from one another the way of nonviolence.** Nonviolence is a translation of the Sanskrit word *ahiṃsā*, and can be defined as being without violence in one's thoughts, words, or actions. Nonviolence can also be defined as living in interdependence with all life. Inherently, nonviolence is freedom from our conditioned tendency to create fundamental separations in our life.

2. **Ongo is a twelve-week journey, while our practice of nonviolence is ever ongoing.** Ongo can be understood as a twelve-week journey with its own beginning, middle, and end. Journeys can happen regularly or as needed. However, the Ongo journey is also a mirror of our lives. Just as we do not "graduate" from our lives (except, perhaps, when we transition from our bodies), there is no completion of an Ongo "course," nor are there any Ongo "expert" certifications. While we do become more experienced through practice, we remain humble and teachable by continuously working with our learning edges and approaching the journey with beginner's mind.

3. **We are not attached to a particular religion or secular modality.** The forms of our practice vary, depending on what's needed. Each form of nonviolence has its own strengths and limitations, which we come to know through ongoing practice.

4. **We consciously choose structures for our gatherings that support our shared purpose, and avoid those that divert us.** Ongo has more explicit structure than many meditation groups, NVC practice groups, and other kinds of spiritual study groups. One example is the use of council rounds on specific topics for open sharing, rather than having unstructured check-ins. This was intentional, because of how often we have seen groups lose energy and focus, or be dominated by a strong personality, when the structures used are not explicit or consciously chosen.

5. **We share leadership, to practice leading and to learn from following each other's lead.** In our lives, based on our role in any given moment, we will lead or follow. We want to be nonviolence in all those contexts. We wrote the book with the intention of cultivating leader-full communities, instead of supporting a few Ongo "experts" to be group leaders. Though experienced practitioners may choose to host Ongo groups, there are no Ongo "teachers." We want everyone to be able to facilitate empathy circles or guide meditations in their wider families, communities, and organizations.

6. **Ongo is a solo and buddy journey, as well as a group journey.** Ongo is a period of intensive practice in the midst of one's life. To fully experience the benefits of that, it's important that practice continues throughout the week, outside of the group gatherings. If your Ongo group chooses to introduce new practices, consider how those practices could also be practiced Solo and with a Buddy during the week.

7. **Ongo Book groups are freely accessible to anyone.** The only fees ever charged for an Ongo Book group are the direct costs for running the group (i.e., Ongo books and venue rental, or online conference platform fees). If those fees prohibit someone from joining, then work to find ways around that. Any other financial requests (i.e., donations for the person organizing) are optional and not a condition for participation in an Ongo Book group.

Guidelines for Introducing New Forms to Ongo

Ongo practices are mutually consented to, shared with integrity, practiced through the body, and used where useful. When introducing new forms to your Ongo practice, we offer these four guidelines:

1. **Seek consent from your Ongo Book group before introducing new forms.** It is important that the group agrees to any modalities that will be practiced together. Consent is inherent in our practices of nonviolence to build trusting relationships in our Beloved Community. You can check consent by sharing with the group what you would like to bring and asking if anyone would be opposed. If even one person is opposed, then it is not group consent.

2. **Learn forms with integrity.** In this day and age, it's easy to go online and quickly download instructions for just about anything. In practice, learning forms with integrity means, whenever possible, learning the form from someone who has a lived practice of it. Perhaps someone in the Ongo Book group is already experienced with another form and can introduce it to the group through practices they initially lead. Every form has its own principles that inform how the form is practiced in order to be effective and not harmful. These principles are not always easily communicated through a short video or text. Integrity also means respectfully acknowledging the people who originated the forms that we practice. These ancestors may have gone to great lengths to preserve and share this wisdom so that we could practice it today.

3. **Practice forms in an embodied way.** It's tempting to think that we know something when we can talk about it. Practicing forms in an embodied way means to limit how

much a form is intellectually discussed or talked about abstractly before actually doing it. If we don't do it first, we quite literally don't know what we're talking about. Talking too much "about" nonviolence is one way we can lose sight of our purpose to "be" nonviolence. All lasting transformation happens through the body. Our thoughts and words are only byproducts.

4. **Use forms where they are useful.** Using forms where they are useful means that we consciously consider where using a form serves our shared purpose, and where it doesn't. The progression of forms in the book aims to balance the limitations of each practice with the strengths of another. For example, we choose to use Needs language throughout Ongo because it is such an effective way to practice nonviolence in our relationships with self and others. However, Needs language also engages the conceptual part of our brain and therefore limits how present we are with our other senses. To give balance, we also incorporate forms like walking meditation, which emphasize awareness of the body. In those cases, we choose not to use Needs language. Similarly, be mindful not to over-rely on any one form unless, for some reason, it is useful to do so.

A Template for Ongo Group Practices

The template below provides a simple format that can be used to introduce other meditations and practices to an Ongo Book group, provided the group has consented to that. This format will be familiar and consistent with the flow of group gatherings from the book.

1. **Open with meditation and, optionally, an empathy circle for those who need it.** The meditation can be a wide range of practices, from sitting in silence to dancing with music. What's important is that the meditation supports participants to bring their hearts, minds, and bodies into alignment, both individually and as a group. Also, it's important that the meditation offers a sense of unconditional safety, acceptance, and belonging to everyone participating. After the meditation, if there is time, an empathy circle for those participants that need it can deepen the collective sense of connection.

2. **Introduce a practice.** When introducing practices, we suggest keeping the introduction simple – just what is needed for participants to dive into the practice. That could include: how you were introduced to the practice and why it's meaningful to you, a quote from one of the ancestors of the practice, brief explanations of any principles that are necessary for the practice, and an overview of what participants are about to do.

3. **Do the practice together.** In doing the practice together, it's important that someone track time for the group. In some cases, it can also be helpful if the person guiding the practice is able to give a personal example of each step, for clarity.

4. **Harvest the experience.**

5. **Take care of any group logistics.**

6. **Close with some form of gratitude together.**

Appendix A

Needs Wheel

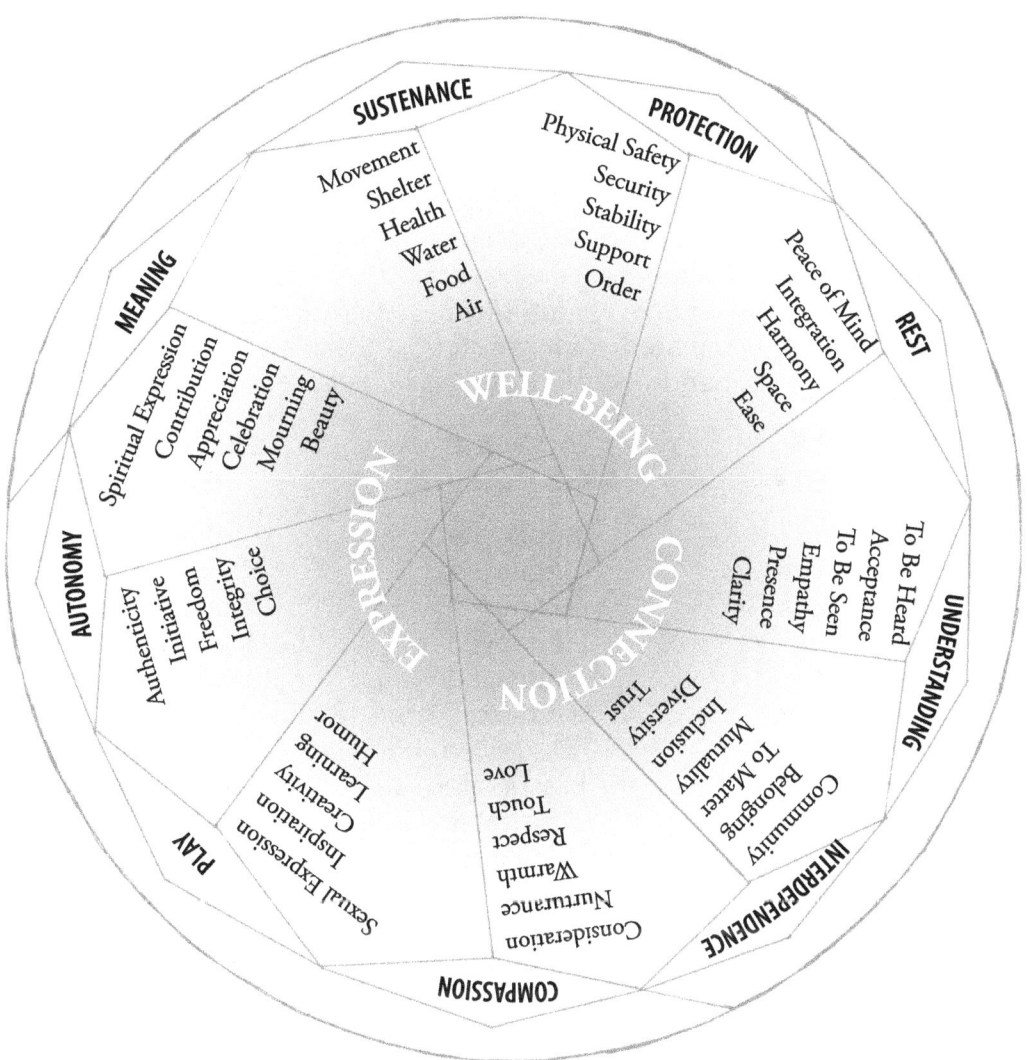

Universal qualities of our One Life together.

Like our heartbeat and our breath, Needs are an essential part of who we are and how we function as living beings. Needs are not something we have or don't have – we *are* them. Every word any one of us speaks, every action any one of us takes, including silence and stillness, expresses a Need. Through deeply hearing, voicing, and embracing these qualities in each moment, in each expression of ours or another, we become more intimate with the One interdependent Life that we all share. The Needs Wheel above is not a definitive list of all Universal Needs but rather a place for us to begin in our understanding and practice.

Based on the work of Marshall B. Rosenberg, PhD | cnvc.org and Manfred Max-Neef | max-neef.cl

Feelings

JOY & CONTENTMENT

Adventurous	Curious	Giddy	Loving	Satisfied
Affectionate	Delighted	Glad	Moved	Stimulated
Alive	Determined	Grateful	Overjoyed	Surprised
Amazed	Eager	Happy	Peaceful	Thankful
Amused	Ecstatic	Hopeful	Pleased	Thrilled
Astonished	Encouraged	Inspired	Proud	Touched
Calm	Excited	Intrigued	Refreshed	Tranquil
Confident	Fascinated	Invigorated	Relaxed	Trusting
Content	Friendly	Joyful	Relieved	Upbeat

FEAR & ANXIETY

Afraid
Alarmed
Anxious
Apprehensive
Bewildered
Cautious
Concerned
Confused
Disconcerted
Disturbed
Dubious
Embarrassed
Impatient
Jittery
Nervous
Overwhelmed
Panicky
Perplexed
Puzzled
Reluctant
Restless
Scared
Shocked
Stressed
Terrified
Worried

ANGER & FRUSTRATION

Aggravated
Agitated
Angry
Annoyed
Appalled
Cranky
Disgusted
Exasperated
Frustrated
Furious
Impatient
Indignant
Infuriated
Irritated
Resentful
Upset

SADNESS & GRIEF

Bored
Depressed
Disappointed
Discouraged
Disheartened
Dismayed
Despairing
Exhausted
Helpless
Hopeless
Hurt
Lonely
Melancholic
Sad
Tired
Troubled

FAUX FEELINGS
Interpretations masquerading as feelings

Abandoned	Ignored	Neglected
Abused	Intimidated	Put Upon
Attacked	Invisible	Rejected
Betrayed	Let Down	Rushed
Bullied	Manipulated	Unappreciated
Cheated	Misunderstood	Used

©2008 John Cunningham | www.empathy-conexus.com

Body Sensations

Inspired by the work of Peter Levine | traumahealing.com

Self-Empathy
(aka "What We're Bringing into the Room")

1. Thoughts - Touching our head and Naming stories, judgments, interpretations, and beliefs we're holding.

Take a DEEP breath!

2. Feelings - Touching our heart and Naming the present body sensations and emotions we feel.

Take a DEEP breath!

3. Needs - Touching our belly and Naming the Needs underlying and being expressed through the Thoughts and Feelings.

Breathe and center

4. Requests - With hands open to receive, Naming any Request for Action that arises out of connecting to the Needs.

Communication Flow Chart

Self-Empathy

What am I:
- seeing or hearing that's stimulating me?
- thinking?
- feeling in the body?
- needing?
- requesting to address those needs?

Check Intention

Am I:

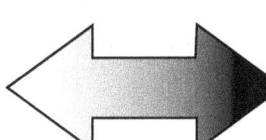

- centered, open, or relaxed?
- curious about connecting?
- knowing that I don't have all the answers?
- open to any outcome that addresses all the needs?

- stressed, scared, or angry?
- wanting to be right?
- wanting to get my way?
- closed to other outcomes?

Empathic Listening

What are they:
- seeing or hearing that's stimulating them?
- feeling?
- needing?
- requesting to address those needs?

Speaking Truth

What I:
- see or hear that's stimulating me
- feel
- need
- request to address those needs

Adapted from The No-Fault Zone | thenofaultzone.com

APPENDIX A

Needs Cards

Needs Cards are one of the simplest and easiest tools we've found to support the learning and practice of empathy whenever people are gathered. In *The Ongo Book*, they are used for Group Gatherings, starting on Week 2. If the group doesn't have a deck of Needs Cards, the Group Guide for Week 2 can follow the instructions below to make them:

If you have access to a computer, printer, and Internet, you can print out a deck of Needs Cards from The Ongo Companion Website (ongo.global). We recommend printing them out on light-colored cardstock, both for beauty and durability. Once you have printed the file, simply cut each page across the dotted lines so that each Need is on its own card, as in the picture below.

If you don't have access to a computer, printer, and Internet, you can make a deck of Needs Cards by hand. There are many ways to do this. Here's one:

1. **Cut 9 sheets of cardstock into 63 cards.** Do this by cutting each sheet of cardstock into 7 strips, width-wise, as shown in the left picture below.

2. **Looking at the Needs Wheel on page 271 in the Appendix, write one Need word on each card.** Write so that they're large and easy to read by others, as in the right picture below.

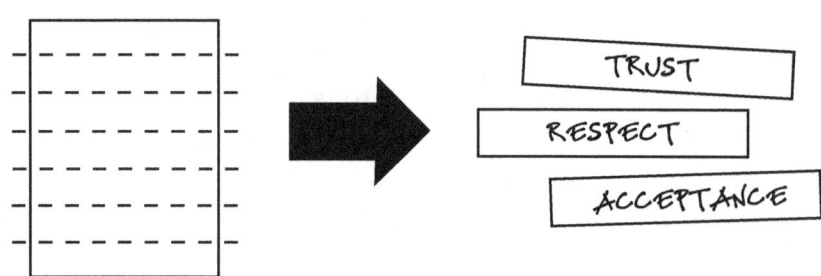

Appendix B

Leading Group Practice Online

"Doing Ongo online allowed for the world to unite around really deep matters that stir us, and awaken a lot of our history and story and legacy - the traumas of war for example. Connecting with my buddy in Poland was beautiful, to be able to heal together and see our unity across the world. None of us is alone - the suffering is still the same - even if materially we have different comforts in life."
– Farida K., Australia

Many of the practices in the Group Gatherings were once practices that we had led for groups online. Because of this, most of the guidance can be followed as-is for online Ongo Book groups. This appendix was written to give guidance for Group Guides on how to work with the Group Gathering instructions that need some adaptation to work well online. This guidance is based on what has worked well in our experience and other online Ongo Book groups. In sharing these recommendations, we are deeply indebted to Wendy Haynes, Jeff Joslin, Laura Sacks, Terry Schiff, and Michelle Towle, whose hard work of testing and writing down their experience helped inform this appendix.

How to Use This Appendix

This appendix is organized by *The Ongo Book's* chapters. Generally, as a Group Guide, you will follow the original instructions in the book. As you do, look for this computer icon: 🖥. It will appear to the left of any section where there is additional guidance in this appendix for online groups. When you get to that section, turn to the page number shown in the icon to find additional instructions that will apply for that section when meeting online. Then, return to the original guidance for the sections that follow. If there is no additional guidance in this appendix for a particular practice, then simply follow the original guidance.

Creating a Circle of Support: How to Start an Ongo Group

Action steps for the group organizer:

- Instead of choosing a physical place to meet, you will need to choose an online meeting platform that's easily accessible for all the participants. The recommendations in this book are primarily from Ongo Book groups that used Zoom as their platform for meeting, but other video and phone conferencing platforms can be used as well (the original Ongo "online" gatherings used international phone conferencing). As technology is constantly changing, we do not have a particular recommendation for which platform to use, though platforms offering the capability for text chat and breakout rooms may be preferable. If using a platform with breakout rooms, we strongly recommend asking a participant who is familiar with the platform to handle the tech each week (i.e., muting and unmuting participants, opening and closing breakout rooms). If using a platform that does not have breakout room capability, we recommend limiting the group size to no more than eight participants so there is enough time for every participant to speak and do the practices at each gathering. We have held successful Ongo groups using everything from free telephone conferencing services to paid professional online video.

Leading Group Practice: Instructions for the Group Guide

Two or three days before the Group Gathering:

In addition to the other instructions:

- Read the Group Gathering instructions for the week that you will be guiding, as well as any additional guidance found in this appendix.

- Remind everyone how to join the online meeting, and the day and time it will take place.

- Ask that participants bring their copy of *The Ongo Book*, the Ongo Circle you sent them (see page 286, Week 1 Group, Preparation – Group Guide), and paper and writing utensils of their choice to the online Group Gathering, in addition to any other preparation requested of participants in that week's Group Gathering instructions.

- **Do any preparation noted under "Preparation – Group Guide,"** also found at the beginning of the instructions for the Group Gathering week you are guiding. Look for the online icon so you can refer to this appendix for any additional preparation that may be needed for online Group Gatherings.

Bring to the Group Gathering:

In addition to the other things, bring:

- The Ongo Circle created by the Week 1 Group Guide, for use as a reference seating chart whenever there are instructions for participants to share "around the circle" (see Week 1 Preparation – Group Guide on page 286 for details).

- For online meetings, you *won't* bring a deck of Needs cards. Instead, each participant will refer to the Needs Wheel in their copy of *The Ongo Book*. The Needs Wheel can also be downloaded or printed from the Ongo Companion Website at ongo.global.

On the day of the Group Gathering:

In addition to the other instructions:

- **Consider sharing an image and/or music that invites a sense of welcome, inspiration, and coming together while participants are arriving to the meeting**, if your online meeting platform has the capability to share an image and/or sound and you feel comfortable with the technology.

- **As participants join the online meeting, put a mark by their name on your copy of the Ongo Circle so you can see who is or isn't present** in this week's Group Gathering. This will give you a visual reference to support participants with ease and flow for going "around the circle," when needed. You can also check with participants as they arrive that they brought their Ongo Circle for reference. It also may be useful at times to share the Ongo Circle on screen if your technology permits.

- **Before the meeting begins, request that participants give the meeting their full focus and refrain from multitasking**, including responding to other messages or notifications on their phone or device during this time.

- **Ask participants to wear headphones if others** (i.e., family members or co-workers) **might wander into their space during the meeting, so that other participants' intimate sharing isn't overheard.**

- **Ask participants to keep their cameras on**, if the technology allows. This will help everyone to stay present and connected to each other during the call.

- **Remind participants to mute themselves when they are not speaking, so everyone can clearly hear whoever is speaking.** During the meeting, there may be times when you or your tech person will need to mute a participant who has forgotten to mute themselves if their background noise is distracting attention from whoever is speaking or during a meditation.

- **When leading the group, use the regular guidance from the Group Gathering instructions for that week, and utilize the additional guidance from this appendix for any section that has the computer icon to the left of it.** When you get to those sections, turn to the page number shown on the icon that's there and follow the instructions for online groups that you find on that page for that section. Use these instructions instead of the original guidance, as it applies. Then, continue with the original guidance for the sections that follow.

During the Group Gathering:

In addition to the other instructions:

- **Use "power-with" leadership.** Silence in an online forum can be misinterpreted, so it can be helpful to offer a bit of narration to what is happening. Consider verbally guiding any silent empathy and taking a collective breath together when things get tough in the group sharing. You might say, "In this moment, let's connect to where we are sitting while we all take three breaths together."

- **If traumatic memories or current trauma reveal themselves for one or more participants ...** Remind participants not to step off the call, turn off cameras, or distract themselves before there is connection and support in place for the participant(s) who are stimulated. You might say, "Being with what rises during our practices can be difficult, and being online can challenge to our ability to stay present to each other. I'd like to invite us take three breaths together." After the three breaths, you might say something like, "I would like to invite (whoever is having the stimulation) to share what would work best for you right now. How can we support you with what is coming alive?" Being online, you may need to take more initiative with words for the empathic connection to be felt by others. At the same time, be mindful and gentle with your empathic guesses.

- **Whenever there's a silent period of meditation** (i.e., "Sit in silence for three more minutes"), **announce how long the silent meditation will be** (i.e., "Now, we will sit in silence for three minutes"), **so those with unstable connections will know when silence is normal, rather than a sign that their connection dropped.**

- **Hold any bells or chimes away from your microphone when striking them to signal the beginning or end of a meditation.** Our experience is that the sound can be jarring for listeners when bells or chimes are struck too close to the microphone. *Note, the sound of bells will also be enhanced if noise suppression is turned off or adjusted to "low" on your conference app audio settings, if you have that option.*

- **Remember to have fun!** Being online can be tiresome and a little more stressful for people, so use your creativity with the technology to create a nurturing space for people. For example, as you wait for people to arrive, you can ask people to introduce their animals at home that are also on the calls, have people write three Needs words in the chat of what is most alive as they step onto the call, or play a song at the end of the call and invite people who want to to dance. Allow the tech barrier to be an invitation for fun that you might not otherwise get to have in person.

WEEK 1 GROUP

Preparation – Group Guide:

🍃 **Create an Ongo Circle and send it to all the participants.**
Prior to the first group gathering, on a piece of paper, draw a circle and write the names of each of the participants in the Ongo Book group around it. Distribute this to everyone in the group. This will be the reference of where each person is on the circle for Ongo. Whenever there are instructions for participants to share "around the circle," this will be the reference seating chart. Having names written in this way allows there to be ease of knowing when participants speak without the need to be called upon and allows a genuine flow of sharing to develop. It also gives everyone the responsibility of knowing when they are sharing rather than depending on someone in the lead.

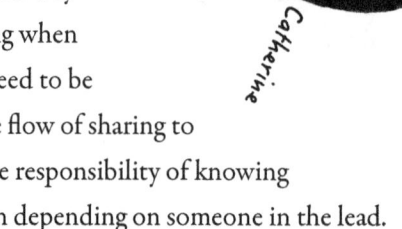

Opening Meditation

Invite everyone to settle into their seat.

Read the following to the group:

Welcome, everyone, to our Ongo Circle. We gather in a circle because on a circle we each have a place and can all be equally seen and heard. Here, we all belong and we all matter. You can look at the Ongo Circle I sent you to get a sense of where you are seated in our virtual circle.

Let us begin by each saying our name into the circle. As each person speaks, welcome them with your presence by silently listening and allowing the length of a full breath before the next person says their name. I will start by sharing my name and taking a breath. Then we will continue clockwise around the circle, in the order written on the Ongo Circle, one at a time. Remember to unmute yourself, take a breath, share your name with the group, and all take a collective breath before the next name, so we can really acknowledge each person's voice and presence.

Say your name into the circle. Take a full breath. Then the participant to your left will continue by sharing their name, and so on, until everyone in the circle has shared.

If there is an extended silence (more than a few full breaths) and a participant has not introduced themselves, gently invite them to speak. Invite them generally *("Would those who haven't yet introduced themselves share their names?")* or specifically *("<Name>, would you be willing to share your name with us?")*.

Now, return to following the original guidance for the Opening, on page 19, beginning with where it says "Once everyone in the circle has shared their name, …."

Sharing and Listening (follow this instead of the original guidance)

Read this guidance to the group:

> We each were invited to bring a written intention that expresses what calls you to Ongo at this moment in your life and what you are hoping to walk away with in your learning by the end of the Ongo journey. Let's go around the circle now and share these. We will start with whoever feels moved to share first, then follow our Ongo Circle as a reference to who will go next, moving counterclockwise this time. You can indicate you are finished speaking by saying "thank you," and the next person will then take their turn. When you share, say your name again and your intention. I ask that we support each other by listening with curiosity and full presence to whoever is sharing, rather than thinking about other things. I also ask that we do not crosstalk, ask questions, comment on each other's sharing, or write in the chat. To support everyone to have time to share, I suggest we keep our sharing to about three minutes each.

Invite whoever would like to start to unmute themselves and share their name and Ongo intention.

After that person shares, if no one speaks up, remind the group to continue to the right of that person, in the order of where each person is "sitting" on the Ongo Circle of names. You can also call the name of the next person and invite them to share.

Setting Up Ongo Buddy Practices
(follow this _instead of_ the original guidance)

Read to the group:

> This week, we will meet with another Ongo member for our first Ongo Buddy Practice. We will continue to meet once a week with that same person through Week 4 of Ongo. Each month, we will change Ongo Buddies so that we will have the opportunity to deepen our Ongo experience by working one-on-one with different community members.

> Today, we will select our first Ongo Buddies. Our only recommendation is that family members and life partners wait until the third month to be partnered together in order to care for the vulnerability at the beginning of the learning process and the deep bond of those relationships. Beyond that, the goal here is not to find "perfect pairings" but rather to let an intuitive process unfold. Let's each take a minute now in silence to breathe and imagine, from this circle, which three people you feel called to practice one-on-one with.

After a minute of silence, if your meeting platform has a chat function, read:

> Now, breathing into the vulnerability that can come with asking someone to be our friend, place in the chat the name of a person in the group that you would like to be your Buddy for this first month. With this as our beginning, let's discuss who the pairings will be until everyone has a Buddy. We will have different Ongo Buddies in months two and three, and magic can happen when we don't over-think this process, so we'll take just five minutes for this discussion.

If your meeting platform does not have a chat function, read:

> Now, breathing into the vulnerability that can come with asking someone to be our friend, we will each take a turn to say out loud the name of a person in the group that you would like to be your Buddy for this first month. With this as our beginning, let's discuss who the pairings will be until everyone has a Buddy. We will have different Ongo Buddies in months two and three, and magic can happen when we don't over-think this process, so we'll take just five minutes for this discussion.

Support the discussion by tracking when two Buddies have agreed to work together and write those two names together on a Buddy List you can refer to.

After everyone has a Buddy:

If your meeting platform allows for breakout rooms, read:

> In a moment, I will move us into breakout rooms to meet our first Ongo Buddies. There, we'll take five minutes to introduce ourselves a little more to our Buddies, exchange contact information, and schedule our first Buddy meeting together.

> **Put each pair of Buddies into their own breakout room.**

> **Bring everyone back into the main room after five minutes.**

If your meeting platform does not have breakout rooms but has a private messaging function, read:

> Please take a moment now to exchange your contact information with your Buddy through private messaging. Please contact your Ongo Buddy soon after this Group Gathering to schedule your first meeting together.

If your meeting platform does not have either breakout rooms or a private messaging function, read:

> After this Gathering, I will send you and your new Ongo Buddy each other's preferred contact information. Please contact your Ongo Buddy soon after this Group Gathering to schedule your first meeting together.

For all platforms (with or without breakout rooms), remind everyone to read "Preparing for Buddy Practice" (page 9) before their first Buddy meeting, if they haven't already. Also let everyone know that they can always reach out to the group and ask if someone else would be willing to be a backup Buddy, if they or their Buddy aren't showing up consistently for Buddy Practice.

Closing

In addition to asking for a volunteer to guide next week's group, ask for a second volunteer to be a tech person next week to handle any breakout rooms, muting, etc.

For the closing sharing, invite whoever feels called to start to share their name and one word that describes what they are taking with them from this first Ongo Group Gathering. Sharing will continue around the Ongo Circle of names until everyone has shared.

After the Week 1 Group Gathering

- **If your group was not able to create Ongo Buddies for any reason, then look at your participant circle and create an Ongo Buddy match for each participant.** We recommend to not pair family members and life partners together until the third month of Ongo, in order to care for the vulnerability at the beginning of the learning process and the deep bond of those relationships. We also recommend pairing more experienced participants with those who might want extra support. Remember to give yourself an Ongo Buddy as well.

- **If Ongo Buddies didn't exchange contact information during the Group Gathering, introduce each participant to their new Ongo Buddy through their preferred method of contact (i.e., email or instant message).** Invite them to connect with each other to schedule their first meeting together.

WEEK 2 GROUP

Preparation – Group Guide:

- Instead of preparing a set of Needs cards, simply remind everyone to have their copy of *The Ongo Book* with them for the gathering.

- Remember to have the Ongo Circle of names with you as a reference and to distribute it again to the participants.

Opening Meditation

Welcome everyone by inviting them to say their names into the circle. Let the group know that you will start and then choose a direction around the Ongo Circle for sharing to continue. Sharing will continue with the person immediately to your left or right, and so on, in order of the names on the Ongo Circle, until everyone has spoken. Ask everyone to unmute when they share their names with the group, and to give presence to each person by taking a full breath of silence between names.

If there is an extended silence (more than a few full breaths) and a participant has not introduced themselves, gently invite them to speak. Invite them generally *("Would those* *who haven't yet introduced themselves share their names?")* or specifically *("<Name>, would you be willing to share your name with us?").*

Then, return to the original guidance for the Opening Meditation on page 40, beginning with where it says "Ring a bell to signal the beginning of the sitting meditation."

Empathy Circles (follow this <u>instead of</u> the original guidance)

For groups of more than eight people, if your meeting platform allows for breakout rooms, let the group know that this next practice will be in small groups.

Ask everyone to open their copy of *The Ongo Book* to the Needs Wheel (page 271) and have it visible during the Empathy Circle.

Read this guidance to everyone:

> One person (in each group) will share for a few minutes about something that is happening in their life. This could be something either painful or joyful. We recommend for this first Empathy Circle that you share something that is alive and meaningful to you today, and something that allows you to practice being vulnerable, without being overwhelmed. In other words, choose to share what you would consider to be a medium weight, not a light weight or heavy weight.
>
> To ensure that there's time for everyone to share, we will each take only three or four minutes to speak. While the speaker is sharing, everyone else in the group listens silently, bringing curiosity, mindful presence, and an intention to connect to the speaker.
>
> After the speaker has finished sharing, the listeners focus on universal needs by looking at the Needs Wheel in *The Ongo Book* and silently guessing which Needs are important to the speaker.
>
> Each of the listeners then offers confirmation to the speaker by unmuting themselves and saying out loud one Need word from the Needs Wheel. People will have a chance to offer more than one word, but it is important to move gently and allow different voices to be heard with each Need word. When saying the Needs, allow a breath of silence between each Need spoken, so the speaker has an opportunity to really receive each word and feel it in their body. Sometimes two or more listeners may speak at the same time. If that happens, each listener will breathe and give space for the other to say their word again.

As the listeners are offering their reflections of Needs, the speaker quietly receives these words by breathing and feeling whatever feelings are touched inside. After the last reflection has been offered, and the speaker has received it, the speaker says "Thank you" to the listeners.

Now, another person in the circle becomes the speaker and the Empathy Circle repeats until, ideally, everyone in the circle has had a chance to share.

Throughout the Empathy Circle, except for the Needs reflections, the only person who ever speaks is the person sharing. Listeners are asked to respect the space by refraining from commenting, asking questions, or offering advice. We will have an opportunity after this practice as a whole group to share about our experiences of listening and speaking.

One last suggestion before we get started: if, at any point, as a listener or speaker, you find yourself getting caught up in your own thoughts, simply breathe and come back to presence with what's being shared. As a speaker, this means bringing your presence to whatever wants to be spoken through you without worrying about whether it makes sense or how it sounds to others. As a listener, this also means that, when looking at the Needs Wheel, you simply make your best guess from a place of curiosity, mindful presence, and intention to connect without worrying about whether or not it's the "right" word or the "right" guess.

Check if anyone is unclear about the practice and needs to hear the instructions again. Once everyone is clear, invite everyone to take a breath together and to bring their presence to the Empathy Circle.

If your meeting platform offers breakout rooms, use that function now to divide the group (including yourself) evenly into smaller groups. If, as host, you need to stay in the main room, your small group can meet there too. Also, if possible, include at least one person who is familiar with Empathy Circles in each small group, so they can offer assistance to their group if any confusion arises about the practice.

If your meeting platform does not have breakout rooms, then do this practice as one large group. In a large group, it's possible that not everyone will have the opportunity to share within the given time.

Invite everyone to begin. Participants can self-select who will be the first speaker in each group.

Keep track of time for the group(s). Allowing at least 10 minutes for "Harvest" and "Closing," let everyone know when they are halfway through their available time for the

Empathy Circle. Ask that each group balance the remaining time so that everyone has the opportunity to share.

Give one more time reminder to everyone five minutes before the start of "Harvest." If participants seem to require more time than is available, suggest to the group that those who would like more support could ask their Ongo Buddies to meet with them after the Group Gathering.

Close by inviting everyone back into the main room (if in breakout rooms).

Return to the original guidance for the Harvest on page 44.

Closing

In addition to asking for a volunteer to guide next week's group, ask for a second volunteer to be a tech person next week to handle any breakout rooms, muting, etc.

For the closing sharing, invite whoever feels called to start to share their name and one word that describes what they are taking with them from this second Ongo Group Gathering. Sharing will continue around the Ongo Circle of names until everyone has shared.

WEEK 3 GROUP

Preparation – Group Guide:

- Remember to have the Ongo Circle of names with you as reference and to distribute it again to the participants.

Opening Meditation

Welcome everyone by inviting them to say their names into the circle. Let the group know that you will start, and then, from your name on the Ongo Circle, sharing will continue around to the right, until everyone has spoken. Ask everyone to unmute when they share their names with the group and to give presence to each person by taking a full breath of silence between names.

If there is an extended silence (more than a few full breaths) and a participant has not introduced themselves, gently invite them to speak. Invite them generally *("Would those who haven't yet introduced themselves share their names?")* or specifically *("<Name>, would you be willing to share your name with us?")*.

Then, return to following the original guidance for the Opening Meditation on page 60, beginning with "Ring a bell to signal the beginning of the sitting meditation."

Practicing Self-Empathy

Follow the original guidance for Practicing Self-Empathy until it is time to form into pairs.

When it comes time to form pairs, read this guidance to the group:

> In a moment we will work in pairs with the Needs that you discovered. You will read the Needs you wrote down to your partner. Your partner will write these down so they can reflect them back to you. After your partner has written down your Needs, they will read them back to you, one at a time, with full breaths in between each Need, so that you can really take them in.
>
> As you are hearing your Needs reflected back to you, simply receive and breathe. Let your hands rest on your belly and feel the body's response to hearing each Need. Breathe and allow those feelings and sensations to expand throughout your whole body. Without any effort, notice if your hands stay on your belly or if they want to open and rest on your lap.

If your meeting platform has breakout rooms, divide people into rooms of two people each (or three if the number is uneven). Remind everyone to switch roles after one person has had their Needs reflected back to them so both people have the opportunity for their Needs to be held. They will have 6 minutes for this practice (9 minutes for groups of three). If, as host, you need to stay in the main room, leave another participant there with you so you can also practice.

If your meeting platform does not have breakout rooms, the practice will take place in the large group, with you inviting in participants by name when it's their turn to do the practice. Participants will take turns doing the practice with the person "next to them" on the Ongo Circle of participant names, one pair at a time, until everyone on the circle, including you, has had the opportunity to experience both roles (the "One Being Held" and the "Supporter"). To do this, step-by-step:

1. Choose one person on your circle and name them out loud as the One Being Held.

2. Name the person who is to the left of the One Being Held on the Ongo Circle of names as the Supporter. Everyone else in the circle will listen and witness with silent empathic presence throughout this process.

3. The One Being Held will read the Needs they wrote down in the Self-Empathy practice to the Supporter. The Supporter writes these down.

4. The Supporter will then read the One Being Held's Needs back to them, one at a time, with full breaths in between, following the guidance you read above.

5. The Supporter will then become the One Being Held, and you will name the person to the left of them as the new Supporter. They will do the practice, and this continues around the circle until everyone has been both the One Being Held and the Supporter.

Once everyone has finished receiving their Needs (and any participants in breakout rooms are back in the main room), return to the original guidance for this practice, on page 64, beginning with "Once everyone has finished receiving their Needs, invite the group to take three breaths together."

Closing

In addition to asking for a volunteer to guide next week's group, ask for a second volunteer to be a tech person next week to handle any breakout rooms, muting, etc.

For the closing sharing, invite everyone to silently choose a Need from their Needs Wheel that describes what they are taking with them from this third Ongo Group Gathering.

After one minute, invite everyone to write the Need they chose into the chat. If your meeting platform does not have a chat function, invite whoever feels moved to share the Need they chose. Sharing will then continue around the Ongo Circle of names to their right until everyone has shared.

WEEK 4 GROUP

Preparation – Group Guide:

- Remember to have the Ongo Circle of names with you as reference and to distribute it again to the participants.
- Ignore any preparation involving the "talking stick" or the Needs cards.

Council Rounds

Read the following instructions for Council Rounds <u>instead of</u> the original:

> Now we will share in Council Rounds. Since we are online, we will take turns speaking by unmuting ourselves, saying our name with a full breath, sharing what we want to say, then signaling we are passing to the speaker on our left with a bow and/or by saying "Thank you."
>
> The person speaking will have our full silent presence. We will keep our cameras on while listening. While they are speaking, we will not comment on or respond to their words, nor will we be thinking about what we will say when it is our turn to speak. We will hold the space of empathy for each speaker. When it is our turn to speak, we will not refer to anyone else's sharing. We will speak from our own experiences and ideas.
>
> We will have three rounds of sharing. For the first round, each person will share on the topic: "Tell us about the suffering you witness in yourself and in the world." We will start with whoever first feels called to speak on the topic, then we will continue to their left on the Ongo Circle of names until we come back around to the first person who spoke, at which point I will introduce the next topic to share on. Given that there will be three rounds of sharing and *<number>* of people here, let us all be mindful about the length of our speaking so that there is time for everyone's voice to be heard. At the same time, honor your own voice by giving it the space it needs to be expressed.

Check if anyone is unclear about the practice and needs to hear the instructions again. Once everyone is clear, invite everyone to take a breath together and to bring their presence to the Council Round. Read:

> Tell us about the suffering you witness in yourself and in the world. Remember to unmute yourself. Who feels called to start this round?

If your meeting platform has a chat function, put "Tell us about the suffering you witness in yourself and in the world" into the chat.

Track the circle. If someone is trying to speak and is muted, remind them to unmute. If there is a long pause between speakers, then check with the next person expected, *"<Name>, would you like to share on this topic?"*

Once sharing has made its way around the circle back to the first person who shared, invite everyone to take a collective breath together, then read:

> For this second round, tell us about what turning toward a power greater than yourself means to you. Remember to unmute. Who feels called to start this second round? This time, we will go around the Ongo Circle to the right.

If your meeting platform has a chat function, put "Tell us about what turning toward a power greater than yourself means to you" into the chat.

Once sharing has made its way around the circle back to the first person who shared, invite everyone to take a collective breath together, then read:

> Before the third round, in silence, let us each look at our Needs Wheel to connect to what our sharing and listening to others has brought alive in us. Breathe as you look over these Needs and see which ones speak to you this moment.

Allow a full minute of silence for everyone to look at the Needs before continuing to read:

> For the third round, tell us about the Needs that you notice have come alive during this sharing. How do these Needs relate to your ideas of suffering and/or the idea of a power greater than yourself? Remember to unmute. Who feels called to start this final round? We will pass to the left this time.

If your meeting platform has a chat function, put into the chat "Tell us about the Needs that you notice have come alive during this sharing. How do these Needs relate to your ideas of suffering and/or the idea of a power greater than yourself?"

Once sharing has made its way around the circle back to the first person who shared, invite everyone to take a collective breath together. Return to the original guidance for the Harvest on page 88.

Closing

In addition to asking for a volunteer to guide next week's group, ask for a second volunteer to be a tech person next week to handle any breakout rooms, muting, etc.

For the closing sharing, invite a person on your circle to share the word they chose that describes what they are taking with them from this fourth Ongo Group Gathering, and to choose a direction for the sharing to then continue around the Ongo Circle, until **everyone, including you, has shared.** If time is short, and your meeting platform has a chat function, you can invite everyone to write their word into the chat instead.

WEEK 5 GROUP

Preparation – Group Guide:

- Remember to have the Ongo Circle of names with you as reference and to distribute it again to the participants.
- Ignore the preparation involving the Needs cards.

Exploring Core Beliefs

Follow the original guidance for Exploring Core Beliefs until it comes time to actually <u>practice</u> in pairs (be sure to read out loud the original guidance for the practice under "Once everyone has settled into pairs ... " before continuing).

In the online version of this practice, the practice is the same, except that participants will begin by giving their partners the three thoughts they wrote down by either saying them out loud to their partners (who will write them down) or by putting their three thoughts into a private message that only their partner can see.

If your meeting platform has breakout rooms, divide people into rooms of two people each for the practice (or three if the number is uneven). They will have 20 minutes for this practice (30 minutes if groups of three). If, as host, you need to stay in the main room, leave another participant there with you so you can also practice. After 10 minutes, send a reminder to all the rooms for participants to switch roles, if they haven't already.

If your meeting platform does not have breakout rooms, the practice will take place in the large group, with you inviting in participants by name when it's their turn to do the practice. Participants will take turns doing the practice with the person "next to them" on the Ongo Circle, one pair at a time, until everyone on the circle, including you, has had the opportunity to experience both roles (the Self-Empathizer and the Supporter). To do this, step-by-step:

1. Choose one person on the circle and name them out loud as the Self-Empathizer.
2. Name the person who is to the left of the Self-Empathizer on your circle as the Supporter.
3. The Self-Empathizer will read out loud (or put in a private message) the three thoughts they wrote down in the first part of the practice to the Supporter. The Supporter writes these down.
4. Both will then do the practice described in the guidance you read earlier, with the rest of the group silently witnessing and offering their empathic presence.
5. After they have completed the practice, the Supporter will become a Self-Empathizer, and you will name the person to the left of them as the new Supporter. They will do the practice, and this continues around the circle until everyone has been both a Self-Empathizer and a Supporter.

Return to the original guidance on page 107, beginning with "Keep track of time" for notes about tracking time and how to complete after everyone has done the practice.

Setting Up Ongo Buddy Practices
(Follow this _instead of_ the original guidance)

If your meeting platform has a chat function, invite everyone to write a quick acknowledgement and thank you to their Buddy in the group chat.

Read to the group (whether your meeting platform has chat or not):

> Today, we will select new Ongo Buddies for the second month of Ongo. As before, our only recommendation is that family members and life partners wait until the third month to be partnered together in order to care for the vulnerability at the beginning of the learning process and the deep bond of those relationships. Beyond that, the goal is not to find "perfect pairings" but rather to let an intuitive process unfold. Let's take a minute now in silence to breathe and imagine that we are sitting next to our current Buddy. From where we sit with our current Ongo Buddy, see two other people in this circle we feel called to continue our one-on-one practice with.

After a minute of silence, if your meeting platform has a chat function, read:

> Now, breathing into the vulnerability that can come with asking someone to be our friend, place in the chat the name of a person in the group who you would like to be your Buddy for this second month. With this as our beginning, let's discuss who the pairings will be until everyone has a Buddy. Remember, magic can happen when we don't over think this process, so we'll take just five minutes for this discussion.

If your meeting platform does not have a chat function, read:

> Now, breathing into the vulnerability that can come with asking someone to be our friend, we will each take a turn to say out loud the name of a person in the group who you would like to be your Buddy for this second month. With this as our beginning, let's discuss who the pairings will be until everyone has a Buddy. Remember, magic can happen when we don't over think this process, so we'll take just five minutes for this discussion.

Support the discussion by tracking when two Buddies have agreed to work together and write those two names together on a Buddy List you can refer to.

After everyone has a Buddy:

If your meeting platform allows for breakout rooms, read:

> In a moment, I will move us into breakout rooms to meet our new Ongo Buddies. There, we'll take five minutes to introduce ourselves a little more to our new Buddy, exchange contact information, and schedule our first Buddy meeting together.

> **Put each pair of Buddies into their own breakout room.**

> **Bring everyone back into the main room after five minutes.**

If your meeting platform does not have breakout rooms but has a private messaging function, read:

> Please take a moment now to exchange your contact information with your Buddy through private messaging. Please contact your Ongo Buddy soon after this Group Gathering to schedule your first meeting together.

If your meeting platform does not have either breakout rooms or a private messaging function, read:

> After this Group Gathering, I will send you and your new Ongo Buddy each other's preferred contact information. Please contact your Ongo Buddy soon to schedule your first meeting together.

For all platforms (with or without breakout rooms), remind everyone to reread "Preparing for Buddy Practice" (page 9) before their first Buddy meeting, if they haven't already. Also let everyone know that they can always reach out to the group and ask if someone else would be willing to be a backup Buddy, if they or their Buddy aren't showing up consistently for Buddy Practice.

Closing

In addition to asking for a volunteer to guide next week's group, ask for a second volunteer to be a tech person next week to handle any breakout rooms, muting, etc.

For the closing sharing, invite everyone to silently choose a Need from their Needs Wheel that describes what they are taking with them from this fifth Ongo Group Gathering.

After one minute, invite everyone to write the Need they chose into the chat. If your meeting platform does not have a chat function, invite whoever feels moved to share the Need they chose. Sharing will then continue around the Ongo Circle of names to the left until everyone has shared.

After the Week 5 Group Gathering

- **If your group was not able to create Ongo Buddies for any reason, then look at your Ongo Circle and create an Ongo Buddy match for each participant.** You may need to contact the Group Guide for the first week of Ongo (often the organizer of the group) to get the names of the first month's Ongo Buddy pairs, to avoid participants being matched again with their existing Ongo Buddies. We recommend not pairing family members and life partners together until the third month of Ongo, in order to care for the vulnerability at the beginning of the learning process and the deep bond of those relationships. We also recommend pairing more experienced participants with those who might want extra support. Remember to give yourself an Ongo Buddy as well.

- **If Ongo Buddies didn't exchange contact information during the Group Gathering, introduce each participant to their new Ongo Buddy through their preferred method of contact (i.e., email or instant message).** Invite them to connect with each other to schedule their first meeting together.

WEEK 6 GROUP

Preparation – Group Guide:

- Remember to have the Ongo Circle of names with you as reference and to distribute it again to the participants.
- Ignore any preparation involving the "talking stick" or the Needs cards.

Council Round

Follow the original guidance for the Council Round, with just one change: instead of using a talking stick, you will invite whoever feels called to start to share, and the round will continue to their right on the Ongo Circle. The "stick" passes when the speaker acknowledges they are done speaking with a bow or saying "Thank you." If needed, remind people to unmute when they speak. If there is a long pause between speakers, then check with the next person expected, *"<Name>, would you like to share on this topic?"*

Practicing Finishing Business

Follow the original guidance for Practicing Finishing Business, with the below change to the structure:

If your meeting platform has breakout rooms:

1. Ask everyone to open their *Ongo Book* to "Practicing Finishing Business" on page 129.
2. Let them know that you will send them in pairs to breakout rooms where they will be doing the Practicing Finishing Business practice. They will take turns reading the instructions aloud to each other while doing the practice together. They will have 30 minutes for this practice (about 15 minutes each).
3. Divide people into rooms of two people each for the practice (or three if the number is uneven).
4. After 15 minutes, send a reminder to all the rooms for partners to switch roles, if they haven't already.

If your meeting platform does not have breakout rooms, pairs of participants will take turns doing the practice with you reading the guidance on page 129, and the rest of the group witnessing. Simply invite two people would like to practice a Finishing Business dialogue to begin. Then, follow the original guidance for this practice. When that pair is done, invite another two people who would like to do the practice to begin. Note that in this format, it's likely that there will not be time for everyone to do the practice.

Closing

In addition to asking for a volunteer to guide next week's group, ask for a second volunteer to be a tech person next week to handle any breakout rooms, muting, etc.

For the closing sharing, invite everyone to silently choose a Need from their Needs Wheel that describes what they are taking with them from this sixth Ongo Group Gathering.

After one minute, invite everyone to write the Need they chose into the chat. If your meeting platform does not have a chat function, invite whoever feels moved to share the Need they chose. Sharing will then continue around the Ongo Circle of names to their right until everyone has shared.

WEEK 7 GROUP

Preparation – Group Guide:

- Remember to have the Ongo Circle of names with you as reference and to distribute it again to the participants.
- Ignore the preparation involving the Needs cards.

Closing

In addition to asking for a volunteer to guide next week's group, ask for a second volunteer to be a tech person next week to handle any breakout rooms, muting, etc.

For the closing sharing, invite everyone to silently choose a Need from their Needs Wheel that describes what they are taking with them from this seventh Ongo Group Gathering.

After one minute, invite everyone to write the Need they chose into the chat. **If your meeting platform does not have a chat function, invite whoever feels moved to share the Need they chose.** Sharing will then continue around the Ongo Circle of names to their left until everyone has shared.

WEEK 8 GROUP

Preparation – Group Guide:

- Bring two Needs cards to the meeting, one with the word *Celebration* and one with the word *Mourning*. You can make these yourself, as long as they are readable by others.
- Ignore the other preparation involving the Needs cards.
- Remember to have the Ongo Circle of names with you as reference and to distribute it again to the participants.

Opening Meditation

Follow the original guidance, with just one change: each person will walk in a small circle in their own space.

Celebration and Mourning Circle

Follow the original guidance for the Celebration and Mourning Circle, with just two changes:

1. **Instead of passing the Mourning and Celebration Needs cards around the circle, you will just show the cards on your camera to the group when you introduce the practice. Invite participants to imagine the card in their hands when they are speaking.** The first round will begin with whoever first feels called to speak to any mourning in their heart by unmuting and saying their name. When they are done speaking, they will signal that they are passing to the next speaker on their left on the

Ongo Circle with a bow, or by saying "Thank you." This will continue until everyone in the circle has had the opportunity to share.

2. **After the speaker has finished sharing their mourning, listeners will look at the Needs Wheel in *The Ongo Book* and silently guess which Needs are important to the speaker. They will then offer confirmation to the speaker in one of two ways:** If there is a chat function, they will silently write the Needs words into the group chat. If there isn't a chat function, the listeners will say the Need words out loud, one at a time, with a breath in between each word. Either way, the speaker will then silently receive these Needs words.

On the second round, as in the original guidance, participants will speak to celebration.

Closing

Follow the original instructions for Closing, with one addition: ask for a second volunteer to be a tech person next week to handle any breakout rooms, muting, etc.

WEEK 9 GROUP

Preparation – Group Guide:

- Remember to have the Ongo Circle of names with you as reference and to distribute it again to the participants.
- Ignore the preparation involving the Needs cards.

Stepping In and Out of Shenpa

Follow the original guidance for Stepping In and Out of Shenpa, with two changes:

1. **Instead of everyone writing their messages on paper to hand to the person they are practicing with, participants will "hand" the message to the other person by reading it out loud, or putting it into a chat message.** During the practice, that other person will then say the participant's stimulating message back to them.

2. **You will invite in participants by name when it's their turn to do the practice.** Participants will take turns doing the practice with the person to their left on the

Ongo Circle, one pair at a time, until everyone on the circle, including you, has had the opportunity to experience both roles (the Shenpathizer and the Stimulator). To do this, step-by-step:

1. Choose one person on the Ongo Circle and name them out loud as the Shenpathizer.

2. Name the person who is to the left of the Shenpathizer on the Ongo Circle as the Stimulator.

3. The Shenpathizer will read out loud (or put in a chat message) to the Stimulator the stimulating message they wrote down in the first part of the practice. The Stimulator writes this down.

4. Both will then do the practice as described in the original guidance.

5. After they have completed the practice, the Stimulator will become Shenpathizer, and you will name the person to the left of them as the new Stimulator. They will do the practice, and this continues around the Ongo Circle until everyone has been both a Shenpathizer and a Stimulator.

6. Follow the same structure again when it comes time for participants to pass the message to the person on their right. This time, you will name the person who is to the right of the Shenpathizer on the Ongo Circle as the Stimulator.

Setting Up Ongo Buddy Practices (follow this <u>instead of</u> the original guidance)

If your meeting platform has a chat function, invite everyone to write a quick acknowledgement and thank you to their Buddy in the group chat.

Read to the group (whether your meeting platform has chat or not):

> Today, we will select new Ongo Buddies for the third month of Ongo. We suggest that any family members or life partners in the group be paired this month as a way to deepen those connections. If you do not have a family member or life partner in this circle that you will partner with, take a minute now in silence to breathe and feel into who you are called to continue your one-on-one practice with – someone whom you haven't already been Buddies with.

After a minute of silence, if your meeting platform has a chat function, read:

> Now, breathing into the vulnerability that can come with asking someone to be our friend, place in the chat the name of a person in the group that you would like to be your Buddy for this third month. With this as our beginning, let's discuss who the pairings will be until everyone has a Buddy. Remember, magic can happen when we don't over-think this process, so we'll take just five minutes for this discussion.

If your meeting platform does not have a chat function, read:

> Now, breathing into the vulnerability that can come with asking someone to be our friend, we will each take a turn to say out loud the name of a person in the group that you would like to be your Buddy for this third month. With this as our beginning, let's discuss who the pairings will be until everyone has a Buddy. Remember, magic can happen when we don't over-think this process, so we'll take just five minutes for this discussion.

Support the discussion by tracking when two Buddies have agreed to work together and write those two names together on a Buddy List you can refer to.

After everyone has a Buddy:

If your meeting platform allows for breakout rooms, read:

> In a moment, I will move us into breakout rooms to meet our new Ongo Buddies. There, we'll take five minutes to introduce ourselves a little more to our new Buddy, exchange contact information, and schedule our first Buddy meeting together.

> **Put each pair of Buddies into their own breakout room.**

> **Bring everyone back into the main room after five minutes.**

If your meeting platform does not have breakout rooms but has a private messaging function, read:

> Please take a moment now to exchange your contact information with your Buddy through private messaging. Please contact your Ongo Buddy soon after this Group Gathering to schedule your first meeting together.

If your meeting platform does not have either breakout rooms or a private messaging function, read:

> After this Gathering, I will send you and your new Ongo Buddy each other's preferred contact information. Please contact your Ongo Buddy soon after this Group Gathering to schedule your first meeting together.

For all platforms (with or without breakout rooms), remind everyone to reread "Preparing for Buddy Practice" (page 9) before their first Buddy meeting, if they haven't already. Also let everyone know that they can always reach out to the group and ask if someone else would be willing to be a backup Buddy, if they or their Buddy aren't showing up consistently for Buddy Practice.

Closing

Follow the original instructions for Closing, with one addition: ask for a second volunteer to be a tech person next week to handle any breakout rooms, muting, etc.

<u>After</u> the Week 9 Group Gathering

- **If your group was not able to create Ongo Buddies for any reason, then look at your participant circle and create a new Ongo Buddy match for each participant.** You may need to contact the Group Guide for the fifth week of Ongo (the one who created the second-month Ongo Buddy matches) to get the names of previous Ongo Buddy pairs to avoid participants being matched again with their previous Ongo Buddies. We also recommend pairing family members and life partners together this third month of Ongo, to support those relationships. We also recommend pairing more experienced participants with those who might want extra support. Remember to give yourself an Ongo Buddy as well.

- **If Ongo Buddies didn't exchange contact information during the Group Gathering, introduce each participant to their new Ongo Buddy through their preferred method of contact (i.e., email or instant message).** Invite them to connect with each other to schedule their first meeting together.

WEEK 10 GROUP

Preparation – Group Guide:

- Remember to have the Ongo Circle of names with you as reference and to distribute it again to the participants.

- Ignore the preparation involving the Needs cards.

Practicing Speaking Truth

Follow the original guidance for Practicing Speaking Truth, with two changes:

1. **Instead of everyone writing their nightmare responses on paper to hand to the person they are practicing with, participants will "hand" their nightmare response to the other person by reading it out loud, or putting it into a chat message.** During the practice, that other person will then say the participant's nightmare response back to them.

2. **You will invite in participants by name when it's their turn to do the practice.** Participants will take turns doing the practice with the person to their right on the Ongo Circle, one pair at a time, until everyone on the circle, including you, has had the opportunity to experience both roles (the Speaker and the Nightmare Responder). To do this, step-by-step:

    1. Choose one person on the Ongo Circle and name them out loud as the Speaker.

    2. Name the person who is to the right of the Speaker on the Ongo Circle as the Nightmare Responder.

    3. The Speaker will read out loud (or put in a chat message) the nightmare response they wrote down in the first part of the practice. The Nightmare Responder writes this down so they can say it to the Speaker during the practice.

    4. Both will then do the practice described in the original guidance.

    5. After they have completed the practice, the Nightmare Responder will become a Speaker, and you will name the person to the left of them as the new Nightmare Responder. They will do the practice, and this continues around the circle until everyone has been both a Speaker and a Nightmare Responder.

Closing

Follow the original instructions for Closing, with one addition: ask for a second volunteer to be a tech person next week to handle any breakout rooms, muting, etc.

WEEK 11 GROUP

Preparation – Group Guide:

- Remember to have the Ongo Circle of names with you as reference and to distribute it again to the participants.
- Ignore the preparation involving the Needs cards.

Closing

Follow the original instructions for Closing, with one addition: ask for a second volunteer to be a tech person next week to handle any breakout rooms, muting, etc.

WEEK 12 GROUP

Preparation – Group Guide:

- Remember to have the Ongo Circle of names with you as reference and to distribute it again to the participants.
- Ignore the preparation involving the Needs cards.

Closing Harvest

Follow the original guidance for the Closing Harvest, with just two changes:

1. **Sharing will continue around the Ongo Circle to the right of the person who began the Harvest.** Participants will know it is their turn to speak when the person to their left on the Ongo Circle signals that they are passing to the next speaker with a bow, or by saying "Thank you." This will continue until everyone in the circle has had the opportunity to share.

2. **Decide, as a group, whether it would feel more connecting in this final Harvest for listeners to offer confirmation to the speakers by putting Needs words silently in the chat or by saying out loud one or two of the Needs they are guessing. Either way, remind participants to use the language of Needs from the Needs Wheel.** If saying

the Needs out loud, allow a breath of silence between each Need spoken so the speaker has an opportunity to really receive each word and feel it in their body. Also, when saying Needs out loud, if the group is larger than six people, due to the limited time, we suggest asking only four or five listeners to offer their guesses of the speaker's Needs.

Honoring Ceremony

Follow the original guidance for the Honoring Ceremony, with three changes:

1. **You will start with the person to the left of your name on the Ongo Circle, and the ceremony will continue around the circle from there.**

2. **You will first say the name of the participant being honored so the group knows whom to honor.** For example, you will say "Lee," then the group will say, "It is an honor to know you, Lee," and Lee will respond, "Thank you for walking with me." Then "Lee" will say the name of the person to their left, and the ceremony will repeat again. This will continue until all the participants, including you, have been honored.

3. **If someone on the Ongo Circle is not present, the group will still say, "It is an honor to know you, <Name>," when it is their turn to be honored on the circle.** To facilitate this, the person to their right on the Ongo Circle will still say their name as if they were there. If your meeting platform offers a recording function, it can be meaningful to record the whole ceremony for the participant who wasn't able to be present.

About the Quotes: In Dedication to Our Teachers

The quotes in this book are primarily from teachers we have studied with, directly or indirectly. For this second edition, we added quotes from leaders in nonviolence who are on the frontlines today, inspiring us by their example. All of these teachers deserve far more attention than we were able to give in the space of this book. Their words come from deep wells of knowledge and experience, in some cases earned through extreme hardship and suffering. Their quotes represent entire bodies of wisdom that, when explored further, can open new dimensions in one's spiritual practice. This chapter offers a place to begin that further exploration. We also attempt to share some of the interconnections among these teachers, as we have found it enriching and insightful for our own spiritual practice to understand how these teachings have evolved.

adrienne maree brown is the writer-in-residence at the Emergent Strategy Ideation Institute, and is the influential author of many books, including *We Will Not Cancel Us and Other Dreams of Transformative Justice*, and *Pleasure Activism: The Politics of Feeling Good*. She is also the cohost of the *How to Survive the End of the World* and *Emergent Strategy* podcasts. To learn more, visit adriennemareebrown.net.

Alice Walker is an internationally celebrated writer, poet, and human rights activist. She won the Pulitzer Prize for her book *The Color Purple*, which she has since described as a "Buddha book that's not Buddhism." We recommend reading *Anything We Love Can Be Saved* and *The Cushion in the Road: Meditation and Wandering as the Whole World Awakens to Being in Harm's Way*. To learn more, visit alicewalkersgarden.com.

Alycee J. Lane is an author, a professor, and a student of Engaged Buddhism. Her work draws from her deep study of Dr. Martin Luther King Jr.'s philosophy of nonviolence, the Civil Rights and Black Power movements, and her own Buddhist practice. We recommend reading *Nonviolence Now!: Living the 1963 Birmingham Campaign's Promise of Peace* and watching the "Where Spirit and Action Meet" clip on YouTube.

Amanda Gorman is an American poet and activist whose work focuses on issues of oppression, feminism, race, and marginalization, as well as the African diaspora. She came to international attention when she delivered her poem "The Hill We Climb" at the 2020 U.S. presidential inauguration, becoming the youngest poet ever to do so. To learn more, visit theamandagorman.com.

Anne Frank was a young German girl and Jewish victim of the Holocaust. The diary that she kept during the two years she was in hiding from the German Secret State Police was published posthumously and became the most well-known diary of the Holocaust. To learn more, read *The Diary of Anne Frank* or visit annefrank.org.

Anne Lamott is a progressive political activist, author, public speaker, and writing teacher. She is known for her humorous and inspiring faith-based writing. As a neighbor of hers at one time, Catherine appreciated their chance encounters on local hiking trails, which often led to inspiring conversations. We highly recommend running into Anne on trail as well as reading *Help, Thanks, Wow: The Three Essential Prayers* and *Traveling Mercies*.

bell hooks defined herself as a "seeker on the path," with the path being "a path about love." She was a practicing Buddhist Christian and a prolific writer on the intersection of race, capitalism, and gender and the resulting systems of oppression they perpetuate. She was one of the most influential cultural critics, feminist scholars, and public intellectuals of the last 40 years. To learn more, read one of her many books, including *All About Love: New Visions*, and *Ain't I a Woman? Black Women and Feminism*.

Bernie Glassman was the founder of the Zen Peacemaker Order and Bearing Witness programs and a disciple of the Zen master Taizan Maezumi. He was known for his "street retreats" in places ranging from New York City to Auschwitz, where participants eat, sleep, and practice bearing witness in public places. His teachings emphasized "not knowing" as the foundation for spiritual practice. We recommend reading *Instructions to the Cook: A Zen Master's Lessons in Living a Life That Matters*. To learn more, go to zenpeacemakers.org.

Bill W. (Wilson) was the cofounder of Alcoholics Anonymous (AA), a nonprofessional, self-supporting, multiracial, apolitical twelve-step program for anyone who wants to do something about their drinking problem. AA is an international fellowship and has no age or education requirements. To learn more, go to aa.org.

Bishop Desmond Tutu was a social rights activist and Anglican Archbishop who received the Nobel Peace Prize in 1984 for his outspoken, vigorous, and rigorously nonviolent opposition of South African apartheid. After the fall of apartheid, he headed the Truth and Reconciliation Commission and became a global activist on issues of democracy, freedom, and human rights. To learn more, read his book *No Future Without Forgiveness* and visit tutu.org.

Brother David Steindl-Rast is a Catholic Benedictine monk who cofounded the Center for Spiritual Studies, with Jewish, Buddhist, Hindu and Sufi teachers, and A Network for Grateful Living. He was also a student of Shunryu Suzuki and other Zen teachers. To learn more, read his book *Gratefulness, the Heart of Prayer* and visit gratefulness.org.

Carl Rogers was one of the founders of humanistic psychology and a pioneer in psychotherapy research. His person-centered approach found wide applications in therapy and beyond, giving rise to learner-centered education and the dialogic approach in politics. He was also a major influence in Marshall Rosenberg's development of Nonviolent Communication. To learn more, read his books *On Becoming a Person* and *Freedom to Learn*.

Chögyam Trungpa was a Tibetan Buddhist master in the Kagyü and Nyingma lineages, the founder of Naropa University and the Shambhala Training method, and a major figure in the dissemination of Tibetan Buddhism in the West. His teachings were deeply inspired by Shunryu Suzuki, whom he considered a father figure. Trungpa's sometimes controversial teaching style helped coin the term *crazy wisdom*. We recommend reading his book *Cutting Through Spiritual Materialism*. To learn more, go to shambhala.org.

Dominic Barter is the developer of Restorative Circles, a community process for supporting people in conflict, and a student of Marshall B. Rosenberg. He is also a friend and colleague who inspires us with his dedication to creative applications of nonviolence in the fields of education, justice, and social change. We recommend watching "Resolving Conflict Through Restorative Justice" on YouTube. To learn more, go to restorativecircles.org.

Dr. Martin Luther King Jr. was an American Baptist minister and internationally recognized for his leadership during the American Civil Rights Movement. He was the youngest recipient of the Nobel Peace Prize until Malala Yousafzai received that title in 2014. His work during the Civil Rights Movement built on and evolved the nonviolence of Thoreau and Gandhi. We recommend reading his speech "A Time to Break Silence" and his "Letter from Birmingham Jail." To learn more, go to thekingcenter.org.

Gabrielle Roth was a dancer, recording artist, theater director, philosopher, and author. Possessed by "a hunger for rituals of the spirit," she was best known for creating The 5Rhythms, her own form of ecstatic dance, a practice that directly addresses the divorce of body from heart and heart from mind by tapping into the natural rhythms of life. To learn more, visit 5rhythms.com.

Greta Thunberg is an environmental activist who, at age 15, started a school strike outside the Swedish Parliament to call for stronger action on climate change. She has become a leading figure among climate activists globally, known for speaking bluntly to world leaders about their failure to act. She is also one of the best-known autism activists, describing having Asperger's as her "superpower." To learn more, read her historic speeches collected in the book *No One Is Too Small to Make a Difference*.

Howard Zinn was an American historian, playwright, and social activist. He is best known for his groundbreaking history book, A *People's History of the United States*. We recommend both that book and the companion volume, *Voices of a People's History of the United States*. To learn more, go to howardzinn.org.

Jack Kornfield cofounded the Insight Meditation Society and Spirit Rock Center, and was a student of the influential Thai Buddhist monk Ajahn Chah. He is one of the key teachers to introduce Buddhist mindfulness practice to the West. We recommend reading his books *After the Ecstasy, the Laundry* and *A Path with Heart*. To learn more, go to jackkornfield.com.

Jiddu Krishnamurti was an influential speaker, author, and founder of the Oak Grove School. He was known for his precise explanations of the subtle workings of the human mind, and for teachings that were grounded in the immediacy of the present moment, while eschewing all religious and philosophical dogma. To learn more, read *Freedom from the Known* or visit jkrishnamurti.org.

Joanna Macy is the founder of the Work That Reconnects, a framework for personal and social change. She was a pioneer in the intersection of Buddhism with contemporary science and a groundbreaking environmental activist. Her work helps people transform despair and apathy in the face of overwhelming social and ecological crises into constructive, collaborative action. We recommend reading her book *Active Hope*. To learn more, go to joannamacy.net.

Koji Acquaviva is a lineage holder in the Sōtō Zen tradition as handed down by Shunryu Suzuki and Zenkei Blanche Hartman. In addition to Zen training, Koji has studied in the Tibetan Buddhist tradition, modern postural yoga, and Pure Land Buddhism. He believes the aim of practicing Buddhism is not to become proponents of an orthodoxy, but rather to discover our innate wisdom and avail ourselves of healing and joy. To learn more, go to kojiacquaviva.com.

Lyla June Johnston is a descendent of Diné (Navajo) and Tsétsêhéstâhese (Cheyenne) lineages. She is a musician, activist, public speaker, and internationally recognized performance poet. We were first inspired by her leadership during a forgiveness walk that she co-led with other Water Protectors at Standing Rock, in 2016, as part of a sustained campaign of nonviolent direct action. To watch her speeches, read her writings, and listen to her songs, visit her website, lylajune.com.

Malala Yousafzai is an activist for girls' education and the youngest-ever Nobel Prize laureate. She rose to prominence at an early age by speaking out for the right to education while living under Taliban occupation, and surviving an attempt on her life. To learn more, watch the film *He Called Me Malala*, read her book *I Am Malala*, or visit malala.org.

Dr. Marshall B. Rosenberg was a psychologist, peacemaker, student of Carl Rogers, and the developer of Nonviolent Communication. His influential teachings were born out of his experience of living through the Detroit race riot of 1943, his deep study of comparative religion, and his work with the Civil Rights Movement. We recommend his book *Speak Peace in a World of Conflict*. To learn more, visit cnvc.org or see YouTube videos of his trainings.

Melody Beattie is an influential author in recovery circles, best known for introducing the world to the term *codependency*. As a survivor of abandonment, kidnapping, sexual abuse, drug and alcohol addiction, divorce, and the death of a child, she brings a deep and empathic wisdom, born out of personal experience, to the topics she writes about. We recommend reading her book *Codependent No More*. To learn more, go to melodybeattie.com.

Mirabai Bush cofounded the Center of Contemplative Mind in Society and was a founding board member of the Seva Foundation, along with Ram Dass. Her teachings bridge contemplative practices with organizational life and social justice. We recommend reading *Compassion in Action* and *Mindfulness in Organizations: Foundations, Research, and Applications*. For more information, go to mirabaibush.com.

Mohandas Gandhi is internationally known for bringing the philosophy of Ahimsa, the principle of nonviolence toward all living things, to civil disobedience and civil rights movements. He was the preeminent leader of the Indian independence movement in British-ruled India. His work, influenced in part by Henry David Thoreau, influenced millions, including Dr. Martin Luther King Jr. and Nelson Mandela. We recommend reading *The Story of My Experiments with Truth*. To learn more, go to gandhiinstitute.org.

Nelson Rolihlahla Mandela was an anti-apartheid revolutionary who became the first freely elected president of South Africa in 1994. He is internationally known for his work in human rights. Mr. Mandela based his life on listening, the principle of dialogue, and joining alliances – even with those considered to be "enemies." We recommend listening to "Address in Capetown," the speech he gave on the day he was released after 27 years in prison, and reading his book *Long Walk to Freedom*. To learn more go to nelsonmandela.org.

Nina Wise founded Motion Theater, a fusion of performance art and spiritual practice. Her work is dedicated to tapping the wisdom that emerges from spontaneity. We recommend reading her book, *A Big New Free Happy Unusual Life*. To learn more, see motiontheater.org.

Norman Fischer is a poet and Zen Buddhist priest in the lineage of Shunryu Suzuki, and founder of the Everyday Zen Foundation. His teachings and writings, known for disarming humor and penetrating clarity, reflect his interests in interreligious dialogue and the intersection of Zen practice with modern life. We recommend his book *Taking Our Places: The Buddhist Path to Truly Growing Up*. Visit everydayzen.org to hear his recorded talks.

Pema Chödrön is a Tibetan Buddhist nun, disciple of Chögyam Trungpa, and resident teacher at Gampo Abbey. She is widely known by Western audiences for her down-to-earth interpretations of Tibetan Buddhist teachings and how they apply to everyday life. We recommend reading her book *When Things Fall Apart*. Visit pemachodronfoundation.org to watch her recorded talks.

Ram Dass was a spiritual teacher, disciple of Neem Karoli Baba, and author of the seminal book *Be Here Now*, a major influence on the Western articulation of Eastern philosophy. He cofounded the Seva Foundation and created the Hanuman Foundation, which developed the Prison-Ashram Project and The Dying Project (conceived with Stephen Levine). To learn more, we suggest the film *Fierce Grace* and his book *Be Love Now*. Also, visit ramdass.org.

Resmaa Menakem is a healer, therapist, and licensed clinical social worker who specializes in the healing of racialized trauma. He is also the founder of the Cultural Somatics Institute and the originator of Somatic Abolitionism, an embodied antiracist practice of living and culture building. We recommend his book *My Grandmother's Hands: Racialized Trauma and the Pathway to Mending Our Hearts and Bodies*. To learn more, go to resmaa.com.

Robert Gonzales was a clinical psychologist, student of Marshall B. Rosenberg, and director of the Center for Living Compassion. He is known for furthering the understanding and practice of Nonviolent Communication as a spiritual practice and way of living. To learn more, visit living-compassion.org.

Robin Wall Kimmerer is a mother, scientist, decorated professor, and enrolled member of the Citizen Potawatomi Nation. She is the founder of the Center for Native Peoples and the Environment. Robin's work emphasizes restoration of our relationships to land. We highly recommend her book *Braiding Sweetgrass: Indigenous Wisdom, Scientific Knowledge and the Teachings of Plants*. To learn more, visit robinwallkimmerer.com.

Shantum Seth is a disciple of Thich Nhat Hanh, social activist, and foremost guide to the sites associated with the historical Buddha. His teaching humanizes the history of Buddhism and Gandhian nonviolence and incorporates his firsthand understanding of present-day social issues in India. To learn more, visit buddhapath.com and ahimsatrust.org.

Sharon Salzberg is a bestselling author and Buddhist meditation teacher, emphasizing vipassanā (insight) and mettā (loving-kindness) methods. She is a cofounder of the Insight Meditation Society, along with Jack Kornfield and Joseph Goldstein. She is widely known for her secular, relatable approach to mindfulness and meditation. To learn more, read one of her many books, listen to her *Metta Hour* podcast, or go to sharonsalzberg.com.

Shunryu Suzuki was a Soto Zen Buddhist monk who founded San Francisco Zen Center and Tassajara Zen Mountain Center, the first Buddhist monastery outside of Asia. His influential teachings emphasized the importance of beginner's mind and "just sitting," rather than promises of enlightenment or spiritual experiences. To learn more, read *Zen Mind, Beginner's Mind*, a collection of his teachings, or visit shunryusuzuki.com to hear his recorded talks

Stephen and Ondrea Levine touched the lives of thousands of people all over the world with their work on forgiveness, finishing business, and boundless compassion. They offered workshops on Conscious Living/Conscious Dying for over thirty years. We recommend reading their books *Embracing the Beloved* (our go-to handbook for our partnership) and *Who Dies?*. To learn more, visit levinetalks.com.

Tara Brach is a psychotherapist, disciple of Jack Kornfield, and founder of the Insight Meditation Community of Washington, DC. She is a leading voice among those integrating Buddhist teachings with Western psychology for emotional healing and spiritual awakening. To learn more, read her book *Radical Acceptance: Embracing Your Life With the Heart of a Buddha*, or visit tarabrach.com to hear her recorded talks.

Tenshin Reb Anderson is a disciple of Shunryu Suzuki and a Senior Dharma Teacher at Green Gulch Farm Zen Center in Muir Beach, California. In addition to his Zen training, his teachings draw from his deep study of both Western and traditional Buddhist psychology and are known for both playful creativity and rigorous discipline. We recommend his book *Being Upright: Zen Meditation and the Bodhisattva Precepts*. Visit sfzc.org to hear his recorded talks.

Tenzin Gyatso, the 14th Dalai Lama, describes himself as a simple Buddhist monk. He is the spiritual leader of Tibet and is internationally known as a man of peace. In 1989, he was awarded the Nobel Peace Prize for his nonviolent struggle for the liberation of Tibet. He has also worked to advance the human understanding of the mind, consciousness, and emotions by fostering dialogues between Western scientists and Buddhist monks. We recommend his book *The Art of Happiness*. To learn more, visit dalailama.com.

Thich Nhat Hanh was a Vietnamese Zen Buddhist monk and peace activist who was nominated by Dr. Martin Luther King Jr. for the Nobel Peace Prize in 1967. He is widely known for his influential teachings on mindfulness and socially engaged Buddhism, based on his own experience as a monk during the Vietnam War. We recommend his book *Peace Is Every Step: The Path of Mindfulness in Everyday Life*. Visit tnhaudio.org to hear his recorded talks.

Toni Packer was the founder of the Springwater Center for Meditative Inquiry after being excommunicated and exiled from the Rochester Zen Center for her rejection of the rituals, forms, and doctrines she had been asked to carry on. She was known for a penetrating, deeply inquiring, and nonreligious approach to meditation, influenced in part by Jiddhu Krishnamurti. We recommend her book *The Silent Question*. Visit springwatercenter.org to hear her recorded talks.

Ven. Ajahn Sumedho is the seniormost Western disciple of the Thai meditation master Ajahn Chah, of the Thai Forest tradition of Theravada Buddhism. His teachings are known for being direct and down-to-earth, focused on practical application rather than intellectual abstraction, and filled with humorous, everyday examples. To learn more, read his book *The Sound of Silence*, or visit amaravati.org to hear his recorded talks.

Viktor Frankl was a neurologist, psychiatrist, and founder of Logotherapy/Existential Analysis; and his work was an inspiration for the humanistic psychology movement (which Carl Rogers was a founder of). As a Holocaust survivor, his teachings on finding meaning in the midst of extreme suffering were based on not just theory, but personal experience. To learn more, read his book *Man's Search for Meaning*.

Zenju Earthlyn Manuel is a dharma heir of Zenkei Blanche Hartman. Her teachings on the nature of embodiment within a boundless life are influenced by her background in Native American and African indigenous traditions, as well as her Zen training. She was raised in the Church of Christ, where she was an avid reader of the Bible and adored the true mystic teachings on Christ's path well into adulthood. To learn more, read one of her many books or visit her website, zenju.org.

Zenkei Blanche Hartman was a disciple of Shunryu Suzuki and one of the first women to lead a Zen Buddhist training temple outside of Asia. She was known for her devotion to zazen (sitting meditation), social activism, and making Zen training accessible to a wide diversity of students. To learn more about Blanche, read *Seeds for a Boundless Life*, a collection of short teachings taken from her talks, or visit sfzc.org to hear her recorded talks.

Gratitudes

Since we first published *The Ongo Book* in 2017, we have witnessed the passing of both close family members and beloved teachers, including many named in this book. We have also been incredibly blessed with the arrival of new life, welcoming two amazing daughters into our lives, and four nephews and five nieces into our wider family. During this time, the world around us has also seemingly woken up to the crises of colonization, racism, and climate change, while undergoing a global pandemic that locked many of us in our homes for over a year.

This second edition represents the deepening of our own practices during these years of tumult and transition, and a conviction that now is the most auspicious of times to be living nonviolence everyday. Each death and birth has brought us to the edges of our own sense of belonging, mattering, purpose, and meaning of living this one precious life. We offer a humble bow of gratitude for every single one of these experiences, without which we could not have written this second edition.

We cannot imagine getting through the last five years without the following people. Thank you, Yeye and Mama G, for continuing to be a force more powerful. Thank you, LN Bethea, Sirena, Mason, and Tom Sawyer. Your friendship, humor, parallel universes, and truth to power have strengthened our resolve, taught us to be better parents, and helped us to realize that the Beloved community is just down the street. We offer a deep bow to Morris Ervin and Venaya Jones for the modeling and support that gave us the mindful foundation we needed as a couple. Thank you, Ben Jensen, for literally, as well as figuratively, carrying us (and all our stuff) through all the transitions of these years. We are blessed to have you, bruddha (that's buddha and brother combined, which you are). We thank Ozella Mei and Gloria DeHaven, our daughters, who have had more patience than any human should ever be asked to have, and they do it with grace, humor, and deep love. All we do is for you.

With all our work, we are blessed by the amazing support of the board of directors of Baba Tree International: Dzebam Godlove, Wendy Haynes, Jiva Manske, Eileen McAvoy, Samuel Odhiambo, and Kate Raffin. Thank you for your dedication to living nonviolence, bringing these practices to the world, and being family.

We wish to thank Magiarí Díaz, whose exuberant perseverance to publish a Spanish translation of *The Ongo Book* led to the collaboration which also brought this English second edition to life. Maya, your dedication made this dream happen! We also want to thank Raed El-Younsi and Enric Gonzalez at simple.cat for jumping into this collaboration with both feet, and for their companionship on the journey of both nonviolence and writing.

Lucy Leu, thank you for your steadfast support of us and being Grandmother Heart-Mind manifest. Shantum Seth, we are deeply honored by your, and your family's, willingness to show up for us on all levels of being. You and Gitu have taken drive-by huggings to the highest level.

We offer gratitude for the incredible team who worked with us to realize our vision for this edition, including: our editor, Dennis Crean, who continues to keep us in (spell)check; Jennifer Hewitson, who created the stunning illustration that graces the cover; our designer, Hadley Gustafson, who formatted all our revisions to perfection; and the team at Booknook, who went above-and-beyond to produce an ebook that far exceeded our expectations. Thank you too to the Ongo Book community, who gave invaluable suggestions for our revisions and additions.

In the years leading up to this edition, we were nourished by the flow of international inspiration provided by Annett Zupke in making the German edition happen, Summer Li and Lisa Kuang in making the Simplified and Traditional Chinese versions happen and, recently, Minako Sudou, Haruno Ogasawara, and Hideharu Endo in bringing Ongo to life in Japanese. In the English-speaking world, Wendy Haynes, Jeff Joslin, Michelle Towle, and Kate Raffin have also moved us immensely with their championing of *The Ongo Book*. We feel both awe and appreciation for each one of your efforts.

We offer deep bows of gratitude to the 300 people from around the world who contributed to the fundraiser to make this and the Spanish edition come to fruition, including these "Young tree", "Mature tree", "Old-growth tree", and "Bodhi tree" donors:

Sonia Bauer	Jeff & Lou Joslin	Kate Raffin
Rebecca Brillhart	Kirsten Kristensen	Matthew Ramsay
Pam Cadden	Roswitha Kröll	Lucy Rodríguez
Alyssa Chen	George LeCompte & Jo Anne Kleinschmidt	Finn Rothacker

Montse Cheta	Leanne Logan	Karen Scott
Marcia Christen	Mika Maniwa	Gram Smith
Philippe Daniel	Joshua Mann	Kendra Smith
Rosie Demmin & Jo Ferneau	Jaya Manske	Leonie Smith
Stacey Dougan	Jim and Jori Manske	Teresa Speakman
R.A. Fedde	Jiva Manske	David & Lynd Steigerwald
Noah Fischer	Ian Mayes	Carol Walsh
Eliane Geren	Eileen McAvoy	Rich Waring
Bren Hardt	Shoko Miyagi	Laura Chu Wiens
Narayana & Wendy Haynes	Eulalia Noguera	Anne Wilson
David Hobbs	The Open-Hearted Practice Group	Thomas Wong
Gail Holmes	Meg O'Shaughnessy	Forté Worthy
Eric Huang	Linda Pittard	

We hope you are as proud of the book that you contributed to as we are. Words don't touch how moved we are by your outpouring of generosity.

Gratitudes Continued

~~~

(The following gratitudes are from the first edition and remain relevant to this second edition.)

The Ongo Book: Everyday Nonviolence is the product of six years of work with the support and input of hundreds of people. It's not an exaggeration to say that this book would not be in your hands today without that support. In particular, we want to thank our online Ongo participants. Your wholehearted dedication to nonviolence inspired us each Ongo week to write these practices, and your feedback refined them. This book is the fruit of our journeys together.

We especially thank Laura Wittke for giving this book legs and a ground to walk on, at a time when it was just an idea in our minds. Without your initial enthusiastic push, *The Ongo Book* might never have been more than an idea.

This book grew with the contributions of dear friends, which we are blessed to be able to include. To our illustrator, and longtime Ongo partner, Kate Raffin, thank you for completely "getting" our artistic vision for this book and bringing it to life. Your steadfast friendship, companionship on the journey, and dedication to the practices is woven deeply into this book and the worldwide Ongo community. To John Kinyon and Jane Lazar, thank you for pouring your hearts into your forewords and consistently supporting us in all that we do. We are honored to walk with each of you in this life.

To our editor, Dennis Crean, thank you for polishing our prose and saving us from any egregious grammar. Thank you to Norman Fischer, Raj Gill, Robert Gonzales, Lucy Leu, Bill McKibben, and Sharon Salzberg for being willing to read our unfinished manuscript and seeing the lotus inside all the mud. And, to Maia Duerr, thank you for believing in this project and generously introducing us to your network. Without you, we wouldn't even have an editor.

Incredible gratitude goes out to our proofreaders, Allison Brown, Dale Donahoe, Jeff Joslin, Leanne Logan, Eileen McAvoy, Sarah McCure, Susan McDowall, Abbey Mitchell, Regina Splees, Sean Watson, Laura Wittke (again!), and Linda Wells. Your encouragement and invaluable suggestions helped shape the final revisions of this book. Special thanks to Kelly Cummings and Paula Schramm for the car ride that inspired both the illustrations and the final cover.

We are incredibly moved by the support of our Kickstarter backers from all around the world:

Abbey Mitchell	Diana Benton	J. J. Jackson
Abbi Jaffe	Dick Moriarty	Jack Lehman
Alicia & Mario Tornero	Dominique Manning	Jack Schott
Allison Brown	Donna King	Jacqueline Gauthier
Amy Diener	Doris Reisig	Jan McCracken
Amy Reyer	Eileen McAvoy	Jane Connor
Angela Walkley	Elena Bernasconi	Janet Trengrove
Ann Louise Emanuel	Elicia Heller Sheldon	Javier
Anna Keller	Elise Levasseur	Jaya Deva Manske
Astrid Schuette	Elkie Deadman	Jean-Philippe Bouchard
Audrey Layden	Elvira Paoletti	Jeanine Hilkens
Barbara Bash	Emily Klamer	Jeannie Sutherland
Barbara Seeley	Erica Davis	Jeannine Murray-Roman
Barbara Slemmer	Esther Gerdts	Jeff and Lou Joslin
Carlene Robinson	Eve Penberhty	Jeff Scannell
Caroline Ader Lamy	Eve Witney	Jennifer Rau
Cate Crombie	Ezzy	Jerry Koch-Gonzalez
Catherine A Pollitz	Fran Hart	Jiva Manske
Cathy Hartman	Frank Maguire	John Corrigan
Chris Wilden	Fredrik Ehnbom	John Covell
Christina Brennan	Garth Knox	John D
Claralynn Nunamaker	Gayano Shaw	Joseph Dowling
Clare Raffety	Gianinna	Julia Baker
Colin Perreault	Gina Cenciose	Julie Michelson
Cornelia Timm	Greg Jenkins	Karen
Crystal Mays	Harriet Slive	Kate Forster
Dale Donahoe	Haruno Nakagawa	Kate Raffin
Dana Goldstein	Hazel Turrone	Kelley Giaramita
Deb Nevil	Hirohisa Shimizu	Ken Anno

Kerry Anne Layden	Melissa Moon	Sarah McCure
Kip	Michal Rock	Sarah Ryterband
Ko WonYeol	Mireille Beaudoin	Sean Watson
Kumiko Kawaguchi	Niko Ant	Sebastien Lemay
Lalli Dana	Noah Fischer	Sherri Boles-Rogers
Laura Wiens	Patricia McMullen	Sherry Chen Yu Shen
Lesley Halliday	Paula Christine	Shinnosuke Kano
Liane Munro	Penelope Newton	Shulamit Ber Levtov
Linda Cheever	Penny Green	Stephanie Morrison
Lindsay Kelley	Peter Welch	Sunny Goddard
Lisa Mundle	R. A. Fedde	Susan Harris
Liv Monroe	Raj Gill	Tad Beckwith
Lucy Rodriguez	Regina Splees	Tara Murphy
Lyne Lajeunesse	Remi Villeneuve	Teresa Speakman
Marie-Elaine Rheault	Renshin Bunce	Tim Herlet
Mark Kennedy	Sage Nagata	Verene Nicolas
Matt Miller	Sarah Barry	Wiene Frans
Melanie Whitham	Sarah Ludford	

After six years of on-and-off progress, it was your support that got *The Ongo Book* to the finish line. Thank you for believing in us and our idea.

Any wisdom found in this book can be attributed to the deep integrity, grace, and skill of our teachers. We offer a humble bow of gratitude to them for their wisdom and the generosity with which they have shared it.

In particular, I, Catherine, honor the Twelve-Step programs of Alcoholics Anonymous and Al-Anon and the thousands of people I have sat in those meetings with, including my first sponsor, Happy, who helped me to find the courage within myself to live a spiritual life; Lee, whose consistent spiritual presence kept me on my path; and Carl Dern, who led me to my first meditation teachers and years of practice at both Green Gulch Farm and Spirit Rock (even before the center was built). I honor Jack Kornfield, whose steadfast and gentle guidance helped me to develop a sitting practice that could weather life's storms; Ed Brown, who showed me that meditation and baking can go hand-in-hand; and Wendy Johnson, who taught me that the garden is the zendo and each interaction with nature is my practice. I offer a deep bow to Ondrea and Stephen Levine, for their teachings on death, dying, and living, and setting the standard of relationship I knew I wanted with a partner, and your immense capacity to be available over the years to receive whatever I needed help with; and Ram Dass, for helping me discover that each moment contains a "YUM!", and that saying "Hi" just isn't that hard. I thank Marshall Rosenberg for naming the language of Needs as it points to what he called Divine Energy, for keeping it real, and bringing in his humor and care when I had challenges in running the alternative school I founded. I offer gratitude to Julie Green, my "user-friendly" Nonviolent Communication teacher, who gave me tangible ways to change the way I communicate with the people I love.

To say I was lucky to hang out with and learn from such an incredible grouping of teachers while in my twenties and early thirties is an understatement. Words aren't sufficient to express the tears of appreciation I touch when remembering all of my moments with each of them. I honor Gloria and Ron Cooper, whom I consider my spiritual parents. Your unconditional patience and love with my growth over the last thirty-eight years has shaped who I am. Anyone who has known me has stepped onto the path of your lineage of wisdom. Thank you for being my life-long teachers and my family.

This book is my bow of gratitude to each of my teachers, in all directions. In that, I include Nature, my first teacher – every tree, stream, animal, bird, insect, and blade of grass that reflected to me a power greater than myself. Because of you, I have the earth under my feet, sky above my head, and sunrise to greet me each new day, reminding me that this life is a miracle.

I also honor my students of all ages who I have been fortunate to learn with on this path. Playing with you deeply influenced how I create "activities" for others' learning and how I manifest my practice each day.

To my whole Cadden family, and all our lineages, thank you for contributing to the life lessons which have helped me to grow spiritually. Dad, I am deeply grateful for those rare opportunities when I accompany you to Mass at your church so we can practice our faiths together. Mom, thank you for giving me this life and loving me no matter what. To all my elders, I offer a deep bow of gratitude for the way of the council and teaching me to listen, even when I am not willing.

To my beloved, Jesse, thank you for this partnership that invites me, daily, to deepen my spiritual journey, reconnecting me to what matters most: the breath, our being, and a life lived in service. Thank you for your incredible dedication to me, to the practices, and to bringing this book into existence. Without your artistic brilliance there would not be such an elegant way to share our work with the world. It is an honor to know you. Thank you for walking with me.

I, Jesse, honor all the teachers who taught at San Francisco Zen Center, Tassajara Zen Mountain Center, and Green Gulch Farm Zen Center during the years that I was a resident, and all those who practiced alongside me. The learning and support I received there is beyond measure. I offer a deep bow of gratitude to Tenshin Reb Anderson, for lighting the fire of bodhicitta in me – a gift which I can never fully repay. I bow to my practice leaders, Gaelyn Godwin and Teah Strozer, for their consistent presence and compassion during my time there. I bow to Shosan Victoria Austin, for encouraging and supporting my early explorations of integrating Nonviolent Communication with Zen practice. I offer deep gratitude to Toni Packer of Springwater Center, for her clear and skillful teaching, which helped me to shed a lifetime's worth of confusion around Zen. I give thanks to my Taoist teachers, Liping Zhu and Michael Belliveau, for helping me to discover the joy of embodied spiritual practice. I credit each and every one of these teachers with any lived understanding I have of Zen Buddhism.

I honor my Nonviolent Communication teachers: Jane Lazar, for introducing me to it; John Kinyon, for humbly guiding me in my practice; and Robert Gonzales, for clarifying and deepening my understanding. I offer deep gratitude to Marshall Rosenberg, for illuminating, through his own being, Zen practice in everyday language. I also appreciate my students over the years for continually inspiring me to go deeper and farther with my practice. Thank you for teaching me through your example.

To my Mom, thank you for sharing the Amitabha mantra with me when I was young and planting the seed of the Buddha Way in my heart. I am grateful for everything you have given to help make me who I am today. To Laura, thank you for your steadfast support of all that I do. I am blessed to have you as my sister.

To my dear Catherine, words cannot come close to my appreciation for you as my partner, my teacher, and my creative collaborator. There would be no *The Ongo Book* without you. Thank you for putting up with my perfectionism and for gently and firmly steering me toward sanity each day. It is an honor to know you. Thank you for walking with me.

We both feel immense gratitude for our board of directors at Baba Tree International: Ashraf Alamatouri, Jiva Manske, Eileen McAvoy, Chrystina Elle Passanisi, Sean Watson, and Melanie Whitham. Your ongoing support helped to make this book real.

We wish to thank our entire team at Play in the Wild!: Emily Manasc, Eve Penberthy, Colin Perreault, Arielle Prince-Ferron, Kate Raffin, Melanie Whitham, and Chris Wilden. Your willingness to practice everything in this book throughout our work and play as a community helped *The Ongo Book* to stay alive in more ways than we can name.

Throughout the creation of Ongo, the writing of this book, and every Ongo online gathering, Tosh, our German Shepherd dog, graced us with his presence. He passed away only months before *The Ongo Book*'s completion, after ten full years of service to us and his community. Tosh, thank you for embodying the bodhisattva way and modeling the unconditional love we all strive for.

About the Authors

CATHERINE CADDEN is a mom, educator, storyteller, and dancer with over 30 years of experience in bringing innovative programs in nonviolence, mindfulness, and conflict transformation to people of all ages, on six continents. She is dedicated to the actionable ideal that world peace is achievable in her lifetime. In 1997, she founded the TEMBA School, a visionary K–8 academic program which integrated nonviolent principles, mindfulness, art, and peace studies. In 2006, Catherine cofounded Play in the Wild! Initiations into Nonviolence for youth, families, and educators. Internationally recognized for her work, Catherine was a keynote speaker at the UNESCO Asia Pacific Education conference in 2012 and a presenter at TEDxTriangleNC in 2010 on Direct Action in L.O.V.E. Her work with her indigenous roots, elders, and teachers taught her to live interdependently with nature, which she shares with all who are willing to learn. She is a Center for Nonviolent Communication Certified Trainer and the author of *Peaceable Revolution Through Education*.

JESSE WIENS CHU is fascinated by life in all its unique expressions and finds joy in supporting people to thrive. He is a dad, artist, advocate, and facilitator. In 2006, he founded ZENVC, an approach to the practice of Nonviolent Communication (NVC) that integrates meditation, mindfulness, and inner work. In this, he draws from his own Chinese-American heritage, seven years of living and practicing in Zen monasteries, and training with NVC founder, Marshall Rosenberg, and Center for Understanding in Conflict cofounder Gary Friedman. Jesse is a Center for Nonviolent Communication Certified Trainer and a former volunteer with BayNVC's Restorative Justice program at San Quentin State Prison. He is also a contributing author to *A Thousand Hands: A Guidebook to Caring for Your Buddhist Community*.

Together, Catherine and Jesse are the devoted parents of two daughters, and live their practices in Beloved partnership, one day at a time.

相看两不厌
只有敬亭山

We sit together, the mountain and me,
until only the mountain remains.
　　　　　– 李白 Li Bó,
　　　　　　translated by Sam Hamill